Discipling the Nations

Discipling the Nations

The Government Upon His Shoulder

Dennis Woods

Legacy Communications

Franklin, Tennessee

To Gary

CONTENTS

ACKNOWLEDGMENTS

I am indebted to many people in the writing of this book. My heartfelt thanks goes to Pastor Norman Jones (RCUS) and Pastors Jim Boardwine, Steve Bicker, and J.A. Tony Tosti (PCA) for their theological review of the manuscript, in part or the whole. The perceptive historical and philosophical insights of Mark McConnell—offered in many long phone conversations—have left an indelible impression on chapters 4 and 6. Likewise, the legal insights of Paul DeParrie (Advocates for Life) and Eugene Saunders (Foursquare pastor and paralegal) are evident in chapter 5. Their reviews and comments do not imply endorsement of every view offered in this book; the ultimate responsibility must rest at my door.

Without the assistance of my "political comrades-in-arms," Mike White and Tim Nashif, I could never have written Part IV: Rebuilding by the Blueprint. This section has been over ten years in the making, as I have labored shoulder-to-shoulder in the political trenches with these charismatic brothers.

Many ideas expressed in this book also reflect the thinking of a broad range of authors who have preceded me. A complete listing would be next to impossible, but the short list would include such names as John Calvin, Martin Luther, Frederic Bastiat, Matthew Henry, Francis Schaeffer, D. James Kennedy, Richard Pratt, J. Steven Wilkins, C.S. Lewis, Herbert Schlossberg, Harold Berman, Gary North, Whitney Cross, and W. Cleon Skousen. These, and many others, have each made their unique contributions.

INTRODUCTION

I recently received a form letter from an old college friend with whom I had been involved in a well-known campus ministry almost twenty-five years ago. My friend is now a regional representative for this para-church group and responsible for more than fifty other staff members.

This individual played a significant role in encouraging my early growth as a Christian, so I share this with a sense of sadness and hope, not of malice. However, his letter conveys an attitude typical of many Christian leaders over the past one hundred years or more—one that I believe has brought America to the brink of destruction.

Most of these leaders, like my old friend, have been totally sincere in their efforts on behalf of the kingdom of God. They have preached the gospel of salvation to countless individuals and helped multitudes in their Christian walk. However, I believe many of them have "dropped the ball" in one extremely important manner. Let me illustrate with a few selected quotes from his letter:

> As I review the moral, spiritual, and economic decline of our nation, I have at times wondered, "Should I change my life mission from the Great Commission to helping reverse our nation's decline?" What is the correct response of a Christian today to the problems that surround us?
>
> As we have prayed about the above questions after 25 years focused on the Great Commission, God continues to give us a crystal-clear calling to "Continue On!" Just as a football team has offensive and defensive strategies, so does ministry. The Great Commission is an offensive strategy of evangelism and discipleship. Meeting the needs of a decaying society is part of a defensive strategy. Both are needed, but someone had better score some points!

My friend has no doubt been positioned by God in exactly that part of the body of Christ best suited for his unique skills as a teacher and leader. However, I believe that his truncated view of the Great Commission has contributed to the very moral evils that he decries.

This attitude on the part of a large portion of America's Christian leadership constitutes a significant ethical failure. It is a failure to acknowledge the comprehensive claims of Christ over all of life. It is a failure to acknowledge Christ as King of kings. It is a failure to call upon the "kings of the earth" to submit their everyday administration of justice to the clear commands of Scripture (see Ps. 2; Acts 4:25–27). It is, in short, a failure to recognize the greatness of the Great Commission.

Martin Luther, the great Protestant reformer, understood the necessity of relating the gospel to the world beyond just the inner "spiritual" life of the individual:

> If I profess with the loudest voice and clearest exposition every portion of the truth of God except precisely that little point which the world and the devil are at that moment attacking, I am not confessing Christ, however boldly I may be professing Christ. Where the battle rages, there the loyalty of the soldier is proved, and to be steady on all the battle field besides, is mere flight and disgrace if he flinches at that point.

Men of God throughout the Bible addressed their message to the sins of the nation and its leaders, not just the individual. For example, the Prophet Micah called the rulers in Israel to repentance with these words, "Hear, you heads of Jacob and rulers of the house of Israel! Is it not for you to know justice? You who hate the good and love the evil, who tear the skin from off my people . . . " (Mic. 3:1–2, RSV).

Psalm 2 calls on the kings of the earth to "serve the LORD with fear, with trembling kiss his feet, lest he be angry, and you perish in the way. . . . " Acts 4:25–27 (RSV) applies this Psalm to the New Testament era just following the triumphant work of Christ on the cross.

We are fond of saying "the Bible has all the answers," yet we systematically ignore or downplay the specific answers the Bible provides for our cultural and political problems. Why do we believe that the Bible has application to our homes and churches, yet deny its application to the life of our nation?

Christ did not limit the Great Commission to an internal "spiritual" kingdom within the hearts of men. To argue in this manner is to follow in the footsteps of Plato, not of Christ. Plato drew the sharp distinction between the "sacred" and the "secular," not Christ. Plato taught that the "physical" realm of existence was less important to man than the "spiritual" aspect of his life, not Christ.

Obviously, the Great Commission must begin within the hearts of individuals. Individual souls must be called to repentance and faith in Christ. But that is just the beginning of the task. Christ went on to declare that His teachings were to extend beyond the individual to the nations themselves. "All nations" are to be discipled and taught to observe all that Christ commanded (Matt. 28:19–20).

What did Christ command? Obviously He based His commands on the whole Bible. Included within those commands are very specific directives for civil magistrates. These directives have been largely ignored by the Church for at least the last century.

God, however, has not ignored or forgotten them. He waits and works for that generation of believers who are endowed with the spirit of Joshua and Caleb. He waits and works for that generation of believers that will not shrink back from total victory. He waits and works for that generation of believers that will not be content to wander in the wilderness of cultural irrelevance and impotence.

The claims of Christ in Scripture are comprehensive. No sphere of earthly activity is outside His jurisdiction. Every sphere of earthly activity is to be subjected to Christ for His glory in history, and that includes "city hall." As Isaiah declares: "the government shall be upon His shoulder." (Isa. 9:6)

When the Church fails to teach and insist that the civil government submit to the directives of Christ, civilization begins to crumble. Culture begins to disintegrate. The age of the barbarians begins to encroach once again. Paganism emerges from its place in the shadows. The Church is driven into the wilderness, and her freedom to preach the gospel is suppressed. The kingdom of God must then wait for another, more noble generation of believers, to press its comprehensive authority over the world.

This book is offered in the hope that this generation of believers will rise to that call. Or if it is too late for this generation, may we instill in our children a vision for what we have failed to do. Then the next generation might emerge from the rubble of a failed humanist culture and begin the task of rebuilding.

My prayer is that my friend and other Christian leaders like him might expand their spiritual vision. I pray they might be endowed with eyes to see that "scoring points" in the kingdom of God is not simply getting more conversions across the goal line—getting them out of the world and into the Church. Instead, may they begin to equip their converts with a comprehensive biblical view of life. This worldview includes bringing every sphere of life, including the political, under the authority of Christ.

My friend is absolutely right about one thing. When it comes to civil government, American Christians clearly have a major remodeling job on their hands. The problem stems from barely discernible cracks allowed to exist at the time the foundation—the Constitution—was laid. Over time these cracks have opened wide to threaten the entire edifice.

Part I: Cracks in the Foundation is a structural analysis. Chapter 1 inspects some of the stunning architectural features of the U.S. Constitution. These include its elegant division of powers, its elaborate republican form, and its intricate system of limited, delegated powers.

Chapters 2 and 3 move in for a closer look at some of the critical flaws in the foundation. Chapter 2 examines faults in the original document—the religious exclusions—which amount to a repudiation of the national covenant with God. Chapter 3 scrutinizes subsequent breaches that developed as a result of ill-advised amendments and Supreme Court rulings.

Chapters 4 and 5 are historical. Chapter 4 highlights major developments between the Puritan settlement and the convention in Philadelphia. It examines some of the key departures from Reformation thought leading up to the founding era.

Part II: The Collapsing Superstructure opens with a panoramic view. Chapter 5 touches briefly on the Civil War and public education, two nineteenth century phenomena which more than anything else have given shape to modern America. Finally it transports us to the present, showing how chaos in the courts has led to chaos in the culture. The superstructure is now teetering on the verge of collapse because the spiritual and legal underpinning has failed.

Chapter 6 examines some of the philosophical tools or blueprints American Christians have brought to the task of remodeling. These include conservatism, traditional values, pluralism, and natural law, among others. Since none has been adequate for the job, we must look for a higher standard.

Part III offers God's Blueprint for Civil Government. Chapter 7 holds forth the Word of God as the only adequate rule for civil government. Chapter 8 lays out the form of biblical civil government, which might be compared to the carpenter's "blueprints." The detailed "specifications" of the plan are spelled out in chapter 9: "The Function of Biblical Civil Government."

Biblical principles of political action are outlined in Part IV: Rebuilding by the Blueprint. These include an overall strategy in chapter 10 and specific details for electoral politics and lobbying, which are based on the author's own experiences in Oregon, in chapter 11. Our ability to work effectively in the civil arena is greatly influenced by our expectation of victory. If we do not believe we can win, we will not. Consequently, chapter 12 develops the glorious meaning of the phrase "King of kings and Lord of lords."

Each chapter concludes with a review quiz, discussion guide, and answer key. These are designed to complete the integration of the material in both an individual and group context.

PART I
Cracks in the Foundation

The Constitution is, of course, the political foundation on which the civil government of the United States of America rests. It is the underpinning on which our society has been constructed. Under the Constitution Americans have enjoyed one of the longest periods of political freedom in the history of the world.

Many glowing accolades have been used to describe the United States Constitution. J. Edgar Hoover portrayed it as "rooted in wisdom, in common sense, and in stern practicality . . . our most priceless inheritance—our bulwark against encroaching tyranny . . . strong, durable, marvelously workable."[1] Some have even gone so far as to describe the Constitution as possessing the marks of divine inspiration[2] or "that Divinely-inspired constitutional document."[3]

The republican government hammered out in the heat of the 1787 summer was in many respects the result of trial and error. The new nation had very nearly floundered in its experimentation with the two extremes in civil government—democracy and monarchy.

During much of the Revolutionary period from 1776 to 1787, the thirteen colonies were governed under the Articles of Confederation. In their attempt to institutionalize the ideals of Jeffersonian democracy, the Articles lacked the necessary authority to effectively govern the nation.

There was, for example, no executive branch under the Articles of Confederation. Furthermore, the absence of a taxing power meant that General George Washington was constantly plagued with shortages of supplies and payroll for the Continental Army. These hindrances to Washington's ability to field an effective fighting force almost cost the colonies the war.

Lack of an honest, uniform currency permitted many of the colonies to flood their economies with unbacked paper money. Inflation was rampant. At one point, the Continental dollar was redeemable at only a hundredth of its face value which led to popularization of the phrase, "not worth a Continental."

To make matters worse, the colonies bickered constantly and erected trade barriers and tariffs, which further aggravated prices. It was this perilous state of confusion and anarchy that led to the cry for revision of the Articles of Confederation in 1787.

On the other hand, the colonies were extremely wary of any centralization of power at the national level. The hazards of weakness in the Articles were obvious. However, they had just emerged after seven long, bloody years from the tyranny of an abusive monarchy. Consequently, they were very jealous of their newly won freedom and extremely hesitant to surrender any of it to a central government.

The challenge was to strike a balance that would preserve state sovereignty, yet grant adequate power at the federal level to permit unified and coordinated action. Of infinitely greater importance was the manner in which the new nation would define its relationship to Jesus Christ—the King of kings. Delegates to the Constitutional Convention met in Philadelphia in 1787 to address these issues. Part I is an analysis of their achievement.

1

The Promise of the Constitution

*T*he promise of the United States Constitution lies in the extent to which it embraces biblical principles of civil government. The Constitution has been admired—and rightly so—for the functionality of its basic doctrinal structure, and some have attributed this to striking parallels with Scripture at key points. We turn our attention first to an examination of these fundamental points of doctrine.

In developing this doctrine, we will assume for the moment that the entire Bible, Old and New Testaments, contains directives for civil government today. This assumption is based on St. Paul's general teaching "that all Scripture . . . is profitable for doctrine, for reproof, for correction, for instruction in righteousness" (2 Tim. 3:16). Chapter 7, "The Foundation of Political Righteousness," elaborates on the question of the abiding relevance of the Old Testament for political righteousness in the present age.

Division of Powers

An important safeguard to ensure that government does not overstep its power is the principle of division of powers. The need for this safeguard lies in the corruptibility of the human heart.

The basis for God's establishing civil government was the evil tendency of human nature to degenerate into total anarchy if left unchecked. The biblical commentary on the condition of the human race prior to the flood is not complimentary. "The Lord saw that the wickedness of man was great in the earth, and that every imagination of the thoughts of his heart was only evil continually" (Gen. 6:5, RSV; see also Judg. 17:6; 21:25).

This depravity led to the judgment and destruction of the human race in the worldwide flood recorded in Genesis. Only Noah and his family were preserved as a righteous remnant in the ark. Following the flood, God established the institution of civil government to hold man's evil nature in check and avoid the necessity of future violent judgment.

One writer observes that,

> The conditions of violence and corruption that occasioned the flood manifested that a new world order was necessary if the human race was to continue and not perish in moral decay . . . . By inaugurating a new one, God recognized the incorrigible sinfulness of the heart of man, and by covenant with the sinful race, He established a stronger basis for social control. If sin's violence to man cannot be kept in check by voluntary controls, then God in His grace would control it by coercive means . . . . The violent tendencies of men would now be put under such restraint that they would never again get so far out of hand.[1]

In establishing civil government, God granted authority to civil officers to punish wrongdoing with appropriate punishment, most notably the death penalty for murder (see Gen. 9:6). The Noahic Covenant, which contained these provisions, was to extend to all generations (Gen. 9: 6, 12, and 13): "Whoso sheddeth man's blood, by man shall his blood be shed. . . . This is the token of the covenant . . . for perpetual generations: I do set my bow in the clouds . . . ."

The granting of such power, however, created the potential for another problem—the abuse of power by civil government. The reality of this problem is clearly acknowledged in Scripture. In fact, the Bible likens the unrestrained power of civil government to that of the brute beasts.

The prophet Daniel was shown that four great world empires would precede the coming of the Redeemer. They were Babylon the lion, Media-Persia the bear, Greece the leopard, and Rome the indescribable beast (see Dan. 7). As wild beasts, unrestrained governments trample on men and their efforts to exercise dominion over the earth under God (see Gen. 1:28). They choose instead to exercise an unlawful dominion over their fellow men.

The beastly image of humanistic civil government is, of course, the divine perspective. From the unregenerate human point of view, civil government is seen as a great statue forged of precious metals. These same four kingdoms appeared in Nebuchadnezzar's dream as a head of gold, breasts of silver, thighs of bronze, and legs of iron (see Dan. 2). It is easy for mankind to overlook the fact that the foundation—the feet—was an unstable mix of iron and clay.

Nonetheless, unregenerate humanity looks to civil government as a great god walking on earth dispensing the blessings of secular salvation. Thus, the tendency is to idolize civil government as the solution to all problems and satisfier of all needs. The testimony of history, as well as Scripture, however, is that this god will turn and devour its subjects if left unshackled.

This has occasioned the concept of "the rule of law, not of men" in Western civilization. A written Constitution based on the Word of God is to check and define the power of the civil magistrate. Deuteronomy 17:18ff (RSV) indicates that the kings of Israel were to be thus restrained:

> And when he sits on the throne of his kingdom, he shall write for himself in a book a copy of this law, from that which is in charge of the Levitical priests; and it shall be with him, and he shall read in it all the days of his life, that he may learn to fear the LORD his God, by keeping all the words of this law and these statutes, and doing them; that his heart may not be lifted up above his brethren, and that he may not turn aside from the commandment, either to the right hand or to the left; so that he may continue long in his kingdom . . . .

The king himself was to be governed and restrained by the revelation of God. Although the U.S. Constitution does not appeal directly to Scripture, it was nonetheless an effort to confine the power of government within a fence of law. However, as we shall see in chapter 2, to achieve this daunting task apart from submission to the Law of God is ultimately impossible.

Another verse that seems to bear on the issue of division of powers is Isaiah 33:22. Here we read that all three of the functions of government are united in the Godhead. These include the establishment or codification of law, the enforcement or administration of law, and the interpretation or application of the law to specific cases: "The Lord is our judge, the Lord is our lawgiver, the Lord is our king: he will save us."

We can infer that any attempt on the part of civil government to unify all of these functions is an attempt to imitate the power of God. God generally frustrates the unity of these and other powers by vesting them in more than a single individual or institution. This is to thwart the constant human striving to "be like God." A case in point was His confusing of tongues and scattering the idolaters at the Tower of Babel. And as we shall see in chapter 8, the representatives of the people in the Old Testament economy were generally distinct from the executive/judicial leadership.

Constitution's Conformity to Biblical Model

The U.S. Constitution employs a similar division of powers. Separation of power is a constitutional device intended to check the tendency of government to go beyond its delegated functions. Under the Constitution, all legislative power was granted to the legislature, all executive power was granted to the executive, and all judicial power was granted to the judiciary. The three branches were to function as a kind of check and balance, each restraining abuses of the others.

Montesquieu was a primary authority to which the founding fathers adhered at this point. The French political philosopher had written: "When the legislative and executive powers are united in the same person, or in the same body of magistrates, there can be no liberty . . . lest the same monarch or senate should enact tyrannical laws, to execute them in a tyrannical manner."[2]

LIMITED, DELEGATED POWERS

In addition to division of powers, another way to prevent abuse of authority is to limit the power of government. There are many ways in which this power may be limited.

In the modern world, when people hear the word "government," they have been trained to think automatically of civil government.

They have been conditioned to think in terms of the power state as the reference point for all of life. In stark contrast, Scripture speaks of many governments regulating human society. Primary among these are church, family, and individual government. Each of these is granted certain powers to govern within its sphere of activity which must not be usurped by the civil magistrate.

At the heart of biblical society is the self-governed individual who is being trained by God to discipline himself morally in accordance with Scripture. The external pronouncements of government reinforce this moral discipline. But ultimately the power of government is limited by the commitment of the individual to obey the law.

Government is also limited in that it must not legislate in areas where the Word of God provides no example of legislation. There is a distinction between crime and sin. Not all sin is crime, to be punished by the state. Hence, the failure of Prohibition, which was the Eighteenth Amendment to the Constitution. Temperance is a matter of personal, not public morality.

However, the ruler must legislate morality. If he does not legislate morality, there is only one other choice: He will legislate immorality. There is no neutrality because any law passed will either conform or not conform to the Law of God.

Jesus said, "He that is not with me is against me" (Matt. 12:30). There is no middle ground; neutrality is a myth. In other words, somebody's morality is going to be legislated because a moral code in one form or another rests at the heart of every system of law. A law is nothing more than a codification of a religious principle. For example, the Sixth Commandment, "Thou shalt not kill," underlies civil law against murder. Consequently, the biblical ruler must confine and conform his legislation to the moral requirements of Scripture.

It should be noted in passing that the legislation of morality does not supply the power to practice morality to individual citizens. It simply sets the standard. Obedience to the law requires strength of character in the lives of officials and citizens.

It is clear in Scripture that God has assigned only certain responsibilities to government, those related to defense and justice. The judicial function of government is clearly seen in Exodus 18, where Moses sat in judgment over Israel. In the New Testament, Romans 13:3–4 highlights the enforcement function of government, ". . . For rulers are not a terror to good works, but to evil . . . for he beareth not the sword in vain." Civil government is not free to legislate in whatever areas it sovereignly chooses. We shall see more on the function of civil government in chapter 9.

Another passage that appears to limit the power of government is Matthew 22:21. Jesus exhorted His disciples to "render unto Caesar that which is Caesar's and unto God that which is God's" (RSV). One implication of this statement is that the power of the government is limited and that it is to receive authority and resources only to function in its legitimate areas of jurisdiction.

In all these ways the legislative power of government is limited by God. Perhaps it would be more appropriate to refer to legislators as "law finders" rather than "law makers." This would signify that their primary task is to search the Word of God for divine law on which to model the laws of the nation.

Constitution's Conformity to Biblical Model

The U.S. Constitution incorporated the principle of limited, delegated power in Article I, Section 8 where it defined the powers of Congress. Congress was limited only to those sixteen functions specified in Section 8. These include among others the power to regulate commerce, coin money, declare war, grant copyrights, and regulate the land and naval forces.

The Tenth Amendment reinforces the fact that the Constitution was not an unlimited grant of power to the federal government. It states that "The powers not delegated to the United States by the Constitution, nor prohibited by it to the States, are reserved to the States respectively or to the people."

Thus, the power of the federal government is limited and originates with the states, which created the central government in the first place. Historian Robert Weaver explains that "Both the people and the States were so fearful that the Federal government might try to seize more powers by usurpation that this amendment was adopted to help prevent such violation of the Constitution. . . ."[3]

The preamble of the Constitution summarizes the legitimate functions of the federal government and introduces the purposes of the document. Notice that these are limited to defense-related functions and those that will promote the good of the nation as a whole. They do not include the authority to make welfare payments to individual citizens.

FEDERALISM

At one time or another, you have probably heard a fellow believer make a statement something like this, "There is no biblical form of government. God doesn't really care what form of government a nation chooses, as long as He is glorified." The assumption is that God has nothing definitive to say on the question of civil government. It is a secular realm, beyond the scope of religious concern. It is presumed that with respect to civil government there are few, if any, absolutes.

If one points to the Old Testament as a biblical paradigm for civil government, he is glibly informed that "a theocracy is a government in which God rules directly over a people." No further discussion, since this is obviously an impossibility today. Case closed.

But the persistent enquirer may be wondering to himself: "Exactly how did God rule His people in the Old Testament? Did the Hebrew state employ principles of government that might profitably be emulated by civil government today?" In short, is the government of Israel under Moses a God-given prototype for civil government in all ages?

A glance beneath the surface reveals that the Mosaic economy was much more than a sort of divine "benevolent dictatorship" with God at the top and Moses a notch or so lower barking out the divine dictates.

To be sure, Moses originally attempted to put this concept into practice. Exodus 18 reveals how the people stood about Moses from morning till evening to inquire of God. Moses wore himself out trying to run the entire nation from a position of central authority.

When Jethro, his father-in-law, took stock of the situation, he immediately advised Moses to decentralize—to divide the responsibility up among rulers of thousands, hundreds, fifties, and tens within the twelve tribes and to let them handle the easier cases. Thus, power is divided vertically as well as horizontally (legislature, executive, judiciary).

Constitution's Conformity to Biblical Model

This principle is seen in the federal—or two-level form—of the American system. This form is best suited for meeting the security needs of a number of small independent states through a strong, but limited central government. It allows simultaneously for local self-government and attention to local needs. Thus, Alexander Hamilton could write: "The proposed Constitution, so far from implying an abolition of the State governments, makes them constituent parts of the national sovereignty, by allowing them a direct representation in the Senate, and leaves in their possession certain exclusive and very important portions of sovereign power."[4]

Under the federal model, the smaller governmental bodies unite and establish a central government with limited, delegated powers. The federal government is a creature of the states and is to remain under their ultimate control, rather than vice versa. When power becomes centralized at the federal level, tyranny and gross inefficiency are not far behind (see chapter 9).

Thus, the thirteen colonies united to establish a dual level of government, republican in form at both state and national echelons. The states as institutional entities maintained direct control of the federal government via their senatorial agents, senators being elected originally by the state legislatures.

Under this system, any number of smaller states may unite to offset certain vulnerabilities they possess because of their size. This may include such things as defense or hindrances to trade that may exist among them or the lack of a uniform medium of exchange. They delegate to the central government specified, limited powers to accomplish these functions, while retaining all other local powers and responsibilities that were better handled on a local level.

REPUBLICAN FORM

The manner in which Moses selected his subordinates sheds further light on the biblical form of government. A very significant detail is added to the story in Deuteronomy 1, which records Moses' farewell sermon to the nation before it entered the promised land. In recounting the Jethro episode, Moses reveals that the people themselves were permitted to select their leaders: "Choose wise, understanding, and experienced men, according to your tribes, and I will appoint them as your heads" (v. 13, RSV). The nominated leaders were then brought to Moses for approval and formal installation at a type of swearing-in ceremony.

The Reverend Thomas Hooker picked up on this idea in one of his election day sermons in colonial Connecticut. He said, "The choice of public magistrates belongs unto the people by God's own allowance."

Shortly thereafter, the freemen of Connecticut adopted a written constitution embodying Hooker's ideal. It was entitled the "Fundamental Orders of Connecticut," which according to Verna Hall became a major prototype for the United States Constitution: ". . . it marked the beginnings of American democracy, of which Thomas Hooker deserves more than any other man to be called the father. The government of the United States today is in lineal descent more nearly related to that of Connecticut than to that of any of the other thirteen colonies. . . ."[5]

Similarly, in the New Testament, church members nominate church officers, who are then vested with authority by the current, sitting officers. In Acts 6:3 (RSV), Peter instructed the congregation to "pick out from among you seven men of good repute, full of the Spirit and of wisdom, whom we may appoint to this duty." A similar protocol was employed for the choice of an elder/apostle to replace Judas in Acts 1:15–23.

In the Bible, qualified civil leadership was identified among the people by the people and selected according to the free suffrages of the people in the sovereignty of God. Jephthah, for example, was recruited for leadership by the people and formally installed by them (see Judg. 11:8–11). Both Kings David and Saul were first anointed by God, but not formally installed as King until the hearts of the people were prepared to accept them. Even God accommodated Himself to the children of Israel and would not impose His Kingship upon them apart from their formal covenantal acceptance of Him.

The general idea is that people will not have deserved confidence in their leaders unless they themselves have selected them. The candidate's intimate associates are the best judge of his character and other qualifications for public office. According to E.C. Wines, "the people, therefore, though in the mass incapable of administration of government, are nevertheless, capable of calling others to this office."[6]

This procedure is the essence of the governmental form today known as "republican," and the vast difference between a republic and a democracy has been lost to most Americans. Most would be shocked to hear that the Constitution did not establish a democracy. Most American Christians would be just as shocked to hear that the concept of democracy is totally alien to the Bible. In a democracy the will of the people is supreme, but in a republic the people choose their governmental representatives, who are then responsible to govern according to God's Word, not primarily according to the will of the people.

Constitution's Conformity to Biblical Model

The U.S. Constitution follows the pattern of the republican form that we have seen modeled in Scripture. The word "democracy" is not mentioned in the Constitution. Rather, each state is guaranteed a republican form of government (see U.S. Constitution 4–4–1). Representatives to the national government are elected by the people to conduct the affairs of state (see 1–2–1). As in Scripture, the primary purpose of constitutional government is defense of its citizens (see 1–8–1ff) and maintenance of justice.

James Madison, the primary intellectual force behind the Constitution, described the republican model in these words in *Federalist #39:* "It is sufficient for such a government that the persons administering it be appointed either directly or indirectly, by the people."[7]

The people's representatives govern in accordance with the written Constitution (see 6–1–2), not primarily the will of their constituents: "This Constitution, and the Laws of the United States which shall be made in Pursuance thereof, and all Treaties made . . . shall be the supreme Law of the Land; and the judges in every State shall be bound thereby . . . ."

This principle is good as far as it goes, but it does not go high enough. As we shall see in the next chapter, the Constitution fails to allow for the supremacy of "the Law above the law"—the commandment of God.

CONCLUSION

We have observed some remarkable parallels between the governmental structure outlined in the U.S. Constitution and that of the Bible. These include federalism, the division of powers, the republican form, and limited delegated power.

It is difficult to determine the extent to which these principles were drawn self-consciously from the Bible by the founders. The *Federalist Papers* are perhaps the best indication of what they were thinking. These were originally a series of newspaper editorials written by James Madison, Alexander Hamilton, and John Jay to promote the Constitution in the colonies. They are widely acknowledged as one of the best sources available on the true intent of the founders. Notes from the Convention were not available in 1787 because the founders had sworn themselves to secrecy. Thus, the *Federalist Papers* contain the arguments by which they justified themselves to the world of that day.

The authors of the *Federalist Papers* are clearly not reasoning self-consciously from Scripture in the derivation of their governmental formulations. The *Federalist Papers* contain no references to Scripture. By way of contrast, there are at least 28 references to the governments of ancient Greece and Rome. Furthermore, the writers of the *Federalist* chose the Roman "Publius," rather than a biblical pen name. Christian historian, Gary DeMar observes that "Athens held sway while Jerusalem was forgotten." He then cites Thomas Cuming Hall:

> Indeed, Alexander Hamilton almost goes out of his way to ignore the Old Testament in his recital of the various republics and their history in "The Federalist," and in his list of republics Sparta, Athens, Rome and Carthage . . . are all reviewed; but of Judaism there is no mention. . . . Indeed it is very striking to observe the authorities that have taken the place of Moses and the prophets . . . . The eighteenth-century conception of Greco-Roman Paganism has completely supplanted Puritanic Judaism.[8]

Many of the founders had received—at least in part—a classical education in addition to instruction in the Bible. That admixture of pagan and Christian thought permeated documents such as the *Federalist*. John Adams' diary, for example, records his resolution to "rise with the sun and to study the Scriptures, on Thursday, Friday, Saturday, and Sunday mornings, and to study some Latin author the other 3 mornings."[9]

Nevertheless, it would appear that the backdrop of the Puritan experiment in biblical government a century earlier had an influence, if only subliminal. Moreover, many of the founders, including Madison, had a keen appreciation for the biblical doctrine of "the depravity of man" via the influence of Pastor Jonathan Witherspoon at the College of New Jersey (Princeton). This resulted in the unique restraints on individual power that they built into the Constitution.

Christianity provided the social context and framework in which men of that day existed, and everyday speech was often sprinkled with religious terminology. To the extent that these biblical concepts have been applied to American government, America may be said to have enjoyed freedom and prosperity, if not the full blessing of God.

REVIEW QUIZ

1. Which form of government best describes the U.S. Constitution?
   a. Democracy
   b. Democratic republic
   c. Oligarchy
   d. Republic

2. Federalism means
   a. Strong central government
   b. Multi-level government
   c. Weak central government

3. The title "father of the Constitution" is usually given to
   a. George Washington
   b. Alexander Hamilton
   c. Thomas Hooker
   d. Thomas Jefferson
   e. James Madison

4. Which of these is not a legitimate function of the federal government under the Constitution?
   a. General welfare
   b. Postal service
   c. Social security
   d. Common defense

5. The source of authority in a democracy is
   a. The will of the people
   b. A written constitution
   c. The Word of God
   d. Congress

6. What event initiated the formation of civil government?
   a. Giving of the Law at Mt. Sinai
   b. The call of Abraham
   c. The flood
   d. Tower of Babel

7. Principle of government whose primary purpose is to protect against the depravity of man:
   a. Republican form
   b. Federalism
   c. Division of power
   d. Limited, delegated power

8. Principle of government which makes central government a creature of the states:
   a. Republican form
   b. Federalism
   c. Division of power
   d. Limited, delegated power

9. Principle of government establishing rule via representatives:
   a. Republican form
   b. Federalism
   c. Division of power
   d. Limited, delegated power

10. Principle of government restricting expansion of government:
    a. Republican form
    b. Federalism
    c. Division of power
    d. Limited, delegated power

11. What political philosopher emphasized the importance of the division of powers in civil government?
    a. Montesquieu
    b. John Locke
    c. Plato
    d. Thomas Paine

12. If authoritarianism is on the left extreme of the political spectrum and anarchy is the right extreme, which of these forms of government is on the right?
    a. Communism
    b. Fascism
    c. Monarchy
    d. None of the above

13. Which of these is not an activity for which the Bible requires a specific penal sanction?
    a. Adultery
    b. Consuming alcoholic beverages
    c. Homosexuality
    d. Incorrigibility

14. (T or F) A sin is a crime with a civil penalty attached.

DISCUSSION GUIDE

1. What is the primary purpose of civil government?

2. What are some of the characteristics of the biblical form of civil government?

3. Can you see any similarities between biblical church government and civil government?

4. What are some of the advantages of the biblical form of civil self-government?

5. At what points does the U.S. Constitution coincide with the form for civil government portrayed in Scripture?

6. Is it possible to justify the American concepts of limited, delegated power; separation of power; and the federal (state and national) form of government from Scripture?

7. A Christian friend advises you that there is no special virtue in any of the various forms of government. (e.g. socialism, aristocracy, republic). "If God is honored," socialism is as consistent with Scripture as is the free enterprise system of self-government. How do you respond?

Answer Key

   1) d   2) b   3) e   4) c   5) a   6) c   7) c
   8) b   9) a   10) d 11) a 12) d 13) b 14) F

2

THE PROBLEM WITH THE CONSTITUTION: THE ORIGINAL DOCUMENT

*G*iven the remarkable fidelity to biblical doctrine described in the previous chapter, what possible fault can we find with the United States Constitution? Was it not birthed at a period in our history when Christian influence was much stronger than it is today? Has it not presided over one of the longest and most prosperous eras of human freedom in the history of the world?

In spite of its many admirable qualities, the Constitution represents a sharp break from the Puritan concept that government must rule by divine authority. It introduced to civil government the radical notion of religious neutrality. With the exception of one oblique reference to deity ("Year of Our Lord, 1787") the Constitution leaves God out of the picture entirely.

Thus, the U.S. Constitution represents an attempt by autonomous man to enjoy the blessings of God, apart from God Himself. There is no higher court of appeal beyond the Constitution itself or its official interpreters in the Supreme Court. This is despite the fact that many of the founders were to some degree "Christian" in outlook, if not in fact.

COVENTAL FORERUNNERS

Earlier documents such as the Mayflower Compact and a number of the colonial constitutions were forthright covenants with the Triune

God. For example, the Mayflower Compact, signed by the Pilgrims aboard the *Mayflower* off Cape Cod, begins with the words:

> In ye name of God, Amen. We whose names are underwritten, the loyall subjects of our dred soveraigne Lord, King James, by ye grace of God, of Great Britaine, Franc, and Ireland king, defender of ye faith, &c., haveing undertaken, for ye glorie of God, and advancemente of ye Christian faith . . . doe by these presents solemnly & mutualy in ye presence of God, and one of another, covenant & combine our selves togeather into a civill body politick, for our better ordering & preservation & furtherance of ye ends aforesaid . . . . [1]

God is clearly acknowledged as party to the covenant and His glory is upheld as the primary interest to be protected. Noted Constitutional historian E.S. Corwin comments on the Mayflower Compact that "Whereas with Locke the ultimate basis of authority is supplied by natural law, here it is supplied by God."[2] Likewise, the *Preamble to the Fundamental Orders of Connecticut* contains these words:

> . . . where a people are gathered together the word of God requires that to maintain the peace and union of such people there should be an orderly and decent government established according to God, to order and dispose of the affairs of the people . . . enter into combination and confederation together, to maintain and preserve the liberty and purity of the gospel of our Lord Jesus which we do profess. . . . [3]

Notice that the authority is the Word of God and that maintenance of the purity and peace of the gospel is the main concern. In like manner, the Magna Carta, the great charter of English liberty, opens with these words:

> Know ye, that we, in the presence of God, and for the salvation of our souls, and the souls of all our ancestors and heirs, and unto the honor of God and the advancement of Holy Church, and amendment of our Realm . . .

have, in the first place, granted to God, and by this our present Charter confirmed, for us and our heirs for ever.[4]

God is here acknowledged as the supreme Partner in the civil covenant.

The Magna Carta was also a good example of the biblical doctrine of interposition (see chapter 8). In 1215 the English barons led a bloodless revolt against the tyrannical and licentious King John. In the meadow of Runnymeade they forced him to sign the Great Charter, defining and limiting the power of civil government.[5]

All of these documents recognized the futility of attempting to erect a civil edifice apart from God. As Benjamin Franklin observed in his famous speech at the Constitutional Convention, "Except the LORD build the house they labor in vain that build it" (Ps. 127:1). Unfortunately, his co-laborers failed to hearken to his summons for a local clergyman to bless the daily proceedings of the convention. In the Franklin manuscript the following note is added: "The Convention, except three or four persons, thought Prayers unnecessary."[6]

CONSTITUTION ABANDONS COVENANT

In contrast to its predecessors, the U.S. Constitution is a secular document with no substantive reference to the God of Scripture. The opening words identify the sovereign covenanting authority: *"We the people* of the United States . . . *do ordain* and establish this Constitution" (emphasis added).

There is no reference to God, His glory, or the authority of His revealed Word. *The people are the focal point,* the locus of authority, and the sovereign grantors of power. Intentional or not, this is undiluted humanism, albeit conservative humanism. Man is the measure.

In effect, this was an attempt to establish a religiously neutral civil government. This attempt was perhaps not self-conscious, but the outcome has nonetheless been the same: political and cultural disaster.

The American Constitution is to civil government what a common law/justice of the peace marriage is to a family. A couple married by a justice of the peace have no higher authority than the state to sanction and bless their union. By contrast, a couple married in a "church wedding" invoke God as the Lord of their union and appeal to His blessing upon it. Under the Constitution, the American people have no higher authority than the state to sanction and bless their union.

The rationalizations offered for this obvious neglect are myriad, but trivial. The usual excuses are to the effect that the various Protestant denominations were jealous of each other and that possibly one or the other would be established as the official state religion. Therefore, the convention left religious matters to be handled by the states.

For example, John Eidsmoe explains, "There was general agreement that the federal government would not establish any one of those state churches as the new federal church thereby creating resentment among the others, or interfere with any of the state establishments. A religious reference could have created divisions."[7]

The problem is that there is no neutrality with God. Jesus said that "he who is not with me is against me, and he who does not gather with me scatters" (Matt. 12:30, RSV). The founders were correct in refusing to establish a particular denomination at the federal level. However, they were not correct in using this as a pretext to evade the covenant responsibilities of the national government to God. By transferring this central issue to the states and refusing to deal with it, the federal government was in effect revoking the national covenant with God—which had been sworn before God years earlier on the *Mayflower* and renewed in many of the colonial constitutions.

On the face of it, the Constitution is a pure expression of the social compact. Following in the footsteps of Locke, Reverend John Witherspoon described the social compact as "an association or compact of any number of persons, to deliver up or abridge some part of their natural rights, in order to have the strength of the united body, protect the remaining, and to bestow others." In Witherspoon's *Lectures on Moral Philosophy,* editor Jack Scott notes, "The central tenet of Witherspoon's political philosophy in common with those of other American revolutionists was the theory of the social contract."[8]

Madison and many others of the founding generation were disciples of Witherspoon, president of the College of New Jersey (Princeton). Witherspoon looked to "sturdy common sense," rather than biblical law as his source of authority in the civil sphere. His rationalistic approach to Scripture as it speaks to the civil magistrate is abundantly evident from his *Lectures on Moral Philosophy,* which were prepared for the senior class at Princeton and considered the culminating course of the college curriculum. They are based far more heavily on human reason and speculation than on biblical exegisis. Madison drank deeply at this well.

Because they do not understand God's covenant dealings with mankind, most Christian writers speak approvingly of the social contract, or else they gloss over it. Some will state in passing that it is simply a secularized version of the covenant as though this was of no consequence. However, this theory is in direct contrast to the biblical covenental model, which invokes God as the primary participant and involves a direct appeal to His law as the standard and source of authority. The Constitution has none of this. It is "We the People"— not God—ordaining "this Constitution for ourselves and our posterity" and there is no reference at all to His law.

Some have excused this on the grounds that the civil authority of God was assumed by nearly all of the leaders of this country in the eighteenth century. Actually, that is the crux of the problem. We assume that they assumed this based on a profusion of religious language and fail to deal with the precise nature of what they actually produced; i.e. a Lockean social contract in all its particulars that overtly excluded the authority of God over the state. This may not have been self-conscious on the part of the founders: they may not have understood the extent to which they were departing from the biblical, covenantal model that was embodied in many of the colonial constitutions.

However, it is entirely possible to enter into or renew a civil covenant with God without establishing a state church. Under the biblical doctrine of separation of church and state both institutions are independent of each other, but equally responsible to God and His Word (see chapter 10). A correct understanding of this doctrine would preclude the establishment and financial support of a particular denomination by the government. It was just as improper for the colonies to adopt this practice as it would have been for the federal government.

However well meaning or ignorant of this principle the founders may have been, it has proven to be a fatal error. God will not be ignored. A nation rejects or neglects God and His Word at its own peril. The founding generation may have assumed the presence of God in the national charter, but subsequent generations obviously have not.

The *Federalist Papers* are generally regarded to be the most authoritative commentary on the Constitution and the intent of the founders. They reveal that Madison and Hamilton were extremely concerned about the leavening influence of "faction." Madison in particular was concerned with the tendency of factions to be "actuated by some common impulse of passion, or of interest, adverse to the rights of other citizens . . ." *(Federalist #10)*. This is a legitimate concern.

But Madison saw faction emanating from a variety of sources, not the least of which was religion: "The *latent causes of faction* are thus sown in the nature of man . . . a zeal for different opinions concerning *religion,* concerning government, and many other points . . . " [emphasis added]. Rather than providing the glue which binds a Christian society together, Madison regarded religion as a divisive and impotent force for social cohesion: " . . . we well know," he said, "that *neither moral nor religious motives* can be relied on as an adequate control [for faction]" (emphasis added). [9]

We also find this in sources other than the *Federalist*. For example, in "Madison's Detached Memoranda" in the 1946 *William and Mary Quarterly* (third quarter), Elizabeth Fleet notes Madison's concerns about "the danger of silent accumulations & encroachments by Ecclesiastical Bodies" and "the danger of a direct mixture of Religion & civil Government." He also lamented, "The establishment of the chaplainship to Congress is a palpable violation of equal rights, as well as of Constitutional principles."

The First Amendment, as well as his earlier "Memorial and Remonstrance" in Virginia, makes it clear that Madison believed government should keep its hands off the church. But he also believed that religion should reciprocate and have little if any influence on civil government. He was committed to the ideal of a secular republic and a strict separation of church and state.

In the place of religion, Madison exalted the republican model as the remedy which "promises the cure for which we are seeking" *(Federalist #10)*. This is a form of idolatry: exalting the design—however excellent—above the Designer, the creature above the Creator (see Rom. 1:25). This would be similar to the Jews rejecting God, while clinging to and relying on the beautifully designed temple and external form of temple worship (see Jer. 7:4–5).

When men reject self-government under God they become slaves. It was not necessarily wrong for the Israelites to ask for a king, for a constitutional monarchy or kingship subject to the law of God (see Deut. 17:18–20) was typologically interwoven with the destiny of Israel. The kings of Israel, David in particular, were used as illustrations of the great King—the Messiah—who would one day deliver the people from their transgressions.

However, their attitude was one of rejecting God as God and establishing civil government in His place—as ultimate source of authority, power, security, and provision. They wanted a king to govern them *like all the nations,* not a king to govern according to God's law (see 1 Sam. 8:5). Samuel warned them that this action would lead to their enslavement. They were being conformed to the world, rather than providing a model to which the world would be attracted:

> Keep them and do them; for that will be your wisdom and your understanding in the sight of the peoples, who, when they hear all these statutes, will say, "Surely this great nation is a wise and understanding people" . . . And what great nation is there, that has statutes and ordinances so righteous as all this law which I set before you this day? (Deut. 4:6–8, RSV)

This passage demonstrates the power of God's law as an evangelistic tool when properly administered by godly civil government. The nations around Israel would be attracted by the justness of God's laws and yield their allegiance to Him.

Just as it was not wrong for the Israelites to ask for a king, it was not wrong for the founders to ask for a republic. However, it was just as devastating for the founders to reject the civil authority of God as it was for the children of Israel (see chapter 5).

In summary, we note that among other things, two key elements of any covenant, are specification of the parties to the covenant and the details of administration. First, as we have seen, if a national organic document is in fact a covenant with God, then it must state this clearly in the preamble. A covenant, as opposed to a contract, includes God as party to the agreement.

Second, there must be a delineation of how the covenant is to be administered. If a covenant is made with God, then it must spell out the nature of the authority to whom God has delegated administration of the covenant. Who represents the people before God? If these two elements are missing, it is impossible to claim that the document represents a covenant with God. In fact, if these elements are absent or distorted, it is possible to argue that the document represents a national break from covenant with God, since this covenant had been established earlier in the Mayflower Compact and the various colonial charters.

We have seen how the Constitution broke with the legacy of earlier civil covenants that were very forthright in their reference to God as the primary Party to the covenant. Next we will examine the issue of delegated authority.

THE BIBLICAL RELIGIOUS TEST

In the Bible God specifies the qualifications of the men to whom He delegates civil authority. The qualifications for public office delineated by the Old Testament were fear of God, ability as evidenced by success in other spheres of leadership, and demonstrated character able to resist pressures (bribes, etc.) to temporize justice. According to Deuteronomy 1:13, judges in particular were to possess wisdom and understanding.

Because successful government moves from the internal to the external through several spheres—self, family, church, civil—we may conclude that the qualifications for success at the inner levels are prerequisites for success in civil leadership. These are detailed as qualifications of elders and deacons in 1 Timothy 3:1–13. They include, among others, commitment to the marriage covenant, temperance, hospitality, gentleness, and dignity.

The civil magistrate is called the "deacon of God" in Romans 13:4. This is one reason why faith was a prerequisite for holding public office in colonial America. Rus Walton notes that "eleven of the first 13 colonies required faith in Jesus Christ and The Bible as basic qualifications for holding public office. In New Hampshire, until 1877, state senators and representatives were required to be of the 'Protestant religion.'"[10] In a sermon delivered at Dedham in 1701, Joseph Belcher insisted, "Piety and the fear of God is the prime and principal qualification in those who sit chief in places of authority."[11]

We have examined the Constitution's adherence to the biblical form in many of its particulars. Among these are the republican model, which is uniquely suited to evaluation of a candidate's religious character traits by the people.

It is impossible, of course, for a government to function in a God-fearing fashion apart from the direction of godly men. Only a people of firm religious character will properly value and tap such men for office. In the Old Testament these characteristics are listed as wisdom, understanding, ability, fear of God, honesty, name recognition, and freedom from covetousness (see Deut. 1:13 and Ex. 18:21).

No system of government—no matter how carefully crafted, no matter how closely patterned after the Word of God—can endure apart from personal purity in the lives of its citizens and its public officials. Only a people whose lives are being molded by the Word of God will produce the quality of leadership that can avoid abuse of governmental power. Thus, true religion is the essential qualification for public office. Apart from the preservative influence of Christianity, government and culture can only deteriorate.

CONSTITUTION ABANDONS RELIGIOUS TEST

The Constitution bluntly rejects this fundamental qualification in Article VI. It states that "no religious Test shall ever be required as a Qualification to any Office or public Trust under the United States." As we have noted, earlier colonial constitutions had required such a test. For example, the Fundamental Orders of Connecticut specified that "the Governor be always a member of some approved congregation . . . ."[12] Likewise, the Massachusetts constitution of 1780 required the following oath: "I _____ , do declare, that I believe the Christian religion, and have firm persuasion of its truth."

We often hear Christians asserting that even though the founders excluded all mention of God from the Constitution, they never intended to separate Christianity and the state. Innumerable Supreme Court briefs, quotes from contemporaries, and legislative pronouncements—spanning one hundred years or more—are cited in support of this assertion. But once again, the only sure source of the founders' intent is the founders themselves, most notably the Father of the Constitution himself, James Madison.

What exactly did the founders mean by "no religious test"? The *Federalist Papers* do not appear to deal directly with this passage in Article VI. However, several references in the *Federalist* indicate that the founders were confused regarding the role of religion and the doctrine of separation of church and state. In *Federalist #57* Madison wrote that "no qualification of wealth, of birth, *of religious faith,* or of civil profession is permitted to fetter the judgment or disappoint the inclination of the people" (emphasis added).

Madison apparently saw faith as somehow blinding the minds (fettering the judgment) of the electorate to more pertinent qualifications for public office. In *Federalist #52* he added that "the door of this part of the federal government [House of Representatives] is open to merit of every description . . . and without regard to poverty or wealth, or to any particular *profession of religious faith"* [emphasis added]. Thus, by his own admission, Madison regarded virtually any qualification except religious faith as requisite for public office.

The key founders were clearly influenced by Christianity. Madison, for example, studied under Reverend John Witherspoon at Princeton, as previously noted. But they apparently believed in a kind of practical, civil religion; this common sense ethic would be inclusive of a fairly broad range of religious faith. Thus, Unitarians Franklin and Jefferson were welcome in the fold.

In addition to Madison, Witherspoon influenced many of the delegates to the Constitutional Convention. He was a Presbyterian minister who gave a big boost to Scottish, common sense rationalism and established it as a credible school of thought within the church. This branch of enlightenment thought advocated a form of common sense politics, not explicitly Christian.[13]

Thus, natural law rules in the public sphere; a common ethic governs all political entities. For example, we seem to find universal laws against murder in all civilized societies.

James Hefley described Madison as one who had attended Princeton and once considered the ministry. However, his commitment to Scripture was problematic: "Though he had been influenced by Voltaire and other European rationalists to believe that the Bible was not divinely inspired, he was assured that a 'high Providence' directed the destinies of nations."[14]

Madison and the Federalists argued in some of the state ratifying conventions that "no religious test" referred simply to a prohibition of one sect's taking precedence over another. Edmund Randolph also expressed this opinion at the Convention in Philadelphia.[15] However, if the text is taken literally it is difficult to escape the implication that the reference is to an individual's qualification for office, such as the requirement of some states that officeholders belong to a Protestant congregation. At the very least, it was an unfortunate and dangerous choice of words, given the familiar use of test oaths by the states and the ease with which the phrase may be extended to religion in general, beyond just demoninational rivalries.

The anti-Federalists certainly believed that it had reference to the undermining of Christian qualification for office. It was fairly obvious from the several colonial constitutions what the phrase was referring to; i.e. a religious qualification for public office. Thus, not just modern pagans have given it that interpretation.

The founders rightly saw the danger of establishing or subsidizing any particular Christian denomination. However, in their zeal to disestablish all denominations at the national level, they also imprudently disestablished religion—and thereby God.

Regardless of what the founders may have meant, latter day heretics have taken their words at face value to reinforce the radical view that Christianity should be excluded from the public square. The seemingly innocuous seeds sown so many years ago by the founding fathers are today bearing a bitter harvest indeed.

For example, Isaac Kramnick, writing for the *New York Times* in an article critical of the "religious right" makes this observation:

> In 1787, when the Framers excluded all mention of God from the Constitution, they were widely denounced as immoral and the document was denounced as godless, which is precisely what it is. Its opponents challenged ratifying conventions in nearly every state, drawing special attention to the stipulation in Article VI, Section 3: "No religious test shall ever be required as a Qualification to any office or public trust under the United States." [16]

He went on to note, "An anti-federalist in North Carolina wrote: 'The exclusion of religious tests is by many thought dangerous and impolitic. . . . Pagans, Deists and Mahometans might obtain office among us.' For another North Carolinian, David Caldwell, the prohibition of religious tests 'constituted an invitation for Jews and Pagans of every kind to come among us.'"[17]

Of course, such statements constitute political heresy for the modern political pluralist. They are the epitome of "political incorrectness."

Authors Frank Rexford and Clara Carson have interpreted this section to mean that "Every official in the United States . . . is on oath to uphold the Constitution. Religion, however, can never have anything to do with the question of eligibility of an officeholder in the United States."[18] This common interpretation means government officials are required to swear allegiance to civil authority, but not to the religious authority of God. This is a key facet of the American civil religion embodied in the secular state. There is therefore no recognized recourse to the court of heaven or the law of God.

PATRICK HENRY'S RESISTANCE

It is rarely mentioned that strong Christian men opposed ratification of the Constitution. Even more rarely mentioned are the reasons for their opposition. Given the desperate position into which we have been driven by the Constitution, it would behoove us to consider the arguments in opposition advanced by such stalwarts of the faith as Patrick Henry.

Patrick Henry was among the most forthright Christian statesmen of the founding era. It may be difficult to criticize the moral fiber of many, if not most of the founders, but it is not difficult to raise questions concerning the essence and depth of their faith. Quotes from the founders on religion and Providence are seemingly endless. Christians thrill to these quotes, but it is rare that the exact nature of their Christianity is examined in detail.

George Washington's Position

Why, for example, did George Washington refuse to take communion for most of his adult life, thereby (in effect) excommunicating himself from the Church of Christ?[19] Why are his public references to the Lord Jesus Christ almost non-existent?[20] Why did Washington aspire and attain to the rank of Grand Master in the Masonic lodge, a lodge in which each promotion requires the applicant to swear to an anti-Christian oath?[21]

When it comes to Washington's religious/philosophical bent, there is simply too much of a mythical or legendary nature to rely on anything other than primary source documents. These would include such things as Washington's own public and private correspondence and the writings of those who knew him extremely well, such as his pastor.

Washington's own pastor during the eight years of his presidency—Dr. James Abercrombie, assistant rector of Christ Church in Philadelphia—had grave doubts about the state of Washington's soul. While his wife went forward to kneel with the communicants on communion Sunday, Washington always walked out the back door. Rebuked indirectly from the pulpit, he acknowledged his offense and promised never to attend church on communion Sunday, a promise that he kept. Dr. Abercrombie left us these words: "That Washington was a professing Christian, is evident from his regular attendance in our church; but, Sir, I cannot consider any man as a real Christian who uniformly disregards an ordinance so solemnly enjoined by the divine Author of our holy religion, and considered as a channel of divine grace."[22]

There is no doubt that Washington thought and spoke highly of Christianity as a socially cohesive force in society. He was convinced of the sovereignty of God in the affairs of men. Further, he strongly encouraged chaplains in the Continental Army and served in a leadership capacity in his local church, attending about once a month. However, we must not confuse "Churchianity" with Christianity. Church attendance for Washington was apparently a social obligation and a means of expressing his humanitarianism.

On the question of Washington's Masonic connections, the only safe ground, once again, are the writings of Washington himself. An oft-repeated statement of Washington from a letter to Reverend G.W. Snyder in 1798, is used to demonstrate his indifference to Masonry: "to correct an error that you have run into, of my presiding over English Lodges in this country. The fact is I preside over none, nor have I been in one more than once or twice within the last thirty years."[23] John Eidsmoe quotes this passage selectively to make it look as if Washington disavowed all Masonic connections: "far from 'Presiding over the English lodges in this country' as Snyder supposed, he had not been in a Masonic lodge 'more than once or twice within the last thirty years.' "[24]

However, J. Hugo Tatsch interpreted that to mean simply that Washington never presided over nor frequented any English lodges in this country, but that this did not exclude the American lodges of which he was an active member. There is too much of a laudatory and sympathetic nature in Washington's private letters to various lodges to deny that he was a lifelong, practicing Mason.

Masonic memorabilia and monuments related to Washington at various sites all over the country are a secondary line of evidence. These might be classified as "archeological" evidence. The Washington monument is, of course, laden with Masonic symbolism.

Some have argued that much of this is from Masonic sources and is therefore unreliable. However, much of what we know about ancient Egypt, for example, is from ancient Egyptian archeological evidence. The Egyptians, of course, worshiped the sun, moon, and various other aspects of the natural world much like the Masons. Do we therefore reject all archeological evidence from the Egyptians?

There are also objective, or at least independent, newspaper accounts testifying to the fact that many of these events in which Washington functioned in his official capacity as a Mason actually occurred. For example, we have a painting of Washington laying the cornerstone of the United States Capital in Masonic garb, as chronicled by the *Columbian Mirror and Alexandria Gazette* of September 25, 1793. This painting was reissued by the White House Historical Association on their *By the People* calendar in 1993, two hundred years after the event.

"Unitarian"—not "deistic"—is perhaps the best way to characterize many of the key founders. While some were members of Trinitarian churches, men like John Adams, Benjamin Franklin, Thomas Jefferson, James Madison, and most likely Washington, were Unitarian in outlook. Unitarianism, or Socianism, is characterized by a denial of the divinity or active lordship of Jesus Christ in the affairs of men.

Patrick Henry's Opposition

Patrick Henry, however, was cut from a different cloth. He was one of the most forthright Christian statesmen of the founding era. Not only did Patrick Henry oppose ratification of the Constitution, he refused the invitation to attend the convention. Why?

Constitutional historian Forrest McDonald makes this observation: "Neither Sam Adams nor John Hancock of Massachusetts nor Richard Henry Lee and Patrick Henry of Virginia chose to come (Henry did not because, he said, 'I smelt a rat'; the others offered no excuses)."[25]

Henry complained of the illegality of the Convention in ignoring the explicit instructions of Congress not to scrap the Articles of Confederation. "The Federal Convention ought to have amended the old system," he protested, "for this purpose they were solely delegated: the object of their mission extended to no other consideration."[26]

Delegate William Paterson of New Jersey had advanced the same objection during the first three weeks of the Convention. "If the confederacy was radically wrong," he argued, "let us return to our states, and obtain larger powers, not assume them of ourselves. . . . If the subsisting confederation is so radically defective as not to admit of amendment, let us say so and report its insufficiency, and wait for enlarged powers."[27] Paterson's plan to correct the weaknesses in the Articles of Confederation was rejected by the Convention after about three weeks.

Further, by calling for independent ratifying conventions in each state the Constitutional Convention bypassed local governmental bodies. In so doing they sidestepped the strong resistance they knew existed in many of the duly constituted state legislatures. The ratification procedure was explicitly illegal because the Articles of Confederation clearly specified that any changes must be approved by Congress and every state legislature (Article XIII).

The delegates had been given writs which authorized their assembly "for the sole and express purpose of revising the Articles of confederation, and reporting to Congress and the several legislatures such alterations. . . ." Article XIII of the Articles forbade that "any alteration at any time hereafter be made in any of them; unless such alteration be agreed to in a Congress of the united states, and be *afterwards confirmed by the legislatures* of every state" (emphasis added). Article VII of the Constitution ignored Congress and the state legislatures, declaring that approval of nine state conventions would abolish the Articles: "The Ratification of the Conventions of nine States, shall be sufficient for the Establishment of this Constitution . . . ."

The states as states were thus completely bypassed in an appeal to "the people"; the state legislatures were excluded from the confirmation process. Were the state legislatures happy about this? Hardly. The procedure specified called for the state legislatures to name the times and places of their corresponding ratifying conventions. Edmund Morgan recounts an instance where nineteen anti-Federalists in the Philadelphia legislature deserted the capitol before the vote. This prevented further business for lack of a quorum. Two of them were located by the sergeant-of-arms and carried forcibly by a mob back to the state house to complete the quorum.[28]

In effect, the procedure chosen amounted to a bloodless coup against the existing order, as some of the anti-Federalist tracts argued. All of the Convention's proceedings were shrouded in secrecy by an oath of silence. The veil of secrecy was not pierced until after the death of the last delegate (Madison) when their notes were finally made public. Looking back from the perspective of two hundred years, Edmund Morgan notes,

> It [ratification] was obtained by the narrowest of margins and by methods that cannot be defended. The prospect was not calculated to please local politicians, and as the convention had anticipated, they were among the loudest objectors to the new plan. Again and again they warned that its adoption would be the death knell not only of the state governments but of the popular liberties which the constitutions of those governments protected.[29]

For twenty-four days in the Virginia ratifying convention, Patrick Henry led the opposition against ratification of the Constitution. According to Long,

> In the Virginia Ratifying Convention in 1788, Patrick Henry protested with vehemence against the proposed new Constitution's lack of sufficient safeguards against governmental abuses due to human weaknesses among its officials, saying: "Show me that age and country where the rights and liberties of the people were placed on the sole chance of their rulers being good men, without a consequent loss of liberty! I say that the loss of that dearest privilege has ever followed, with absolute certainty, every such mad attempt."[30]

He recognized the danger of establishing power—even ostensibly limited power—in the hands of men apart from the possibility of recourse to God and divine law. This is the essence, indeed the very definition, of tyranny: ruling apart from any reference to the law of God.

Hamilton and others downplayed the threat that the new government would not respect the limits placed upon it "as was being asserted by those who were extremely fearful of any central government with substantial powers and were arguing in favor of stricter and clear limits on Federal power. Chief among these were Patrick Henry, Richard Henry Lee and Samuel Adams."[31] The prophetic foresight of these Christian statesmen is all too obvious as we survey the wreckage of the American Republic over two centuries later.

John Eidsmoe calls attention to the fact that "Henry did succeed in persuading the delegates to approve resolutions calling for amendments to the Constitution in the form of a bill of rights. Henry also advised those of his supporters who threatened violence if the Constitution was ratified, to peaceably submit to the new Constitution, and to work for passage of amendments which would safeguard personal liberty."[32]

Unfortunately, even the safeguards of the Bill of Rights, for which Henry so eloquently argued, have been inadequate to overrule the inherent secularism of the body of the Constitution. These bulwarks have failed to withstand the winds of twentieth century skepticism because they are built on a foundation of sand (see Matt. 7:24–27). In the teeth of this intrinsic secularism, modern Christians protest in vain that the First Amendment was never intended to separate God and government.

OTHER PROBLEMS

Treaties Supersede National Sovereignty

Under the Constitution the authority of a treaty passed by two thirds of the Senate takes precedence over state and national laws. According to Hamilton Long, "In the Virginia Ratifying Convention, Patrick Henry voiced the fears of many when he took the position that the language of the Treaty Clause was not sufficiently clear in limiting Federal power with regard to treaties."[33]

Once again the voice of Henry proved to be prophetic. This provision has led on occasion to a compromise of national sovereignty and individual freedom. A good example is the North American Free Trade Agreement, passed in November, 1993. This treaty does violence to the commerce clause of the Constitution by subjecting U.S. environmental and labor regulations to the oversight of regional government.

According to former Congressman Ron Paul, "The commerce clause of our Constitution was intended by the Founders to mandate free trade in the United States, and it worked for more than 100 years. Then it was turned on its head to justify restrictions of trade by the federal government. NAFTA is an extension of that horrible principle."[34]

The commerce clause has also been used to justify other federal mischief. The right to regulate *inter*state commerce was one of the sixteen powers granted Congress to ensure free trade among the states. However, the courts have now extended this power to include *intra*state commerce and production, thus granting the federal government almost unlimited authority over economic activity within the states.

Confusion and Compromise on Slavery

Article 1, Section 2 of the Constitution assumed the ongoing presence of chattel slavery in the newly formed United States. It specified that slaves shall be counted as three fifths of a person for purposes of representation. Slaves were the absolute property of their owners, with none of the rights and protections specified in Scripture.

The slave system remained intact until the War Between the States. In seeking to correct this institution, the Thirteenth Amendment went too far in banning biblical modalities of indentured servitude. We will deal with the subject of private household "slavery" in greater detail in chapter 5 and chapter 9. For now we should note that the Peonage Act, passed subsequent to the Thirteenth Amendment, forbids indentured servitude to the private sector but authorizes it for the state. As W. Cleon Skousen comments:

> Under this amendment the Congress passed the Peonage Act in 1867 under which it has been held unconstitutional for a criminal to have his fine paid by someone with whom he agrees to work until the fine is paid. However, the court has allowed cities and counties to assign prisoners to work out their fines on the roads or elsewhere.[35]

This ruling is patently unbiblical, contradicting the fundamental principle that the convicted lawbreaker is responsible to make restitution to his victim. Ostensibly to promote individual freedom, the state has used this occasion to consolidate its own power.

Judges Appointed for Life

The founders envisioned a weak judiciary, never suspecting the extent to which judicial tyranny would subsequently encroach. James Madison, for example, argued that there was no danger the federal courts would be a threat to states' rights since their power "was small and limited."[36] The constitutional provision that federal judges be appointed for life has only served to exacerbate the problem of judicial activism that has plagued the twentieth century.

CONCLUSION

The United States Constitution breaks with the tradition of previous civil documents that were forthright covenants with the God of the Bible. The Constitution is a secular document, ignoring God and representing therefore a breach in earlier national covenants with Him. Reinforcing the secular nature of the Constitution is its denial of a religious test for office. This was a basic feature of most of the earlier documents and a biblical imperative. These fundamental flaws were recognized by strong Christians of the founding era, mostly anti-Federalists, who strenuously resisted its passage.

It is well known that many of those attending the Constitutional Convention were church members and Christian, at least in the nominal sense. However, because of their failure to reason self-consciously from the Bible, we are forced to conclude that their Christianity was seriously compromised by the natural law humanism of the eighteenth century Enlightenment. Noted social commentator Otto Scott put it this way:

> The United States was a government whose constitution claimed no higher authority than its own laws. That was essentially a lawyer's concept of civilization, and could be traced not to the church, but to Roman tradition.

> The novelty of a nation without an official religion was not fully appreciated in 1830—for no land was as crowded with churches and no people more prone to use religious terminology and Christian references in everyday speech in their writings, and in their thinking, than the Americans. There was no question of the piety of millions. There was equally little doubt that they did not fully realize that a land with no religious center is a land where religion is what anyone chose to claim.

> Far from being the ideal document hailed and heralded in a sea of campaign oratory, the Constitution was a lawyer's contract that claimed no higher law than its managers, who represented themselves as reflecting the will of the people. Since such a will was undefined and undefinable, lawyers made up the rules and procedures of government as they went along, within limits that were often ignored, slyly subverted, or poorly guarded. In effect, the Founders had recklessly placed the government in the position of what ancient Greeks called a "tyrant" which, in its original sense, meant a rule without divine authority.[37]

We gain little by clinging to an interpretation of history that pretends the founders and the document they produced are something other than what they really were. We need to take what is good from the Constitution, admit the problems, and then move forward to correct them. Until we acknowledge the problems, we will never be able to move on to the desperately needed solutions.

In the current political climate, it would be obviously risky to call for a convention to introduce sweeping changes in the Constitution. This is especially true given the precedent of the first Convention in exceeding its legal authority. However, as Christians regain the ascendancy in American political affairs, it will be imperative to amend the Constitution to reaffirm the national covenant with God. God and the authority of His Revelation must be ensconced in the Preamble and the religious test oath must be established once again as the essential qualification for public office.

Review Quiz

1. What is the most prominent feature of the biblical court system?
   a. A bottom-up appeals court system
   b. No *ex post facto* laws
   c. Government by the consent of the governed

2. Which early American patriot opposed ratification of the U.S. Constitution?
   a. Patrick Henry
   b. George Washington
   c. Benjamin Franklin
   d. Thomas Paine

3. Which of these is *not* a problem with the U.S. Constitution?
   a. Social contract theory
   b. No religious test
   c. No *ex post facto* law
   d. Supremacy of treaties

4. Which of these is not an essential ingredient of a covenant?
   a. Specification of parties to the covenant
   b. Legal terms of covenant
   c. Third party witnesses
   d. Specification of hierarchial administration
   e. Disposition in event of death, dissolution, or change
   f. Binding oath

5. Which governmental document did not specify the triune God as a party to the covenant?
   a. The Mayflower Compact
   b. The Virginia Compact
   c. The U.S. Constitution
   d. The Magna Carta

6. What school of theology best characterizes many of the key
   founders?
   a. Presbyterian
   b. Unitarian
   c. Deist

DISCUSSION GUIDE

1. Were the founding fathers justified in ignoring their commission
   from the Continental Congress to simply revise the Articles of
   Confederation? Explain your answer.

2. Were the founding fathers justified in the procedure they specified
   for ratification of the Constitution? Explain your answer.

3. At what points does the main body of the U.S. Constitution depart
   from Scripture?

4. How does a nation reject God from ruling over them?
   (see 1 Sam. 8)

5. How would you describe the religious faith and philosophical worldview of the key founders of the U.S. Constitution? How did these factors affect the document that they produced?

6. In what ways did earlier national covenants acknowledge God? What happens when God is excluded from a nation's founding covenant?

7. What are some of the biblical qualifications for public office?

Answer Key
  1) a   2) a   3) c   4) c   5) c   6) b

3

The Problem with the Constitution: Amendments and Judicial Misinterpretations

*S*omeone has observed that perhaps no other piece of human literature has been more praised and less practiced than the U.S. Constitution. At many points subsequent officials have proceeded directly contrary to the clearly stated intent of the founders. In so doing, they have reversed the fundamental principle of the "rule of law, not of men."

In their rejection of God, modern leaders have found it expedient to reject the Constitution at those points where it has reflected the biblical model (see chapter 1). Over a long period of time, statutes, amendments, and Supreme Court rulings have virtually reversed most of the major doctrines of the U.S. Constitution. This has been in direct opposition to the clearly stated intent of the founders spelled out in the *Federalist Papers*.

THE "ELASTIC CLAUSE"

The Tenth Amendment reinforces the fact that the Constitution was not an unlimited grant of power to the federal government. It states that "The powers not delegated to the United States by the Constitution, nor prohibited by it to the States, are reserved to the States respectively, or to the people."

Unfortunately, some have taken the last paragraph of Article I,

Section 8 to authorize just such a grant. The so-called elastic clause grants Congress power: "To make all laws which shall be necessary and proper for carrying into execution the foregoing powers, and all other powers vested by this Constitution in the government of the United States, or in any Department or officer thereof."

This clause has been interpreted to mean that the federal government may appropriate power to do almost anything it desires. This misinterpretation has paved the way for the expansion of the welfare state in twentieth century America. For example, a modern General Education Degree (GED) prep book uses the word "enumerated" rather than "delegated" to describe the sixteen powers of Congress, then states that the elastic clause grants other powers not enumerated or listed:

> These powers are called enumerated powers because they are listed in Article One of the U.S. Constitution. In addition to enumerated powers, the Constitution provides for powers that are not listed. The elastic clause enables the legislative branch to stretch its authority to meet the needs of specific situations that the Founding Fathers could not foresee.[1]

This is clearly a novel interpretation, in direct conflict with the intent elucidated by the founders in the *Federalist Papers*. The *Federalist Papers* were written originally as anonymous editorials to persuade the thirteen colonies to ratify the Constitution. James Madison, the principle architect of the Constitution, explained his true intent in *Federalist #41*:

> It has been urged and echoed that the power "to lay and collect taxes . . . and provide for the common defense and general welfare of the United States," amounts to an unlimited commission to exercise every power which may be alleged to be necessary for the common defense or general welfare . . . .

> Had no other enumeration or definition of the powers of the Congress been found in the Constitution than the general expressions just cited, the authors of the objection

44

> might have had some color for it; . . . but what color can
> the objection have, when a specification of the objects
> alluded to by these general terms immediately follows and
> is not even separated by a longer pause than a semicolon?
> . . . For what purpose could the enumeration of particular
> powers be inserted, if these and all others were meant to
> be included in the preceding general power? Nothing is
> more natural nor common than first to use a general
> phrase, and then to explain and qualify it by a recital of
> particulars.[2]

In other words, Madison and the founders clearly spelled out what specific, delegated powers they meant to be included within the general powers: to provide for the common defense and general welfare. These powers, and only these powers, were assigned by the states to the Congress.

Hamilton in *Federalist #33* and Madison in *Federalist #44* made it very clear that the "sweeping clause"—as detractors then called it—referred only to "particular powers." These were defined as the means necessary to the execution of the delegated powers. Even then, the necessary signatures were not obtained until the Bill of Rights was added, the capstone of which was the Tenth Amendment. It limited the powers of the federal government only to those specified in the Constitution itself.

Congressman Davy Crockett was an early exponent of Madison's strict interpretation of the Constitution. When the House of Representatives was debating an appropriation for the benefit of the widow of a distinguished naval officer, Crockett rose to speak:

> . . . we must not permit our respect for the dead or our
> sympathy for a part of the living to lead us into an act of
> injustice to the balance of the living. I will not go into an
> argument to prove that Congress has no power to
> appropriate this money as an act of charity. Every member
> upon this floor knows it. We have the right, as
> individuals, to give away as much of our own money as
> we please in charity; but as members of Congress we have
> no right so to appropriate a dollar of the public money.[3]

Sadly, it takes only a casual survey of the contemporary political scene to recognize that the voice of both Madison and Crockett have been drowned in a flood of twentieth century socialism.

GENERAL WELFARE EXCUSE FOR SOCIALISM

The Constitutional Approach to Welfare

The Constitution's general welfare clause has been violently twisted to mean exactly the opposite of the founders' intent. The phrase appears in two places. The Preamble states that one purpose of the Constitution was "to promote the general welfare." In addition, Article I, Section 8 defines the taxing power of Congress to include "Power to lay and collect Taxes, Duties, Imposts and Excises, to pay the Debts and provide for the common Defence and general Welfare of the United States . . . . "

Throughout the *Federalist Papers* both Hamilton and Madison expressed concern to secure both the public good and the rights of private citizens. However, they were disturbed by the possibility that factions and special interests might misuse the power of government for their own welfare at the expense of the general welfare.

Herein lies one of the most misunderstood and misconstrued passages in the Constitution. The general welfare clause was interpreted by the Supreme Court early in the twentieth century, contrary to all precedent, to represent a virtually unlimited grant of power to the federal government to spend money for any welfare scheme it desired. Even a casual reading of the *Federalist Papers,* however, reveals this interpretation as foreign to the intent of the founding fathers.

The function of law is to be an impartial standard of justice. But when law is manipulated to confiscate the property of one class of citizen for transfer to another, the law itself becomes an instrument of injustice. The biblical pattern of welfare consists of individuals, churches, and private organizations responding in genuine compassion to the needs of their neighbors. The poor should be encouraged toward a lifestyle of responsibility and financial self-sufficiency, as opposed to the dependency and laziness fostered by the welfare state (see chapter 9).

In its original context, promoting the general welfare meant that all expenditures from the public treasury must benefit the public at large. Twentieth century liberals have twisted this to justify the erection of a massive welfare state which serves special interests and indigents.

The Biblical Approach to Welfare

Thus, justice has come to refer not to adjudication in the courtroom sense of determining right and wrong, but to a fair distribution of scarce resources. However, in Scripture the Hebrew word for justice in nearly all cases is *shapat*. The primary sense of this word is to exercise the processes of government. It means to judge with righteous justice or to determine right and wrong or to rule as God would rule. The same word can also mean "to rule" as in Psalm 96:13 and Genesis 18:25.

Thus, the meaning of the Hebrew word alone contradicts liberation theology, which attempts to justify socialist doctrine from Scripture—not to mention the clear biblical teaching against the doctrines of socialism intertwined in the very fabric of Scripture. Liberals and social gospel advocates superimpose a Marxist view of justice on Scripture when they define biblical "justice" as "the fair distribution of scarce resources."

It is impossible for government to protect individual life and property and, at the same time, involve itself in wealth redistribution programs. In order to redistribute wealth, government must violate the property rights of some individuals in society to aggrandize itself or those it nurtures in dependence. It is no more right for governments— who are commissioned to uphold the law—to steal than it is for individuals (see Ex. 20:15). Taxation is authorized only for God-ordained functions.

The Bible consistently teaches that God has entrusted the dominion mandate, and as a consequence the stewardship of private property, to individuals, not to government (see Gen. 1:28). Civil government has, in fact, been instituted to protect the property of individuals and to ensure just dealing in all their relationships. Hence, any use of government power to deprive individuals of their property or inheritance is proscribed. Such abuse, coming usually in the form of illegitimate taxation, leads directly to slavery (see next section).

Most often there are enticing words of a common purse and wealth for all (see Prov. 1:14). By uniting together, men are told they will have power to institute necessary economic "reforms." Such actions are based on the threat of violent assault, whether they be conducted by mob rule or the more "respectable" electoral process.

When men vote money for themselves out of their neighbor's pockets, they gradually, but surely, transfer control of property and the tools of production into the hands of the government. This is the critical distinction between socialism and capitalism. In the former, the state owns the tools of production; in the latter, the individual does. Capitalism can, of course, become idolatrous if it is not tethered to the Ten Commandments.

PROGRESSIVE INCOME TAX

In the *Communist Manifesto* Karl Marx called for a graduated income tax as one of the ten steps needed to dismantle a capitalist society. Since 1913 Marx's dream has been enshrined in the Sixteenth Amendment of the United States Constitution. It states simply that "Congress shall have power to lay and collect taxes on incomes, from whatever source derived, without apportionment among the several States, and without regard to any census or enumeration."

This amendment superseded the original requirement of Article I, Section 2 that all taxes be proportional to the census. Taxation was initially tied to population: "Representatives and direct taxes shall be apportioned among the several States . . . according to their respective numbers . . . . "

Biblical Taxation

This leads to the question of the appropriate form of taxation. Does the Bible provide substantive instruction for how the state is to finance its legitimate activities?

Most of what we can learn is from a logical principle of negation. By a process of elimination we can strike down most modern forms of taxation as patently unbiblical. In fact, several are blasphemous attempts to usurp the divine prerogatives of Christ as King of kings. Their secondary effect is to steal the freedom of men because property rights are essential for the exercise of biblical freedom.

Particularly heinous are property and inheritance taxes. Both are direct attacks on God-given liberty, since private ownership of property is the tangible evidence of liberty. Via inheritance, property is passed from one generation to another and serves to build up the capital base of a nation and increase the capacity of godly citizens to "fill the earth and subdue it." Rulers are therefore forbidden to indulge in either form of taxation because they directly short-circuit this process by denying private property. For example, King Ahab was severely judged by God for unjustly confiscating Naboth's vineyard (see 1 Kings 21).

The property tax is a direct assault on God's claim to ownership of all the earth: "The earth is the Lord's and the fullness thereof" (Ps. 24:1). The mere existence of a property tax is the denial of private property and freedom. It means, in effect, that government is landlord of all private holdings. The reality of this becomes obvious when a person becomes incapacitated by age or infirmity and is unable to pay the tax. Government forecloses.

In like manner, the inheritance, or death tax, is an assault on the biblical recommendation for a good man to "leave an inheritance to his children's children" (Prov. 13:22, RSV). Likewise, the apostle Paul tells us that it is good for parents to lay up for their children (see 2 Cor. 12:14).

As of 1993, any estate over $600,000 is taxed at very high rates in the United States. There was even a strong effort underfoot to lower this exemption to $200,000. In many cases, families are forced to liquidate the estate at "fire sale" prices in order to pay the tax. The labor of a lifetime disappears into a government-made "black hole." This malevolent tax is a bald governmental assault on "widows and orphans," two groups whom God has singled out for special protection in the Bible.

The graduated income tax discourages work, productivity, and thrift (see 2 Thess. 3:10; Gen. 3:19) and encourages dependence and sloth, which are forbidden in Scripture (see Prov. 26:14, 24:33). It destroys incentive and motivation to produce because higher levels of productivity are taxed at higher rates. The graduated income tax was, in fact, one of the ten planks of the *Communist Manifesto,* a prescription for the destruction of a free society.

As noted above, the U.S. Constitution authorized only a head tax proportional to the census, determined in a manner similar to assigning the number of representatives. Each citizen was to pay an equal amount derived by dividing the total cost of government by the total number of taxpayers. The Sixteenth Amendment annulled this provision by providing for an income tax, unrestricted by the requirement of proportionality.

Some have attempted to build a case for the head tax from Scripture by citing the temple tax of Exodus 30: 11–16. However, this theory is built on a rather cryptic argument.[4]

49

When the British attempted to levy a national head tax in the late 1980s it met with stiff resistance because of its perceived unfairness. A low-income family, who can least afford it, is forced to pay a much higher proportion of their income than a high-income family.

In like manner, the sales tax would appear to be a direct attack on a low-income family's ability to sustain itself, with the penalty at the point of purchase. Moreover, it enlists the businessman as the government's collection agent, usually without just compensation.

By the process of elimination, therefore, we are left with a simple flat rate income tax. The flat rate tax is intuitively fair because everyone pays an equal proportion of their income. Furthermore, it finds biblical warrant in God's model for church taxation, the tithe.

The flat tax should not be permited to rise above 10 percent. To do so is to rival and exceed God's claim on man's productivity, thereby constituting an implicit claim to deity on the part of the state. With this, the founders were in general agreement. For example, in 1758 Benjamin Franklin wrote, "It would be thought a hard Government that should tax its People one-tenth Part of their *Time,* to be employed in its Service" (emphasis original).[5]

Such a tax was the direct consequence of Israel's rejection of God as their King in 1 Samuel 8. This passage reveals how the people of Israel rejected the rulership of God and sought to have a king. The sin was not in asking for a king (see Deut. 17), but in asking for a king *like the nations.* They were looking for security in civil government, seeking to have their various needs met by government rather than God.

God granted their desire, but He sent leanness into their national soul. Samuel warned them of the consequences of rejecting God's rulership. The king, he said, would take the tenth of all their produce, the same as God. The passage goes on to describe this presumptuous act of confiscatory taxation as the essence of slavery and tyranny.

Tax Resistance

This raises the question of the legitimacy of a tax revolt against an oppressive ruler. The Bible makes it fairly clear that taxation is not a legitimate focal point for resistance to an ungodly government. Scripture indicates that Christians are to pay taxes—even taxes that violate biblical and Constitutional principles. There are several premises behind this conclusion.

First, the biblical mode of transforming culture is not revolution, but regeneration and reformation. Individuals are not permitted the liberty to indiscriminately disobey government. The primary response of a people suffering under oppressive leadership is to repent, cry out to God, and trust Him to raise up a deliverer.

Second, Christians are commanded to work—not revolt—in order to take dominion in the earth. There are many indications in Scripture that a work-oriented society will overcome an oppressive society (see Judg. 3:31; Zech. 1:18).

Third, on the question of oppressive taxation, Jesus specifically commanded "to avoid giving offense" (Matt. 17:27) and promised to miraculously provide the tax money. Elsewhere He said not to resist him who is evil.

The line is to be drawn only at those points where the ruler is forcing us to disobey the command of God. Resistance should come at the point of worship or evangelism or other activities which directly affect our relationship to God.

It should be remembered, however, that the appetite of the humanistic power state for taxes is practically insatiable. These are necessary to fuel its idolatrous drive to become "God walking on earth." For example, rates on the original 1913 Federal Income Tax Form ranged from 1 percent for those earning not more than $50,000 to 6 percent for those earning over $500,000. Dire warnings that rates could some day rise as high as an unconscionable 10 percent were laughed down in Congress. By the mid-1980s rates for the highest income levels stood at 70 percent.

Furthermore, the response of the church should be far different from the response of the individual Christian to state demands in the area of taxation. In Ezra 7:24 (RSV), we read the charge of Artaxerxes to his officials in order to avoid the wrath of the God of heaven. He notified them "that it shall not be lawful to impose tribute, custom, or toll upon any one of the priests, the Levites, the singers, the door keepers, the temple servants, or other servants of this house of God."

Officers of the church are to resist unlawful attempts of government officials to impose taxes or other regulations on the church. The church is the embassy of heaven on earth. As such, the church enjoys the same immunity as the embassies of other foreign nations in the United States.

Abandonment of Gold-Backed Currency

The abuse of governmental power is most apt to manifest itself through manipulation of a nation's currency. Control of the medium of exchange is no doubt the most effective and efficient means of controlling the lives of other people. In fact, said Karl Marx, "give me power over a nation's currency, and I care not who makes its laws." The abuse of the power to manipulate money leads to all sorts of other evils (see 1 Tim. 6:10). It is one of the subtlest forms of coercion, whereby a people may be enslaved gradually and scarcely notice the hand of tyranny tightening its grip until it is too late.

Federal Reserve Bank

Private European banking interests historically twisted the power to control money supply and interest rates to their own advantage, and the framers of the Constitution were determined to prevent this abuse in the new nation. They took this power out of private hands and gave it to Congress, which was then to administer it even-handedly to serve the best interest of all citizens.

However, with the establishment of the Federal Reserve, Congress shifted this responsibility back into the hands of private bankers, the most powerful of whom exploited it for their own benefit. Many of our present-day economic problems can be traced to this abuse.[6] The responsibility of Congress is to follow the example of Nehemiah in putting a halt to this exploitation on the part of "the nobles and the officials" (Neh. 5:1–13).

Men turn to a monetary economic system to avoid the inconveniences associated with barter. A relatively portable but universally valued metal, such as gold or silver, is readily accepted as a uniform medium of exchange. At a further stage of development paper "receipts" may be substituted for gold as an additional convenience, but always with the assurance that the paper may be redeemed for the metal at any time. As men become accustomed to this system they tend to forget the metal backing and impute value to the paper receipt itself.

This forgetfulness opens the way for government manipulation of the currency. Manipulation may take a variety of forms. For one thing, the metal may be diluted by dross, or less valuable metals, as in Isaiah 1:22. Worse, the gold backing may be completely removed, as in the United States today. This opens the way for government to indulge in unrestricted printing or inflation of the money supply. Prices rise as the amount of currency in circulation increases relative to the goods on the market. The true value or purchasing power of the currency is diminished to the detriment of the bearer.

The Bible condemns this kind of dishonest "weights and measures." The only remedy is disciplined adherence to the "gold standard" as a backup to the paper. This means that each unit of paper currency be representative of, or redeemable for, a fixed weight of precious metal. Under the Constitution, the states are forbidden to accept anything other than such metal-backed money as legal tender. This important provision of our Constitution is currently ignored by our elected representatives.

Fractional Reserve Banking

Another related form of money manipulation is fractional reserve banking. Under this system, financial institutions may lend out on credit as much as seven or eight times the value of their cash reserves. This practice is based on the observation that only about one fifth of bank customers will withdraw their funds at a given time.

Originally this practice was recognized as fraud, but over the years it was legalized in most Western nations. The system feeds on the covetous desire of bank customers to go into debt to buy goods they cannot afford in the present. The result is inflation of the monetary supply and economic fraud perpetrated against investors and those who avoid debt. This too is forbidden by Scripture.

OTHER PROBLEMS

Marshall's Judicial Review

The decisions of Moses and the rulers of Israel were based on the law of God, not their own fallible human wisdom. Likewise, under the U.S. Constitution, judges are not granted the power to legislate judicially. Contrary to popular wisdom, the Constitution is *not* "whatever the Supreme Court says it is."

The judiciary is to interpret the law as it relates to the circumstances of a particular case in dispute and pass judgment on the basis of that law. Judges are forbidden by both Scripture and Constitution to assume the role of God, passing judgment on the higher law. By doing so they make themselves the final arbiter of right and wrong.

The Constitution itself binds the judiciary by this principle: "This Constitution and the laws of the United States which shall be made in pursuance thereof . . . shall be the supreme law of the land; and the judges in every State shall be bound thereby . . . " (Art. VI, Sec. 8).

In the early years of the Republic, however, the first chief justice, John Marshall, returned a decision that began to erode this principle. In this case, which involved a number of inconsequential judicial appointments, Marshall articulated the doctrine of judicial review. Under this doctrine it is "the power and duty of the Court to pronounce null and void, and refuse to enforce, legislation in conflict with the Constitution."[7]

The Supreme Court thereby assumed authority as custodian of the Constitution above that of the executive and legislature. This was in violation of the spirit of the Constitution, which actually limits the jurisdiction of the Supreme Court to "such Exceptions, and under such Regulations as the Congress shall make" (3–2–2). Unfortunately, Congress has meekly acquiesced to the Court's assertion of supremacy.

Having enthroned itself above the Constitution, it goes without saying that the Supreme Court has not hesitated to place itself above the authority of the Bible itself. The impact of Marshall's legacy is well summarized by Steve Wilkins:

> A "strict construction" of the Constitution which denied "implied powers" was viewed as essential to the maintenance of liberty. Jefferson and those presidents who followed him were firm believers in this. But there were forces in the country which held the contrary view—chief among them, the new Chief Justice of the Supreme Court, John Marshall. Marshall was a convinced nationalist and constantly concerned to preserve the central government's supreme authority.[8]

States' Rights Nullified by Fourteenth and Seventeenth Amendments

The Fourteenth Amendment is the most convoluted and difficult to interpret of the Constitution's twenty-six amendments. Of the three Civil War amendments this one is most destructive of states' rights. One fundamental issue at stake in the War Between the States was the right of the states to secede from the union. The contention of the

South was that the states had voluntarily entered into the federal union on condition of certain stipulations which were specified in the Constitution. It followed, therefore, that they could voluntarily leave the union if the terms of the covenant (Constitution) were violated by the federal government.

The right of secession was forcibly suppressed on the field of battle. The Fourteenth Amendment was drafted by the victors to ensure subjugation of the vanquished and to consolidate additional power at the federal level. A number of provisions served to accomplish this end.

In the first place, Section 1 provides that from that point forward priority would be given to U.S. citizenship, with state citizenship secondary. This is derived from the stipulation that "No state shall make or enforce any law which shall abridge the privileges or immunities of citizens of the United States." This shift to a federal focus was reflected in the diction used to describe the United States. Prior to the War Between the States, it was customary to say "the United States are . . . . " After the War the usage shifted to "the United States is . . . . "

Furthermore, the amendment went on to state: "Nor shall any state deprive any person of life, liberty, or property, without due process of law: nor deny to any person within its jurisdiction the equal protection of the laws." On the surface this sounds fair enough. However, subsequent interpretations have construed this to mean that the states are now subject to the restrictions of the Bill of Rights. Such an interpretation completely circumvents the original intent of the Bill of Rights which was to limit the power of the federal government.

The Seventeenth Amendment, which took effect on May 31, 1913, completely obliterated the Connecticut Compromise—known as the Great Compromise—of the Constitutional Convention. The early weeks of the Convention had been marked by rancor because of an inability to arrive at agreement on the question of representation in the new Congress. The large states favored representation based on population while the small states naturally favored an equal number of representatives for each state.

Under the Great Compromise the representation in the lower chamber was to be based on population. In the higher chamber two Senators were to be selected by the state legislatures of each state. The latter provision ensured that the states *as states* had an important mechanism of control—two personal representatives—at the federal level. Under the Seventeenth Amendment senators are elected by popular vote and the states as political entities are left to the mercy of the federal juggernaut.

CONCLUSION

Not content with the Constitution's religious neutrality, modern humanists have distorted the document at nearly every point wherein it reflects the biblical pattern. They have done this by departing from or ignoring the clearly stated intent of the founders. Instead, the Constitution is assumed to be a "living" document, readily adaptable to the changing times.

In practice this has meant that the power of the federal government has expanded in response to a variety of cultural crises. The triggering mechanisms have sometimes been broad based, resulting in ill-advised constitutional amendments. More often, the catalyst has been individual litigation, providing the judicial environment in which an activist Supreme Court may gradually subvert the Constitution.

REVIEW QUIZ

1. What is the biblically imposed upper limit on taxation?
   a. 100 percent of increase in personal productivity
   b. 50 percent of increase in personal productivity
   c. 9 percent of increase in personal productivity

2. (T or F) The Thirteenth Amendment to the U.S. Constitution has made indentured servitude legal in the United States.

3. Paul's return of what runaway slave is evidence that household slavery (indentured servitude) in the New Testament era is not inherently evil?
   a. Demas
   b. Onesimus
   c. John Mark
   d. Philemon

4. Which Supreme Court justice established the principle of judicial review in *Marbury vs. Madison?*
   a. John Marshall
   b. William Jennings Bryan
   c. Oliver Wendell Holmes
   d. James Madison

5. Which form of taxation appears to come closest to the biblical model?
   a. Head tax
   b. Sales tax
   c. Death tax
   d. Flat tax
   e. Progressive income tax
   f. b & d

6. Which constitutional amendment obliterated states rights?
   a. Tenth Amendment
   b. Eighteenth Amendment
   c. Seventeenth Amendment
   d. Thirteenth Amendment

DISCUSSION GUIDE

1. What is the meaning of the elastic clause?

2. What power does the phrase "promote the general welfare" grant to the federal government?

3. What does the word "justice" mean in Scripture? What bearing does this have on the concept of "social justice" as it is used by some left-leaning organizations today?

4. Can a particular type of taxation be justified from Scripture? Explain.

5. What is the essence of tyranny as defined in 1 Samuel 8?

6. How does the response of the church differ from that of the individual when it comes to taxation and regulation?

7. Why is a metal-based currency so important to a sound economic and political system?

Answer Key

1) c   2) F   3) b   4) a   5) d   6) c

4

FROM PLYMOUTH TO PHILADEPHIA: THE DECLINE FROM PURITANISM

A text without a context is pretext. To fully apprehend the significance of the United States Constitution it is necessary to understand the historical context from which it arose. That context is incomplete apart from a consideration of the rise and decline of Puritanism in the seventeenth century and the Great Awakening in the first half of the eighteenth.

THE MAYFLOWER COMPACT

The story of the Pilgrims and their miraculous voyage to the new world is well known. These true heroes of the faith risked death and separation from all they held dear to establish a beachhead for God in the New World.

The hand of God clearly rested on the Pilgrims during the Atlantic passage. Originally bound for the Virginia coast, a violent storm providentially drove the *Mayflower* northward toward Massachusetts. In the midst of the storm the main beam of the ship buckled, threatening to sink her. Falling to their knees in prayer, the Pilgrims remembered a giant printing screw that for some obscure reason had been carried aboard. It proved to be just what was needed to jack the main beam back into place and save the ship.

Unknown to the Pilgrims, God had used a dreadful plague to rid the Cape Cod area of a violent Indian tribe a few years prior to their landing. In their place, He arranged for the friendly Indian Squanto to greet the Pilgrims and serve as their mentor. Incredibly, Squanto had spent several years in England, mastering the English tongue and learning the ways of the British.

The Mayflower Compact was drawn up and signed on the *Mayflower* prior to landing. According to historians Peter Marshall and David Manuel, "it marked the first time in recorded history that free and equal men had voluntarily covenanted together to create their own new civil government."[1]

To the Pilgrims went the honor of establishing the beachhead in New England and providing the example of courage for those who would follow. However, the main task of colonizing the New England wilderness fell to their Puritan brethren just up the coast around Boston.

THE PURITAN EXPERIMENT

Perhaps less well known than the Pilgrims are the Puritans. What we know of the Puritans is often handed down in the form of caricature or negative stereotype. They are usually presented as stern, austere, authoritarian, and joyless. What really characterized the Puritans?

One of the distinctives of Puritanism is the regulative principle of worship. It is based on the Second Commandment: "Thou shalt not make unto thee any graven image . . . " (Ex. 20:4). This principle holds that God must be approached in worship only in the manner He has specified in Scripture. Any departure from this formula, no matter how attractive it may appear from a human perspective, leads ultimately to rejection by God and death. "There is a way that seemeth right unto a man," says the proverb, "but the end thereof are the ways of death" (Prov. 14:12).

The greatest example of this principle is, of course, the atonement of Christ. Without the sacrifice of His life on behalf of the sinner— appropriated by faith as a garment of righteousness—it is impossible to approach a Holy God. This principle also finds expression in a host of other details of worship, such as the administration of communion, clerical garb, church architecture, and music.

The Puritans were one of the few groups in history who self-consciously attempted to extend the regulative principle into all of life. They were also one of the few groups who by virtue of historical circumstance had the opportunity to do so. To their credit, they sought to bring every sphere of their earthly existence—family, work place, magistery, economics, etc.—under the direct authority of Scripture.

For example, the Puritans believed that the equity (essential principle or meaning) of the Mosaic legislation applied directly to the administration of public justice. Even before their arrival in the New World, Elniff notes that they "began to search the Scriptures for the very forms and models they should use in reforming England, especially the church and its relation to the state, as well as the government of the church itself."[2]

The Puritans are often vilified as tyrannical and abusive. However, the governmental structures they erected in New England were based on the concepts of limited, delegated power. This power was to be dispersed among a variety of institutions. "John Cotton was one of the most vocal of the Puritans in articulating the idea of limitation on power, 'that all power that is on earth be limited.' "[3]

One of the key features of Puritan government was the limitation of the franchise (vote) to church members. These "freedmen" of the society elected their civil leaders in a republican format. While such a restriction may sound incredulous to modern ears, it is impossible to maintain true liberty in any society apart from it. We will return again to the biblical rationale for the limited franchise in chapter 8, "The Form of Biblical Government." The Puritan allegiance to Scripture extended even to statutory law. In describing the Puritan system of servitude, Morgan notes, "When a man stole from, or otherwise damaged another and could not make restitution in cash, he might be sold for a number of years to pay the bill."[4] This is a direct application of Exodus 22:1–3 (see chapter 9).

THE DECLENSION

The great migration of Puritans from England to Massachusetts began in 1628 and lasted about sixteen years. The founding generation established a biblical commonwealth which flourished briefly. However, according to historian Thomas Wertenbaker, "Before the end of the seventeenth century, although the ideals of the founders still exercised a powerful influence upon the minds and hearts of the people, the experiment of a Bible commonwealth had definitely failed."[5]

Why did the Puritan experiment in Christian culture falter after the first generation had passed from the scene? This is a complex question which has filled the pages of many books. We can do little more than attempt a summary in this brief chapter. One of the goals of this manual is to demonstrate how the seeds of autonomy sown by the Puritans have plagued every subsequent generation and contaminated our founding document, the U.S. Constitution.

Fatal Inconsistency

The first generation of Puritans obviously held the Bible in high regard. Unfortunately, they also relied on human reason and natural law to demonstrate or establish the authority of God's Word. Perry Miller observed, ". . . in the Puritan mind confidence in the certainty of God's Word was matched by an equal confidence in the infallibility of logic."[6] He concluded: "the latent conflict in their theory of reason engendered conflicts in other realms as well, in their theory of human psychology and in ecclesiastical practice, and was perhaps the one glaring weakness in their otherwise perfect system, the single but fatal inconsistency in an otherwise monumental consistency."[7]

The temptation to indulge in this inconsistency comes when we observe that the unbeliever resists the authority of the Bible. However, we note that the unbeliever can reason with his mind just as the believer can reason. Therefore, why not appeal to the unbeliever on the basis of that which we seem to have in common: human reason? Can we not use human reason to demonstrate that Scripture is reasonable?

In accepting this approach, the Puritans became locked into an enlightenment frame of mind on the rationalistic side. Consequently, they failed to go far enough with the regulative principle, by failing to assert the ultimate authority of the Bible.

We are all to some extent prisoners of the times into which we are born. The Puritans were no exception. Especially in the second and third generations, their outlook was tainted with the idea—inspired by the Enlightenment—that reason is sufficient in defending the supreme authority of the Bible.

> They accepted knowledge as an ally . . . . The ministers and other educated men sent to England for the latest works of Newton, Halley, Kepler, Boyle . . . sought to use the new light which they shed on the wonders of God's world to buttress Christian faith.

> They seem to have been unaware that the advance of science was transforming thought both in Europe and New England, their own thought . . . and weakening the entire structure of the Bible community.[8]

This is a subtle, but critical shift in the locus of authority. If we rely on human reason and natural law as the fundamental authority to defend Scripture, we thereby diminish the authority of Scripture. Ironically, if we trust in anything other than the Bible to establish the authority of the Bible, we thereby assert the ultimacy of that "anything other"— whatever it may be. We will develop this theme further in chapter 6.

Human reason is clearly a gift of God and a tool to be used in unlocking the mysteries of God's Word and God's world. However, we must not forget that it is a creaturely, derivative tool. Reason always operates from, or on the basis of, some source of authority. If that authority is the Word of God, well and good. However, if the source of authority is the autonomous mind of man or nature, we quickly run into trouble. This is reason run amok.[9]

The Puritans did not arrive at this calamitous juncture through any conscious effort to subvert the authority of Scripture. On the contrary, their high regard for the Bible led them to appreciate the order, regularity, and majesty of God's creation. Ironically, this appreciation led them to shift their focal point—in the space of a few short years—from the authority of the Word of God to the alleged authority of natural law as apprehended by logic.

Therefore, if the primary ground of authority resides in human reason, it was only natural that the children of the Puritans would begin to question why they even needed the Scripture at all.[10] And so, in the space of a single generation, Satan succeeded in subverting the grand experiment in biblical culture by undermining its foundation.

The declension (as it is known) was gradual. The Halfway Covenant drawn up by the Boston Synod in 1662 has been criticized by many; however, it probably served to delay the declension. It was an accommodation in which the infants of unbelieving parents were granted baptism. At the same time the families were denied communion and voting rights in the community on the basis of church membership. The intent was to grant unbelievers the benefit of association with the church, while denying full membership in order to maintain the purity of the church.[11]

Nonetheless, religious practice gradually became divorced from religious profession. As men launched into the wilderness on their own, the faithful, covenanted Puritan was gradually transformed into the prosperous and self-reliant Yankee. They gradually became hardened to the urgent pleas of the ministers to repent and return to the Lord according to the example of their forefathers.

Roger Williams and the Quakers

Controversy over the immigration of Roger Williams, the Quakers, the Anabaptists, and finally the Salem witch trials gradually weakened the authority of the clergy. The Puritans objected to the claims of Anne Hutchinson and the Quaker missionaries that they were recipients of direct revelation from God via an "inner light" or an "immediate voice."[12] They viewed these claims as heretical and dangerous, but they were willing to tolerate them as long as they were kept private. When individuals insisted on broadcasting their heresies, however, the Puritans viewed them as destructive of the biblical, social order and moved to suppress them. In most cases they were sentenced only after all other means, including counsel, gentle exhortation, and exile from the colony had failed.

Roger Williams was something of a unique case. An ordained Congregational minister, Williams actually occupied the pulpit for a time in Salem. Williams was loved by the Puritans for his winsome personality and zeal for the Lord. However, they were driven to distraction by his extreme perfectionism over minor points of doctrine and practice. For example, he harped incessantly on the king's alleged lack of authority to grant Indian lands to the settlers. The Puritans feared that his attacks on the Crown would lead eventually to revocation of their charter.[13]

After repeated attempts at counsel and persuasion, the Puritans finally moved to deport Williams by ship. At that point he fled into the wilderness and went to Rhode Island.

New England suffered a brief period of repression when Charles II revoked the original charter. Freedom was restored during the Glorious Revolution of 1688, when William and Mary drove James II from the throne. However, William abolished church membership as the basis for the franchise, substituting in its place ownership of property.[14]

The loss of Harvard University to the liberals in 1700 was a final, fatal blow. Harvard University had been established in 1636 to train young men for the ministry in Puritan churches. This loss ensured that the pastors supplying New England pulpits would no longer be sympathetic to the way of life of the Puritan founders.

Lessons from the Puritan Experiment

It is common for moderns to point a finger at the Puritans as an example of the tyranny that is unleashed when men try to rule under biblical law. Although it is impossible to know for certain, the number of Quakers and accused witches unjustly sentenced to death by the sixteenth century Puritan magistrates is probably well under fifty.

The witch trials were conducted in the context of hundreds of documented cases of demon possession and satanic attack. The demons apparently assumed the form of innocent neighbors in their attacks on the "bewitched."[15] Contrary to the advice of the ministers, the magistrates erroneously accepted this "spectral evidence" and sentenced about twenty persons to death. A number of the magistrates, most notably Samuel Sewall, later confessed to their error in deep, public humiliation.[16]

It is not our intention to excuse any miscarriages of justice, especially the unjust taking of life. However, it would be well to remember that humanism, in all of its manifestations, has resulted in untold millions of tyrannical deaths in the twentieth century alone. The Puritans' occasional excesses pale in significance to the Stalin purges, the Maoist massacres, the Auschwitz ovens, and the American abortion mills. Such is the terrible toll exacted by the doctrine of "freedom of conscience" unrestrained by the law of God. This was the legacy of Roger Williams. When every man does "that which is right in his own eyes," tyranny follows hard on the heels of anarchy (Judg. 21:25).

The task of the Christian scholar is to study the Puritan experiment to identify its biblical strengths as well as those points at which it departed from the biblical standard. We must use the lessons learned to build on the foundation they laid as God gives us opportunity.

THE GREAT AWAKENING

The Great Awakening which peaked in the second quarter of the eighteenth century brought revival, but it also reinforced the strain of frontier individualism bred into the American pioneer. The Awakening was characterized by itinerant preachers and a message of individualistic revival. It stressed a personal, experiential decision for Christ.

This was fine as far as it went, but it worked to divorce the believer from the sense that he was a citizen in a Christian culture. When the itinerant preacher rode into town, he often ignored the authority of the local church(es) in the area. Thus, he inadvertently undermined the established covenantal structure.

For the most part, that was what the controversy between the Old Lights and the New Lights was all about. The Old Lights felt that the Awakening was destroying respect for the institutional foundations of society. The New Lights stressed the freedom of the individual in direct relation to God through the new birth.[17]

Consequently, Christians began to lose sight of the fact that they were heirs to a grand historical movement known as Christendom. This was not a light matter, for there were blessings and cursings attendant on observance of covenant obligations in the family, church, and nation. These were not emphasized in the Great Awakening. The new believers were not presented with the standard of biblical law on which to base their new life, and consequently many fell away after a short time.

It was assumed that if people's lives were changed, society would change automatically as a by-product. However, this is not the case if Christians are not instructed in the whole counsel of God as it relates to every area of life and culture. Sadly, this instruction in the law of God was not often provided.

The believer's vision was focused inward on a subjective emotionalism, rather than outward on his responsibilities within the covenantal framework of Christian society. Thus, the Great Awakening must be viewed as a revival and not a true reformation of the totality of life and culture in terms of the law of God.

This is more easily understood when we think of the Great Awakening in the shadow of the Protestant Reformation. The latter had a profound impact on every aspect of society in addition to salvation of the individual soul. The Reformation unfolded in patterns which saw Christ redeeming and subduing the entire creation unto Himself, not just men as individuals. It took a century or more to run its course, recasting government, art, music, work, law, and much more in the biblical mold.[18] The Reformation finally dissipated around 1700 with the decline of the New England, Puritan republic, and the onset of the Great Awakening.

The Great Awakening took a different course. Some have argued that the enthusiastic tendencies of the Great Awakening led to deterioration in theology, morals, politics, and society in general. For example, they point out that the percentage of babies born less than eight months after marriage skyrocketed to 49 percent in one Rhode Island district during the revival era.[19] A similar pattern was seen in the wake of revivals up and down the coast.

It may be going too far to lay all these excesses at the door of the Great Awakening. However, the Awakening clearly unleashed cultural forces with repercussions far different from the Protestant Reformation. These reverberated well into the next century, when the revival was rekindled as the Second Great Awakening (1800 to 1830).[20]

To the extent that it has found expression in the public arena, the Awakening has typically assumed the form of a moral crusade against a variety of evils. The litany of crusades includes temperance, abolitionism, reclamation of prostitutes, prohibition, and even the modern anti-abortion and abstinence movements. Here again, the hallmark has been a focus on a revived individual, as opposed to covenantal, institutional reformation.

There is much talk of moral outrage against the evil, but little talk of restructuring the culture biblically so as to deal with the root causes. The call to morality is usually in terms of a pietistic emotionalism, rather than the objective standard of the law of God. The mentality of the participants is defensive or reactive, their involvement terminating once the preceived threat is seemingly subdued.

Historian Whitney Cross offered the following analysis of the Second Great Awakening in the *Burned-Over District* of Western New York. A similar dynamic was at work in the first Awakening.

> Its venturesome proponents were thus heavily responsible for its own demise . . . . Unfortunately their unparalleled vitality and courage aided mankind to make slight, if any, progress along the wearisome road toward Utopia. For the assumption that sin must be attacked primarily in the individual, rather than in society, misled these zealots into a futile expenditure of their energies. The wastage, in channels leading only to self-destruction, of a potent motivation which if applied to the political, economic, and social problems of the era might have accomplished

great things, is probably the chief debit in the account of religious enthusiasm.[21]

Jonathan Edwards personified and legitimized the First Awakening, as Charles Finney did the Second. Although Edwards' messages were typically powerful expressions of biblical truth, even he did not escape the influences of the Enlightenment. As C. Gregg Singer notes, "Edwards was tremendously impressed with the empirical philosophy of John Locke and tried to work it into his theology—without too much success."[22]

CONCLUSION

The Puritan heritage and the Great Awakening combined to produce a generally religious populace in the closing quarter of the eighteenth century. This religious conviction steeled the American people in the face of British imperialism and firepower, and this faith prevailed in the War for Independence of 1776.

However, the colonial religious outlook was not fully attuned to the ways of God in dealing covenantally with a culture. As a consequence—and in spite of anti-Federalist warnings—Americans failed to recognize the anti-covenantal nature of the Constitution presented to them in 1787. Thus, as we have seen in chapter 2, they were prevailed upon to accept a document having "the form of godliness, but denying the power thereof" (2 Tim. 3:5).

REVIEW QUIZ

1. The Pilgrims differed from the Puritans in
   a. Their use of the Book of Common Prayer
   b. Their desire to separate from the Church of England rather than reform it
   c. Reliance on corn and turkey rather than tobacco as the primary cash crop
   d. A Congregational as opposed to Presbyterian form of church government

2. The Puritan philosophy of life was an extension of
   a. Their unique view of the separation of church and state
   b. The rationalism of the Enlightenment
   c. Economic determinism
   d. The regulative principle

3. Puritan civil government may best be described as
   a. Congregational
   b. Oligarchy
   c. Republican
   d. Democratic

4. Puritans extended the franchise to
   a. Women
   b. Freeholders
   c. All men
   d. Christian freedmen

5. Which of these was *not* a reason for the decline of New England Puritanism?
   a. Rationalism
   b. Their stern, austere, and joyless outlook on life
   c. The rise of Yankee individualism
   d. Franchise based on property ownership

6. The weakness of the Great Awakening was
    a. Failure to rely on the preached Word
    b. No strong leaders to guide the revival
    c. Anti-covenantal individualism

DISCUSSION GUIDE

1. Why did the Puritans limit the right to vote to covenanted church members?

2. How did the Puritans apply the regulative principle to the colonization of New England?

3. What were some of the key features of Puritan civil government?

4. What factors led to the decline of New England Puritanism?

5. When God provides the next opportunity to construct a Christian culture, in what ways should it be the same and in what ways should it differ from the New England Puritan society?

6. Describe the one "glaring weakness" in Puritan theology.

7. Compare and contrast the Great Awakening and the Reformation of the sixteenth century. Discuss the difference between a revival and a reformation.

Answer Key
   1) b   2) d   3) c   4) d   5) b   6) c

PART II
A Collapsing Superstructure

At 7:05 P.M. on the evening of July 17, 1980, more than 1,600 people were gathered in the atrium of the Hyatt Regency Hotel in Kansas City, Missouri. Most of the them were dancing to the music of a well-known band for a tea dance competition, including observers on the second and fourth floor walkways stomping in rhythm to the music. Suddenly a sharp sound—like a thunderbolt—silenced the crowd. Without warning the overhead walkways gave way, releasing their human cargo to the crowded dance floor below.

It was the worst construction failure in American history. One hundred and fourteen people died and over two hundred were injured. An on-site design change intended to simplify construction was determined to be the cause of the collapse. The change resulted in the lower walkway being supported almost entirely by the upper walkway, which was then carrying twice the load of the original design. This fatal error was overlooked by the design engineers supervising the project.[1]

In like manner, critical details overlooked at the design phase of a governmental edifice will lead inevitably to cultural collapse. Sadly, modern America is experiencing just such a structural failure.

5

FROM PHILADELPIA TO THE PRESENT: THE DESCENT INTO JUDGMENT

*I*t is beyond the scope of this book to describe the complete history of our decline since Philadelphia. We merely pause to point out a few of the major trends, events, and institutions that have done the greatest damage. We will also take a quick look at the cultural breakdown resulting from an accelerating erosion of the American legal order.

NINETEENTH CENTURY PRELUDE

The War Between the States

Bloody revolutions almost always set the stage for further advances toward tyranny. The Civil War was no exception. Amazingly, slavery was abolished in England by the stroke of a pen. This came about through the untiring legislative labors of a Christian parliamentarian named William Wilberforce over a period of thirty years.[1] The slave holders were compensated and the slaves went free without a shot being fired.

There was a different spirit abroad in America: a spirit of extreme impatience, self-righteousness, instant perfection, and belligerence. This was typified by the writing of William Lloyd Garrison, editor of the *Liberator,* who probably more than any other man stirred up the climate for war. This paragraph was typical of his writing:

I unreflectingly assented to the popular but pernicious doctrine of gradual abolition. I seize this opportunity to make a full and unequivocal recantation, and thus publicly to ask pardon of my God, my country, and of my brethren the poor slaves, for having uttered a sentiment so full of timidity, injustice, and absurdity . . . .

I am aware, that many object to the severity of my language; but is there not cause for severity? I will be as harsh as truth, and as uncompromising as justice. On this subject I do not wish to think, or speak, or write, with moderation. . . . I am in earnest I will not equivocate I will not excuse I will not retreat a single inch AND I WILL BE HEARD . . . . [2]

This was a spirit that refused to tolerate a variety of Southern proposals to phase out slavery gradually. This spirit insisted on the sacrifice of over 600,000 American lives as brother took up sword against brother.[3] There were for example, almost as many men killed at Gettysburg in three days as died in the entire Vietnam War.[4]

Although the Southern system of slavery has been grossly misrepresented, it was nonetheless unbiblical. In the first place, no more than 20 percent of Southern families ever owned any slaves. Furthermore, public opinion served to keep most abuses in check and the vast majority of slaves were, in fact, well treated.

In the 1930s the federal government compiled over 10,000 pages of interviews with former slaves in its 40-volume *Slave Narratives*. Eighty-six percent of the former slaves described their masters as "good masters," according to Steve Wilkins in *America: The First 350 Years*. Ten percent described their masters as "hard masters," and only four percent said they had "cruel masters."

However, the slaves had few rights or protections under the law. They had the legal status of commodities. Thus, slave families were on occasion split apart, and physical punishment was not subject to biblical restraints. And obviously the slaves were not released after seven years or provided the opportunity to earn their freedom, as specified by Scripture. Biblical laws of slavery and indentured servitude will be discussed in some detail in chapter 9, "The Function of Biblical Civil Government."

It should not be forgotten, however, that the system was used by God to deliver the slaves from African paganism into a generally Christian culture. Further, the practitioners of African voodoo were just as culpable in ensnaring their black countrymen as were the slave traders.

Nevertheless, in the providence of God a coterie of Unitarian Boston abolitionists funded the revolutionary John Brown to fan the flames of judgment against the Southern culture.[5] This was similar to His use of ancient Babylon to judge Judah. Pro-life activist Paul deParrie notes that Brown "continually affirmed that slavery would not end without bloodshed."[6] His bloody activity in Kansas and at Harper's Ferry provided the necessary spark to ignite the conflagration.

The emancipation of the slaves in 1863 should have torn down the final barrier standing in the way of human freedom and dignity. Instead, the Civil War marked the beginning of a long decline wherein the black man simply exchanged his old slave holder for a new master, a paternalistic national state. Incredibly, the white man took a place beside the Negro, meekly accepting the chains of statism and the loss of local self-government and sufficiency.

For example, passages of the Constitution clearly designed to limit the power of the federal government were reinterpreted by the Supreme Court to mean exactly the opposite—an unlimited grant of power to Congress. The damage initiated by the Supreme Court was compounded by a series of debilitating amendments—worst of all the fourteenth, sixteenth, and seventeenth. These have largely succeeded in crippling local self-government and transferring its power to Washington, D.C.

The Fourteenth Amendment turns the Bill of Rights on its head, applying its restrictions to the states rather than the federal government. The Sixteenth Amendment authorized the progressive income tax and the Seventeenth wiped out state government representation at the federal level with the direct election of senators (see chapters 2 and 3 for additional detail). Over the years the cumulative impact of these radical changes has staggered the American Republic until today political liberty in the United States is now in serious jeopardy.

The Public School System

The revolutionary changes that brought us to these perilous times would not have occurred if the biblical principles of government that guided the Puritans had remained enshrined in the hearts of the American people. Unfortunately, they have been erased through years of secular, public education.

Much, of course, has been written on the anti-Christian nature of the government school system. The words of Martin Luther almost five hundred years ago have proven to be prophetic:

> I am much afraid that schools will prove to be great gates of hell unless they diligently labor in explaining the Holy Scriptures, engraving them in the hearts of youth. I advise no one to place his child where the Scriptures do not reign paramount. Every institution in which men are not increasingly occupied with the Word of God must become corrupt.[7]

Karl Marx drafted the blueprint with his *Communist Manifesto* in the early 1800s. He called for "a heavy progressive or graduated income tax" and "free education for all children in public schools."[8]

However, education was not among the powers delegated to the federal government by the Constitution. In fact, Jefferson challenged the very basis of the compulsory education system when he wrote, "To compel a man to furnish contributions of money for the propagation of opinions which he disbelieves and abhors is sinful and tyrannical."[9]

During the mid-1800s Horace Mann was the key figure in a movement which introduced socialized, "free," public education to America. With this foundation stone in place, the way was open for John Dewey to complete the process of secularizing American education. To Dewey, God and biblical absolutes were mythical and in any event had no place in a government or public classroom. R.L. Dabney, later to become Stonewall Jackson's chaplain in the Army of the Confederacy, sounded the alarm:

> On the other hand, it is an Atheistic outrage on the Christians, who compose the larger part of the citizens, to intrude between them and their children, and then give them a godless, which, as we have shown, must be an ungodly education . . . . The practical result will surely be, that the attitude of our constitutions will enable the infidel party to triumph everywhere, to expel the Bible

and Christianity from all the schools, and to rear us (so far as State schools go) a generation of Atheists.[10]

Herbert Schlossberg in his landmark book *Idols for Destruction,* points to the idol of historicism, or the human tendency to absolutize the flow of history. Because the tide of history happens to have dumped public schools on our doorstep, we feel we must work to improve them.[11] For example, James Hefley writes, "By necessity or by choice, however, the educational stake of many Christians will continue to be in public schools . . . . We must try to reverse secularistic trends."[12]

Instead, we should judge the public schools, as prophets, according to the Word of God. Nowhere does the Bible assign authority for education to civil government. That responsibility is assigned solely to parents (see Eph. 6:4), who may choose to delegate it in part to the church and private schools. For us to try to clean up the government schools is to fight against God and to become accomplices to a great evil that has been perpetrated on our land. In our political activism we must learn to judge every human institution according to the law of God.

The government school system is based on an ungodly, socialistic base of support. A case in point is Oregon, where about 70 percent of personal property taxes goes to support government education. This, of course, is pure socialism: forcing someone else to pay for the education of your children. It is becoming clear to many that socialism does not work any better in education than it does anywhere else. What many Christians fail to see is that the system would be just as immoral and unworkable if the government schools were teaching pure Christianity. It is an unbiblical and unconstitutional establishment of religion.

Currently we see a great movement of Christians running for and attempting to control the school boards of America. This may or may not be a laudable effort, depending on the motives. If the motive is to gain leadership experience and credentials for future campaigns for higher office, well and good. If the motive is to defund public schools from within, well and good. If the motive is evangelism in a generally non-Christian "mission-field," well and good.

However, if the motive is to "clean up" the public schools and "restore them to the glory days of yesteryear," the movement is destined for futility. God simply will not permit socialism to be "cleaned up." This is akin to the Israelites moving into the promised land and attempting to "clean up" the temples of Baal!

In accounts of reform in the Old Testament, the good king of Israel would reform the temple and the society and would destroy all the idols, with one exception—he would leave the high places intact. I have often wondered, "Why in the world didn't he destroy those terrible high places?" Now I think I know. It is possible for an idol to become so entrenched in the fabric of society that even the people of God fail to recognize it for what it is and to take steps to get rid of it.

Our modern idols are not always easy to detect. They often take the shape of ideas and institutions woven into the warp and woof of our culture. Like a piece of hologram art work, they escape the casual gaze. It takes a concentrated exercise of visual acuity to look beyond the surface veil and see the dragons lurking in the background.

The government schools have taken on the character of an idol in American life. We have assigned to them a Messianic quality that rivals that of God Himself. We idolize education as the source of the "good life," usually defined in terms of increased earning power. This idolatry has brought us to the brink of national destruction. How can we be so naive as to think that God will bless any effort to restore such an idolatrous program? God cannot bless legalized theft, and He cannot bless any institution that sets itself up as His rival.

Our energy would be far better expended running for offices in city, county, and state government. To try to resuscitate the public school system is to fight against the judgment of God. Instead, we should work hard to set up an alternative system of Christian schools and home schools and encourage Christian fathers to accept their biblical responsibility for education.

CHAOS IN THE COURTS

Having lost its moorings in the Bible and common law, our criminal justice system is now more criminal than just. This manifests itself in a profusion of legal aberrations.

In general, the system places a greater emphasis on procedural technicalities than on guilt or innocence based on written law. Consequently, legalism and the exponential multiplication of law on the books has hamstrung American society.

The very definition of justice has been obscured in American jurisprudence. For example, the judicial process often starts with plea bargaining, rather than attempting to determine guilt or innocence based on a clearly defined offense.

Jurors are not selected at random, but rather they are disqualified for special knowledge that would supposedly prejudice their decision. There is a false assumption of neutrality. In Scripture special knowledge of a case does not disqualify the ability of a Christian to pass godly judgment on an alleged offense. In fact, such knowledge often makes him better equipped to pass judgment. Even intimate family members are called upon to pass judgment on one another for capital crimes (see Deut. 21:19).

Jurors must prove intent and are thereby required to read the defendant's mind. Thus, it matters not if an offense occurred; it matters only if the defendant "intended" to commit the offense. This has opened the door to psychological testimony and the plea of not guilty by reason of insanity for some of the most heinous crimes.

Furthermore, jurors are instructed by judges to decide only the facts of the case, not the law. Thus, the time-honored doctrine of jury nullification of unjust law is denied. Under jury nullification, jurors evaluate the law itself in light of higher constitutional and biblical law. If they determine that the law is unjust, they may return a "not guilty" verdict. Were it not for this doctrine, hundreds of escaped slaves would have been returned to their masters in the years prior to the Civil War.

This is one of the problems inherent in an adversarial system, rather than an advocacy system in which there is a concern on the part of all to arrive at truth. Defense attorneys are concerned only with acquittal of their defendants rather than simply ensuring that they get a fair trial. Instead of emphasizing a judgment based on the full disclosure of evidence, an adversarial system focuses on who can best present their case. Elocution triumphs over truth.

In fact, more attention is given to criminal rights than to victim's rights. The victim's input in the sentencing process is virtually unheard of in most states. In addition, compensation to the victim is almost non-existent. The system disregards the rights of the widow and orphan in such matters as probate. Probate lawyers sometimes end up with as much as 20 percent of the estate, which can be tied up for years.[13]

Double jeopardy has been permitted in both state and federal courts since the Civil War. A celebrated case of this nature was the retrial of acquitted Los Angeles policemen in the 1993 Rodney King beating case, which triggered massive riots. The government bowed to the pressure of the mobs and the media in having the case retried in federal court. In the subsequent trial two of the police were found guilty.

Moreover, a defendant who has been found innocent of a criminal offense may then be sued for damages by the supposed victim in a civil court. The Bible does not recognize a sharp distinction between civil and criminal law since all crime is ultimately against God. Part of David's confession to the crime of murder and adultery included these words, "Against Thee and Thee only have I sinned" (Ps. 51:4).

The deterrent value of punishment is denied and criminals are coddled. For example, separation of juvenile law from adult criminal law fosters the growth of youth gangs. The Bible recognizes no such contrast, holding the incorrigible son fully responsible for his crimes (see Deut. 21:18–21).

One *Wizard of Id* comic strip, drawn by Parker and Hart, depicted a little boy and a learned doctor in front of a statue of Lady Justice. The little boy immediately wonders why Lady Justice is blindfolded. As the doctor explains, the reason is that justice is blind. Next, the little boy notices that the statue carries a sword. The doctor then responds that she does so to ensure that justice is upheld. The little boy ponders the answer for a moment, but he cannot resist one more question. Could the doctor tell him the reason why Lady Justice is shown holding a scale? To this, the doctor answers ruefully, "Justice ain't cheap, son."

The cartoon illustrates an unfortunate fact of American life: attorneys, with their immoderate fees, make the price of justice all but unaffordable for most Americans. Rather than serving justice they seem to be serving their own pocketbooks. In addition to very high hourly rates, we find astronomical monetary awards in civil cases due to percentage compensation of liability attorneys.

Currently, these prices may be simply the result of free market forces. That may be true, although price fixing at artificially high levels is far from uncommon within the judicial fraternity.[14] Free enterprise or no, the fact remains that to attain justice, the average person must pay through the nose. Almost everyone can cite a horror story of an acquaintance who has been sued for frivolous reasons, was subsequently acquitted, but ended up with a $10,000 attorney bill. Is this justice?

One possible remedy would be to require the losing plaintiff and attorney to pay all court fees. Ultimately, the best solution may be to remove the administration of justice from the marketplace altogether, making the work of legal representation a ministry of either church or state. This was apparently the case in ancient Israel, where one of the tasks of the Levites was to serve as a legal expert and teacher in the courts, compensated by the tithe (see Deut. 17:9; 1 Chron. 23:4; 2 Chron. 17:8–9; 19:8).

But today attorneys use the law for their own personal aggrandizement, rather than champion the law. They risk the judgment of Christ on their ancient forerunners: "Woe to you lawyers also! for you load men with burdens hard to bear, and you yourselves do not touch the burdens with one of your fingers" (Luke 11:46, RSV).

With some notable exceptions, this is a fairly accurate description of today's attorneys. Lawyers comprise the majority in many state legislatures and are responsible for weaving a complex web of unbiblical laws. They then posture as legal experts in private practice, who alone are able to extirpate the hapless layman who gets caught up in the web. This is contrary to biblical law, which is contained in a very small corpus and was read to the entire nation every seven years (see Deut. 31:11–13). Even children are capable of comprehending and obeying the laws of God.

For these and many other reasons, justice in the United States is no longer blind, it is cross-eyed. Greater concern and legal protection is afforded the law breaker under the American system than is afforded his victim. Rather than looking to the courts for justice, Americans now sense the inherent injustice of the system and avoid it whenever possible.

CHAOS ON THE STREETS

Crime

The danger in such a humanistic legal system is the total breakdown of all law. Sensing the inherent injustice of the system, men come to despise and disobey the law. With the breakdown of law comes a descent into anarchy. Law abiding citizens become prisoners in their own homes, afraid to come out at night. Then arises a hue and cry for more and more dictatorial measures—such as gun control—in the name of public safety and order. Gradually control replaces freedom.

This is all part of God's judgment on a society that refuses to adjudicate His law in the exercise of public justice. When the represent-atives of a culture refuse to execute God's law in the administration of justice, God begins to execute that culture. This execution may come in the form of anarchy in the streets, totalitarianism, war, famine, or disease.

Because God's penalties for criminal activity are not enforced, career criminals are released to claim more innocent victims. Incorrigi-bility is no longer punished with death: the three-time loser penalty is no longer enforced (see Deut. 17:12). A misplaced sense of mercy for the criminal has resulted in total lack of mercy for his current and future victims.

Former Congressman Ron Paul reports that in 1968, the worst year of the Vietnam conflict, 14,618 U.S. soldiers were killed. This figure is dwarfed by more than 25,000 murders on the streets of the United States in 1992. "A violent crime is committed every 17 seconds," he says. "There are 78 women raped every hour." The average time a convicted murderer spends in prison is six years and seven months, less than the average terms of non-violent drug dealers. Many crimes are not reported and thus do not appear in these statistics.[15] According to Bureau of Justice Statistics, males, younger persons, blacks, Hispanics, residents of central cities, and the poor tend to have higher rates of victimization than persons who do not possess these characteristics.[16]

Although the number of felony convictions has risen dramatically, the certainty of punishment remains low.[17] For example, between 1986 and 1990 the number of felony convictions increased 42 percent in state courts. However, in 1990 state courts imposed a prison sentence on only 46 percent of convicted felons. In general, a felony is defined as a crime that has the potential of being punished by more than one year in a state prison.

Culture

How has the explosion in crime affected the broader culture? As we have seen, religion is the foundation of law. Law in turn undergirds and provides stability for virtually everything else that constitutes a nation's culture. As the legal system in America erodes, other institutions of society begin to rock and teeter. The result is a cultural earthquake.

As of 1993 the destructive effects of this earthquake were felt on every hand. For example, a crime like homosexuality (Lev. 20:13) not only goes unpunished but is actually encouraged by our legal system. In 1992 a Seattle judge placed a three-year-old boy with a homosexual couple, over the objections of his mother. "I truly believed they [the state] would place my son with a good family," said Megan Lucas, "This isn't what I want for my son." [18]

In Washington, D.C., the government actually recruited homosexuals as adoptive parents in accordance with federally prescribed quotas. Recruiting for the first ten-week training program was initiated in the summer of 1993 when not enough sodomites volunteered. The homosexual facilitator said that "if the social worker objected to delivering a child to a sex pervert, the social worker would be removed from the case and that no judge in D.C. has ever refused to deliver children to adoptive sex perverts." [19]

How could our courts have become such bastions of corruption? For one thing, crime and immorality have been trivialized for years by television and other major media. The tenderest ages are now defiled via cartoons and comic books. In this genre is a comic called *Flatbush Native,* the name taken from New York's black Flatbush district. One issue features a man who nonchalantly witnesses a rape from his apartment window and later kills a dozen cops during a convenience store holdup. The editors say they are simply "reflecting urban reality" and that the "heroes use their powers to help themselves instead of saving the world." [20]

As noted earlier in this chapter, the breakdown of law and order provides the opportunity and the rationale for imposition of dictatorial controls. The Clinton administration moved rapidly in that direction with its drive to nationalize the health care industry in 1994. This blatant power grab was designed to deliver 14 percent of the American economy into the hands of the federal government. The ability to parcel out health care is a frightening tool for controlling a people.

Furthermore, "health care" was redefined to encompass a broad spectrum of activity, including such things as food and tobacco, violence and gun control, sex education and teenage pregnancy. The administration planned to consolidate the unconstitutional powers of such agencies as the EPA, OSHA, and BATF under a super-regulatory agency with power to control nearly every area of American life. [21]

Perhaps most absurd, and troubling, was the President's linking of gun ownership and health care. He stated that the nation will never be able to get its health-care costs down if the streets continue to be a battleground for armed teenagers. Thus is created a further emotional rationale for passage of gun control laws in violation of the Second Amendment: "A well regulated Militia, being necessary to the security of a free State, the right of the people to keep and bear arms, shall not be infringed."

The result of such an approach can be nothing other than an escalation in crime as law-abiding citizens are systematically disarmed. Unaffected by gun control laws, the criminal element can easily obtain the "tools of the trade" needed to assault an increasingly defenseless populace.[22]

As was the case in Nazi Germany and the Soviet Union, efforts are constantly made to silence the growing voices of dissent in America. In the five years following the repeal of the so-called "Fairness Doctrine" by Ronald Reagan (1987), Christian and conservative radio commentators proliferated.

The Fairness Doctrine was imposed in 1949 by the FCC to ensure a balanced ideological mix among what was then a limited number of radio frequencies. The idea was to give groups of opposing ideological outlook "equal time" to express their views.

In practice, the doctrine led to nearly four decades of stifled debate. Dubbed by some the "blandness doctrine," it was used by the government to squelch voices contrary to the dominant media. According to Don McAlvany, this was accomplished by pressuring "station owners into neutral, pabulum-like noncontroversial, milquetoast-type programming with the Fairness Doctrine's loss-of-license penalty hanging (like a sword of Damocles) over their heads."[23]

During the six-year period 1987 to 1993, the reinvigorated freedom of expression resulted in increasing numbers of Americans becoming informed and taking action against the liberal agenda. Subsequently, Democrats in Congress introduced bills that would, in effect, reimpose the "Fairness Doctrine" and derail this challenge to the airwaves.

To illustrate, Rep. Bill Hefner said, "Talk radio scares me. The negative attacks on Congress are getting to the point where we are not able to govern." Thus in the name of fairness, the government moves to stifle freedom of expression, contrary to the first amendment: "Congress shall make no law . . . abridging the freedom of speech, or of the press . . . ."[24]

CONCLUSION

It is becoming more and more evident that America is on the verge of serious collapse—spiritually, politically, and economically. Once undiscernible cracks in the philosophical foundation have opened to cripple the American system of law and government.

Within the past ten years or so, American Christians have finally awakened to the danger and have cast about for a solution. We have searched in vain for some "blueprint" that would enable us to fill the cracks and shore up the collapsing system. Nothing seems to work. The next chapter explores some of the faulty "blueprints" with which we have attempted to rebuild.

REVIEW QUIZ

1. What is the primary cause of crime?
   a. Poverty
   b. Poor family life
   c. Lack of education
   d. A human predisposition toward disobedience to the law of God

2. The fact that evil men are in leadership is an indication that:
   a. God uses bad government to chastise His people
   b. Conspiracies control the movement of history
   c. Things must get worse and worse before Christ returns
   d. Christians have no business in politics

3. (T or F) When attorneys dominate a culture, formal legal procedure pushes out law and morality. The practice of law takes precedence over the law.

4. The statement that in the American judicial system "victims are robbed twice" refers to the fact that:
   a. The prohibition of double jeopardy is not enforced by the courts
   b. Criminals are quickly released to rob again
   c. Victims must pay taxes to support criminals in prison

5. The British Parliament abolished the slave trade in 1808 as the result of whose labors?
   a. William Wilberforce
   b. Oliver Cromwell
   c. Charles II

6. Whose pen did the most to spark the War Between the States?
   a. Abraham Lincoln
   b. The apostle Paul
   c. William Lloyd Garrison

7. Which of these was *not* a feature of the system of chattel slavery that existed in the antebellum South?
   a. Slave marriages had no basis in law
   b. No legal protection for slaves
   c. Slave given his own plot and released after forty-nine years
   d. No system for earning freedom

8. What was the root cause of the War Between the States?
   a. Refusal to obey biblical requirements for slavery resulted in judgment of Christians by Unitarian abolitionists from Boston
   b. The economic necessity of slavery in conflict with man's inalienable right to liberty
   c. The conflict over state's rights and centralized government
   d. Southern Calvinism vs. New England Unitarianism

9. (T or F) The jury is able to determine the defendant's heart motives by making inferences from external evidence.

10. Which of these was *not* a power assigned to the government by the Constitution?
    a. Set up the court system
    b. Regulate interstate commerce
    c. Provide for well-educated populace
    d. Punish counterfeiting

11. Under jury nullification juries try
    a. The facts only
    b. The facts and the law
    c. The law only
    d. The judge
    e. b and d

12. What system underlies public education?
    a. Socialism
    b. Free enterprise
    c. Humanitarianism
    d. Sado-masochism

13. The father of the public education system was
    a. William Lloyd Garrison
    b. John Dewey
    c. Herbert Schlossberg
    d. Franklin Roosevelt

14. Who gets preferential treatment under the American system of justice?
    a. Widows and orphans
    b. Attorneys
    c. Criminals
    d. Victims
    e. b and c

DISCUSSION GUIDE

1. How could the War Between the States have been avoided?

2. What were the root causes of the War Between the States?

3. In what ways was life in America different following the War Between the States?

4. What is the basic problem with government education?

5. To whom does the Bible assign primary authority for education?

6. What are some of the most pressing problems in the American criminal justice system?

7. What are some specific ways in which breakdown of the law order has led to deterioration of American culture?

Answer Key

1) d	2) a	3) T	4) c	5) a	6) c	7) c
8) a	9) F	10) c	11) b	12) a	13) b	14) e

6

REMODELING WITHOUT
A BLUEPRINT

*I*n the early 1980s, Christian writer Os Guinness noted that two dangers faced American Christendom: 1) failure to reenter the political realm, and 2) reentering the political realm with a standard tainted by humanistic thought. In recent years, Christians have begun to take a more active role in public life; unfortunately, they have not for the most part carried a clear biblical standard into the political arena.

God has not forgotten the covenant that our forefathers established with Him in the Mayflower Compact and the several colonial constitutions, whether we remember it or not. Obedience to God's revealed law lies at the heart of God's covenant with this nation. The Word of God applies as much to modern nations as it did to ancient Israel (see chapter 7). Thus, He will bless or curse our political efforts to the extent that we implement His law in our national life:

> And if you obey the voice of the LORD your God, being careful to do all his commandments which I command you this day, the LORD our God will set you high above all the nations of the earth. And all these blessings will come upon you.
>
> But if you will not obey the voice of the LORD your God or be careful to do all his commandments and his statutes

which I command you this day, then all these curses shall
come upon you and overtake you. (Deut. 28:1–2, RSV)

Christians today have quite a bit of zeal for tearing down the
"idols of Baal" (such as abortion, sodomy, pornography, etc.).
However, we have very little zeal for rebuilding a civil order based on
the authority of God's law. We are willing to accept almost any
standard for political righteousness except the law of God: conscience,
majority rule, conservatism, common sense.

It is as though we have fallen into the trap of Jehu. He received
praise from God for his wholehearted destruction of the house of Ahab,
which was addicted to idolatrous Baal worship: "Thou hast done well
in executing that which is right in mine eyes, and hast done unto the
house of Ahab according to all that was in mine heart . . . " (2 Kings
10:30).

But the next verse says that he "took no heed to walk in the law of
the Lord God of Israel with all his heart." Sadly, many believers today
commit this same error. We are very fond of saying that "the Bible has
all the answers," but we then proceed into the political realm as
though the Bible were completely silent.

Reliance on common sense and human logic has led Christians
into a number of blind alleys down through the centuries. The
twentieth century seems to have more than its share of these dead
ends. Let us first examine how human logic can lead us astray. Then
we will look at some specific erroneous standards for political
righteousness that have been erected on the foundation of human
logic.

COMMON SENSE AND HUMAN LOGIC

The first principle of logic was driven home to me a few years ago at a
pro-life debate seminar. At the time an initiative was being floated that
would require parental notification of pending abortions for teenage
girls. The seminar was taught by a man flown in from out-of-state to
train the pro-life debate team. Ironically, I did not learn the first
principle of logic from anything the instructor taught us directly.
Rather, I learned it from what he left out of his presentation.

Our speaker was acclaimed as a brilliant man, and for the most
part he was. He had even debated the notorious atheist Madalyn

Murray O'Hair. He, of course, accepted these accolades with the appropriate degree of humility. In that Saturday seminar we learned many excellent principles of logic and debate. For example, we were taught to ask our opponents three critical questions when faced with an illogical statement:

1) What does it mean?
2) How do you know? and
3) So what?

When the humanist said, "You right-wing Christians are trying to impose your version of morality on the rest of us," we were taught to challenge him with questions like these:

1) What do you mean by "impose"?
2) Oh really, where did you get your information on that?
3) Is that really so different from what you're trying to do to us?

All argumentation consists of three basic elements—the words, the facts, and the logical presentation. These questions are designed to expose the flaws in these three basic elements of our opponent's reasoning.[1]

These questions are excellent verbal weapons which we should learn to handle with skill. They are, however, a two-edged sword, which can do much damage to our cause if used without discretion.

Common Ground

A basic flaw in the model surfaced during the question-and-answer period when an elderly woman asked a question something like this: "Everything we've talked about today is centered on human logic and reasoning. Where does the Word of God enter into all of this?"

At this point our learned instructor revealed his ignorance of the first principle of logic. He replied in words to this effect: "I have found that the non-believer is usually not ready to accept the Word of God. I always try to use logic to expose the errors in his thinking and bring him to a point where he can accept the Bible."

The search for common ground in human reason is a trap that many brilliant Christian men have fallen into down through the centuries. It is a futile search. The only common ground we have with the unbeliever is the "word of the law" written in his heart (Rom. 2:15). This does not refer to the written Word, but rather to the divine signature that God has left impressed on all of his created handiwork. When a man's conduct fails to conform to the divine impression, he is said to have a "guilty conscience."

However, fallen creation or human reasoning cannot be relied upon to interpret that innate signature and unspoken testimony because man's reason is fallen and distorted. Rather, the revealed Word of God in the Bible—illuminated by the Spirit—alone can provide the correct context for interpretation of the evidence. The problem is not intellectual because the existence of God is obvious in His creation. On the contrary, the problem is moral, a dishonest rejection or distortion of the irrefutable evidence. The only corrective is the Voice of God.

The First Principle

The first principle of logic is simply this: Human logic is fallible and must always be informed by the revealed Word of God. Apart from God's revelation, human logic quickly goes awry. Furthermore, some of God's revealed truth is beyond the capacity of human logic to fully comprehend (see Isa. 55:8–9).

Adam and Eve found this out the hard way. Their basic sin was to set themselves up as independent judges of truth. This was in essence an attempt to play God. Unfortunately, most of us are no better than Adam and Eve in our attempts to reason with the natural man. We fail to remember that the natural man "suppresses the truth in unrighteousness" (Rom. 1:18).

You can build an airtight case and argue the natural man into the corner with your brilliant logic and he will still not believe. Only as the Spirit of God applies the Word of God to his heart will he believe and understand. Right reason can be exercised and evidence properly evaluated only in the context of faith and the Word. Thus, theologian Cornelius Van Til has warned: "We do not first defend theism philosophically by an appeal to reason and experience in order, after that, to turn to Scripture for our knowledge and defense of Christianity. We get our theism as well as our Christianity from the Bible."[2]

As we go forth to "bring every thought captive to Christ" (2 Cor. 10:5), our appeal must not be to the independent reason of our opponents. We dare not encourage them in the notion that they are the autonomous judge of the truth of God. This is to encourage them in the temptation of Eve.[3] Rather, we must wield the truth like a sword.

Doubtless, this should be done in a discreet manner lest we be guilty of "casting our pearls before swine." In public debate we need not preach a sermon or thump our Bibles; nor must we always quote chapter and verse. However, on occasion we may choose to paraphrase or summarize the Scripture.

Nonetheless, we must remind the natural man that he has no right to set himself up as the judge of the Word of God. He must be confronted with the fact that the only reason he refuses to accept the Bible is that he has presumptuously decided to play the role of judge of his Creator.

Questioning techniques such as those mentioned above may be effective, if they are used in this context. For example, if the unbeliever objects to our unembarrassed use of the Bible in the public arena, we may ask him questions about censorship, book burning, and freedom of speech. However, our human reasoning should never replace the sword of the Spirit.

More importantly, we must not train our children to think and debate in this autonomous fashion. As adults, most of us can offer the excuse that we are products of the government school system and therefore do not know any better. But let us not repeat the same mistake with the next generation. The "arrows" that come forth from our quivers in the years ahead must be sharpened with the Word of Truth, not the rationalism of the ancient Greeks.

Ramifications

The ramifications of this error extend far beyond the individual. Ideas have consequences. All attempts to appeal to fallen man on the basis of a supposed "common ground" in reason apart from revelation lead to frustration. Ultimately, they will lead a society to either anarchy or statism.

Christian philosopher John Locke, for example, developed his secularized version of human rights and the social compact—apart from a biblical base[4]—apparently to appeal to a broader spectrum of humanity. Working from this foundation, humanist philosopher Jean-Jacques Rousseau developed the idea that society has corrupted the natural instincts of man in his pristine state. Thus, he venerated the "noble savage" and called for a return to the state of nature. His theories led to the dismantling of French society and the terror of the French Revolution—the guillotine. This carnage was justified on the grounds that it would clear the way for a new social compact, emancipated from the superstitions of religion and tradition. The French Revolution became the prototype for the even more brutal Bolshevik Communist Revolution a century later.

Shortly before the French Revolution, the Declaration of Independence was written by American patriots as a skillful piece of wartime propaganda. It too was based on Lockean social compact theory. The Declaration's phraseology was ambiguous enough to appeal simultaneously to the American Calvinists and the French humanists.[5] Both sides could read into the vague, but exhilarating language their own perspective and rally to the cause.[6]

Today the Declaration is still a favorite of radicals at both ends of the political spectrum. The right uses it in their appeal for autonomous individualism. At the same time, the left uses it to justify an egalitarian, socialistic society. These errors might have been avoided if the Declaration had been a more forthright expression of civil government's obligation to the law of God as revealed in Scripture. Instead these truths were held to be self-evident. But are they?

This predilection to trust in "self-evident" common sense and human logic has led us to adopt any number of other mistaken standards for political righteousness. These include a variety of traditions, philosophies, and so-called laws. They often have a surface appeal, but on closer examination we discover that they are resting on a foundation of sand.

HUMAN RIGHTS

One such erroneous standard masquerades under the banner of "human rights." Modern humanists have used the rubric of "human rights" to justify all sorts of perversions and atrocities. Human rights rhetoric is a remarkable illustration of how the power of language may be twisted and harnessed for evil ends.

If by human rights we mean the equal protection and responsibility of men and women under the law of God, we are on solid ground. By nature we are all "dead in trespasses and sins," "children of wrath" with no merited rights before God. By the grace and mercy of God, Christians have been quickened and delivered from the wrath of God (Eph. 2:1–4). Thus, only believers are truly free, possessing "rights" in the ultimate biblical sense. These rights are contingent upon a right relationship to God through Christ. A sentence of death rests on the heads of all others. For this reason, franchised—voting—believers were referred to as "freedmen" by the New England Puritans.

As an aspect of this grace toward mankind, God has given His law as a safeguard for the rights of His people. The law of God also serves as a guide for the responsible exercise of these rights in the service of God.

Furthermore, God's mercy and common grace extends the protection of the law to the unbeliever who dwells in geographic proximity to the believer. God told the Israelites that "One law shall be to him that is homeborn, and unto the stranger that sojourneth among you" (Ex. 12:49). This law restrains the unbeliever's lawlessness and serves as a tool of evangelism, protecting him and drawing him to the grace and mercy of God (see Deut. 4:6–8). Therefore, only by the grace and longsuffering of God is the unbeliever said to enjoy equality or human rights under the law in the political context.

Some Christian writers believe that this biblical concept is encapsulated in the Declaration of Independence.[7] The opening words of the Declaration are familiar to all: "We hold these truths to be self-evident, that all men are created equal, that they are endowed by their Creator with certain unalienable rights, that among these are life, liberty and the pursuit of happiness."

However, the source of authority for these stirring words—the Creator—is not the God of the Bible. The author, Thomas Jefferson is best described as a Unitarian, who denied the authority of Scripture. Although his true beliefs were checked by the bridle of public opinion, in later life he went so far as to produce his own version of the New Testament. The so-called *Jefferson Bible* deleted all reference to the miracles of Christ. Thus, Jefferson did not derive these truths from the Bible; rather on the basis of his own autonomous reason he declared them to be self-evident.

What was the source of human rights according to Jefferson? The following paragraph clearly states that the source of authority for the safeguarding of human rights resides in the social compact: "That to secure these rights, Governments are instituted among Men, deriving their just powers from the consent of the governed."

The just power of government is here said to derive from the consent of the people, not from God. This paragraph is taken directly from Lockean social compact theory as demonstrated in chapter 8. Under the social compact men give up some of the freedom they enjoy in the natural state to create a government. This government is invested by the people with power to secure their rights and freedoms. There is no reference to God.

By contrast, in a theocratic republic the people are granted the privilege by God of nominating or selecting their leaders. However, they are not granted the authority to constitute or create a government independent of God. The just power of government comes from God alone (see Rom. 13:1; Acts 17:26). But under the Declaration, this compact is entered into apart from any reference to the God of the Bible.

Herein lies the evil of modern human rights theory. When we divorce the source of our rights from God, we may start out with lofty goals: life, liberty, and the pursuit of happiness. However, apart from the divine reference point, it is not long before these noble virtues degenerate into all manner of perverted "rights." The list is endless.

Today we find the spiritual heirs of Jefferson clamoring for the right to privacy, the right to abortion, the right to sexual preference, the right to health care, the right to full employment, the right to welfare, the right to disseminate hard core pornography, ad nauseam. They use the "pursuit of happiness" phrase to justify these demands. Jefferson would no doubt be appalled at this development, but it is the logical extension of his autonomous position—his belief that man is free to create his own system of ethics. The result is not a free society; rather it is a free-for-all society.

About all it takes to get added to the list is to declare yourself a persecuted minority whose human rights are being trampled—unless, of course, you happen to be a born-again Christian. Christians play under a different set of rules with one hand tied behind their backs.

Anyone who would dare challenge these rights is stridently accused of discrimination, a cardinal offense in the lexicon of modern social sins. In former times the discriminating man, the man who could tell the difference between good and evil, was admired. Today he is vilified. Thus, there is tremendous pressure to defend our neighbor's practice of evil as his pluralistic right because we do not want him to interfere with our practice of righteousness.

All of this is a futile effort to divorce liberty from the law of God. It assumes that men by nature have certain things owed to them simply by virtue of their humanness. However, we have observed that the natural man, as sinner, stands condemned before God, devoid of any inherent rights. Rather than insisting on his illusory rights, modern man needs to face up to his responsibility as a sinner who stands condemned by God. Only then can he enter into the glorious liberty of the children of God.

Thus, we find that the language of liberty is used to justify all manner of licentiousness. Nowhere was this more evident than during the French Revolution of 1789. Its call to arms was "liberty, equality, fraternity." Its elegant *Declaration of the Rights of Man,* with its lofty elocution, was a masterpiece of human rights oratory.

Never did performance fall so miserably short of promise. In a few short years the situation in Paris degenerated into the barbarity of the Reign of Terror, with tens of thousands of the "enemies of the people" falling under the blade of the guillotine. Guilt was established by the euphemistic "Committee of Public Safety" merely on the basis of belonging to a particular social class. In the end it took Napoleon's "whiff of grape-shot" and a military dictatorship to restore order.

The reason the French flirtation with human rights degenerated more rapidly than the American version was that they were more forthright and brutal in their suppression of Christianity. The American attack on religion—a declaration of religious neutrality—was much more subtle and oblique. Thus, it has taken America two hundred years to self-destruct, rather than the two or three required of the French Revolution. But self-destruct we will, unless we learn the lesson that human rights are non-existent apart from God.

TRADITIONAL VALUES

It is quite remarkable to hear American Christians appealing repeatedly to something called "traditional values." The Pharisees of Jesus' day were also firm believers in traditional values. However, as they clung tenaciously to their manmade traditions over the centuries, they gradually loosened their grip on the Word of God. Jesus rebuked them soundly: "You forsake the commandment of God and hold fast the tradition of men" (Mark 7:8, RSV).

What is a traditional value, anyway? And what could be more traditional than the family? One man's traditional value, however, is another man's immorality. Consider, for example, the Carter administration's "Year of the Family." In addition to the biblical model of husband, wife, and children, the term "families" was not so subtly redefined to include fornicating couples and homosexual partners.

The rhetoric of the Nazi movement in Hitler's Germany was laced with the language of "traditional values." The Nazis spoke often of "our Christian heritage," "getting back to spiritual values," "our traditional values," and "the divine will for our nation."

Christians can fall into this trap too. We tend to use such phrases because we don't want to refer directly to the Bible. Over time the words are drained of their biblical content and we become vulnerable to the ideas of almost any demagogue who appears to be "speaking our language."

A big part of the problem is that the term "traditional values" is too often left undefined and nebulous. Tradition may be good or bad, depending on its base of authority. Noah Webster's original 1828 dictionary defined *tradition* as "that which is handed down from age to age by oral communication. The Jews pay great regard to tradition in matters of religion, as do the Romanists. Protestants reject the authority of tradition in sacred things, and rely only on the written word."

Webster did make this acknowledgment: "Traditions may be good or bad, true or false." For example, Paul exhorted the Thessalonians to "stand fast, and hold the traditions which ye have been taught, whether by word or our epistle" (2 Thess. 2:15). In this sense, "tradition" is synonymous with the written Word of God.

But in its more common usage tradition refers to oral custom handed down from parent to child, from generation to generation. The Jews placed great emphasis on precise memorization, but apart from a written transcript, deterioration is inevitable. This may occur by accretion, reduction, or distortion.

You have probably played the parlor game called "gossip." The first player whispers a secret in the ear of the second player who then repeats it in the ear of the third. By the time the message has traveled all the way around the room, it bears no resemblance to the original. This same process occurs in the broader cultural context via tradition.

In addition, tradition is a means by which heresy enters into and destroys a theological doctrine or a legal principle over time. Its mental state of mind is "we've always done it that way!" Problems enter as traditions gradually become divorced from the authority of God's Word and degenerate inevitably toward humanism.

We find it easy to think that that could never happen to us or that "we are too firmly grounded in the truth for that to happen." However, the weight of church history is against us. Consider the rapid decline of some of the most solid denominations in America over the past 150 years.

Today, in the name of traditional values, many Christians want to arrest the death throes of the socialistic public school system. Earlier in this century Christians attempted to forbid the consumption of all alcoholic beverages in the name of traditional values or "fundamentals" of the faith.

In the last century they jumped on the abolitionist bandwagon being pulled by New England Unitarians. As a result they ended up rejecting the crucial biblical doctrine of indentured servitude when chattel slavery was abolished (see chapters 5 and 9). Before that they were sold on the concept of public education because it was allegedly "free" and on the penitentiary model of criminal justice. In each case the problem came when Christians had "heard it said" according to the tradition of men rather than "seen it written" according to the Word of God.

Too often in pluralistic America, Christians have hidden behind the banner of "traditional values" to avoid a direct appeal to the Bible or to biblical values. In the process their political/cultural vision has become blurred, and their message has been diverted from the Word of God. In the words of theologian and author, Carl Henry: "We hear much today about the need for values, but values are not absolutes—at least not necessarily. They are the preferred ideals of individuals and societies. We need again to have the commandments of God emblazoned on our consciences and the redeeming grace of God throbbing in our hearts."[8]

Because American Christians have not held firmly to the authority of God's Word in the public arena, the American legal system has degenerated into a hodge-podge of tradition. Our once proud legal system originally derived its authority from the objective standard of the Bible as it found expression in English common law.[9]

Today the basis of authority is nothing more than the precedent established in earlier cases. These change constantly because they are based on the shifting tide of legal opinion apart from the Word of God. Instead of searching the Word of God, or even the Constitution, legal technicians wade through endless volumes of legal commentary for a precedent—a tradition—on which to rest their case.

CONSERVATIVE PHILOSOPHY

Conservatism is another lame horse to which American Christians have hitched their philosophical wagon. A common stratagem of the Devil is to present two false ideas as though they were opposites, one being false and the other therefore "true." The real truth is thereby excluded from the field of debate. Political conservatism has served well in this capacity in twentieth century America.

The biblical standard is found in the Proverb: "Do not swerve to the right hand or to the left" (Prov. 4:27, RSV). Conservative humanism is as bad as liberal humanism since both seek humanistic solutions. Both reject or ignore the authority of the Word of God. Liberalism stresses state solutions while conservatism stresses the autonomous individual.

Neither effectively addresses the philosophical problem of "the one and the many." That is, how can the rights and freedom of the individual be balanced with the legitimate needs of society and the state? The answer to that question is found ultimately only in the person of God. He is at once one and three—an individual and a community of Persons. The delicate balance between the one and the many is reflected in God's Revelation, the standard for all of human life and activity. Thus, apart from Scripture, it is impossible to define the proper relationship between the one and the many, the individual and the state.

In addition, we must be careful not to deify the past. Not everything in the past is worth conserving, carte blanche. We must scrutinize the past through the lens of Scripture, accepting and conserving what is good and rejecting what is bad. For example, it is easy to idolize the founders of America and accept without question everything they said and did.

Because there is an apparent or partial coincidence between some points of Scripture and conservative philosophy, we must be careful not to accept all conservative teaching without careful examination. Because conservatism is not firmly rooted in the Bible, its tenets are ambiguous and unstable. Consider this scathing analysis of conservatism by Robert Dabney:

> This is a party which never conserves anything. Its history has been that it demurs to each aggression of the progressive party, and aims to save its credit by a respectable amount of growling, but always acquiesces at last in the innovation. What was the resisted novelty of yesterday is to-day one of the accepted principles of conservatism; it is now conservative only in affecting to resist the next innovation, which will to-morrow be forced upon its

timidity and will be succeeded by some third revolution, to be denounced and then adopted in its turn. American conservatism is merely the shadow that follows Radicalism as it moves forward towards perdition. It remains behind it, but never retards it, and always advances near its leader. This pretended salt hath utterly lost its savor: wherewith shall it be salted? Its impotency is not hard, indeed, to explain. It is worthless because it is the conservatism of expediency only, and not of sturdy principle.[10]

An example of how conservatives are just a step behind liberals is seen in a 1985 article by Sally Reed on how the NEA is ruining education in America. "The way to save education," she wrote, "is to return control of schools to the parents and local communities where it belongs."[11] This is a band-aid approach to a terminal condition. From the conservative humanist standpoint, the socialized education system is worthy of being saved and can be saved. All that is needed is the restoration of parental control. The Bible, of course, makes no allowance for collectivist education.

In a similar vein former Congressman Ron Paul bemoans the lack of consistent principle displayed by many conservative legislators:

Texas has two conservative Republican Senators, and they show why we have fiscal problems in Washington, D.C. For example, in the debate on the disastrously expensive construction welfare project, the Super Collider, Sen. Phil Gramm asserted: " . . . opponents of the project were selfishly thinking about the next election rather than the future of the nation."

Columnist Bill Thompson of the Ft. Worth Telegram remarked: "Talk about chutzpa and hypocrisy. Phil Gramm never thinks about anything but the next election." Until we see a willingness by conservatives to vote against their own state's pork barrel projects, we can expect the spendarama to continue.[12]

We could multiply examples endlessly, but one more will suffice. The front page of the Spring 1990 *Homeschool Court Report* trumpeted this headline: "Conservatives Declare War on Religious Freedom." As attorney Michael Farris wrote,"The conservative bloc on the Supreme Court (with the heroic exception of Sandra Day O'Connor) has voted to eradicate the traditional protections of free exercise of religion."[13]

The ruling to which he referred was "Smith II." It permitted vast new authority for the government to overrule religious conviction when it conflicted with (even trivial) bureaucratic rules.[14] Ironically, it took a liberal Congress and President to overturn this ruling, according to the winter 1993 issue of the same publication.

Conservatism has "advanced" to the point where it now sees the civil state as the solution to most problems. This is sadly the case even with some of our finest Christian political organizations and lawmakers. For example, a brochure of the American Coalition for Traditional Values states: "We favor governmental assistance for the deserving poor, but only through programs which encourage individuals to be self-reliant, thus strengthening the family rather than weakening it."

Likewise, Christian Congressman Jim Bunn, swept into office in the 1994 Republican landslide, was described by the Portland *Oregonian* as "one of the strongest conservatives in an increasingly right-leaning Oregon GOP" (January 22, 1995). However, the same piece noted, "Bunn defended many social services programs, including welfare and school breakfast programs. He argued that conservatives could not oppose abortion on one hand and, on the other, hurt programs that help children." Can you imagine Davy Crockett advancing such an argument (see chapter 3)?

The difference between conservatism and liberalism is one only of degree, not of kind. It is only a question of how far and how fast we allow the state to intrude into our lives, not whether we allow the state to intrude. Regardless of which humanistic ideology we follow, the state will eventually absorb everything.

LAW OF NATIONS AND NATURAL LAW

The law of nations and the natural law are two closely related concepts. According to the law of nations, some supposed common standard for political righteousness exists that nations can agree upon apart from God's Word. This standard may supposedly be derived from a careful scrutiny of nature.

For example, C.S. Lewis held such a belief. According to a David Reinhard editorial in the Portland *Oregonian,* "Lewis believed in a public morality based on the publicly accessible rule of natural law. The natural law—the tao, he called it—transcended different cultures and religions."[15]

William Blackstone was the great exponent of natural law legal theory on which the American colonists relied heavily. He believed that the "immutable laws of human nature" are woven into the fabric of the universe and that God "gave him [man] also the faculty of reason to discover the purport of those laws." Furthermore,

> These are the eternal immutable laws of good and evil, to which the Creator Himself . . . conforms; and which He has enabled human reason to discover . . . the discovery of these first principles of the law of nature depended only upon the due exertion of right reason . . . .

> He has not perplexed the law of nature with a multitude of abstracted rules and precepts referring merely to the fitness or unfitness of things, as some have vainly surmised; but has graciously reduced the rule of obedience to this one paternal precept, "that man should pursue his own substantial happiness," This is the foundation of what we call ethics, or natural law.[16]

Thus, according to Blackstone, the law of nature may be found out merely by the exercise of right reason, without reference to revelation. Moreover, in this passage he downplays statutory law and makes man's "substantial happiness" the ultimate standard of right and wrong.

But what if my "substantial happiness" happens to derive from taking other people's money without having to work for it? Or what if I get "substantial happiness" from molesting little children? Or what if I determine that the "substantial happiness" of mankind is best advanced by the elimination of a certain class of citizens like Jews—or unborn babies?

Elsewhere, Blackstone paid lip service to the authority of the Bible, but only rarely in his four-volume legal commentary does he refer to Scripture. Even then it is only to illustrate a point, not as an appeal to supreme authority.

In Blackstone's system, the only real difference between the law of revelation and the law of nature is the clarity of the former. "If we could be as certain of the latter [law of nature] as we are of the former [law of Scripture], both would have an equal authority," he wrote, "but till then they can never be put in any competition together." But rather than aggressively asserting the superiority of Scripture, Blackstone concluded paradoxically, "Upon these two foundations, the law of nature and the Law of Revelation, depend all human laws." Since the two are therefore of essentially equal authority, the way is left open for man to attempt to clarify the law of nature using human reason.

Like Locke, Grotius, and others, Blackstone felt compelled to mention in passing the supremacy of revealed law, but then he proceeded to develop his political theory primarily in terms of natural law. He did very little biblical exegesis of the law of God. The intent was probably not malicious or sinister, but the effect was to elevate natural law to a par with Scripture. Thus "baptized," natural law largely displaced revelation as the base of authority.

This religious syncretism differed only in degree from that existing in Israel during times of national apostasy. Even on the verge of the Babylonian captivity, the apostate kings of Israel never formally rejected the worship of Jehovah. However, they introduced rival gods and religions—idols which provoked the judgment of the true God.

Do we look to natural law for guidelines in governing the church? Do we look to natural law for guidelines in governing our families? Why then do we believe that natural law is the rule when it comes to governing our nation? Where in the Bible do we hear God calling His rebellious people to return to natural law? Always the call to repentance is couched in terms of a return to the revealed law of God in Scripture. We have accepted Satan's myth of neutrality, as if there were some area of creation that is independent of the authority of God's Word. Natural law leaves man conveniently unaccountable to any objective moral standard.

As we have seen earlier in this chapter, men by nature reject whatever truth about God they observe in the world around them (see Rom. 1). Thus, they have an inherent predisposition against natural law, muted though it may be in its testimony to truth. This partiality has been exacerbated by Darwinism, which militates against absolute laws in nature because nature is supposedly evolving.

Allusions to natural law are sometimes akin to childish references

110

to "Mother Nature." The underlying assumption tends toward Deism; God has wound up the universe like a clock and left it to run on its own, governed by natural laws. This view of God as an absentee landlord conveniently leaves man unaccountable in any definable way to the objective moral standard of the Bible when it comes to government. It is contrary to the biblical doctrine of the sovereignty of God and His immediate, personal governance of the universe.

Even when this naive perspective is not present, many Christians forget that the specifics of natural law are undefined and undefinable. Whatever correspondence one man's interpretation of natural law may have with Scripture is coincidental. Or, more likely, it is derived from preexistent biblical influences on the culture that have colored the man's outlook.

Apart from this biblical backdrop and influence, man in either the savage or "civilized" state loses his moral bearings and is quickly led astray by his sin. The Nazi atrocities of the Second World War are an obvious example of the latter.

The unbeliever who subscribes to natural law theory puts too much faith in the normalcy of nature. He assumes that whatever is natural is good; that whatever "is" therefore "ought" to be. Thus, Neitzsche looked at nature, saw violence, and assumed it to be normative for human society. The Nazis used his writings to bolster their theories.[17]

But man in the uncivilized state is closer to nature and should, therefore, be better equipped to discern the edicts of natural law, right? No less a theologian than C.S. Lewis has challenged us in *Mere Christianity* to "think of a country where people were admired for running away in battle, or where a man felt proud of double-crossing all the people who had been the kindest to him."[18]

The missions film/book *Peace Child* provides just such an example. This film is set in a primitive jungle tribe where treachery and betrayal were regarded as the highest of virtues. The film graphically relates how a man from a neighboring village was lured into a false sense of friendship on his first several visits to the tribe. They feasted him royally and sent him home with their blessing. On a subsequent visit they brutally murdered and cannibalized him. When missionaries first related the gospel story, they thought Judas was a great hero for betraying his friend Jesus.[19] So much for the efficacy and nobility of natural law.

So we find that natural law theory is inadequate at its best, lethal at its worst, at both the individual and cultural levels. The natural law advocate is thwarted at two points: 1) the inability of fallen nature to provide a reliable standard, and 2) the inability of his fallen reason to properly interpret that standard.

The appeal to natural law is too often a crutch on which embarrassed Christians have come to rely in the public arena. In the modern secularized world, references to the Bible seem quaint or somehow out of place. Instead of standing forthrightly on the authority of Scripture, it is all too easy to fall back on natural law. We must learn more and more to stand with Moses and the prophets who were not ashamed to declare, "Thus saith the Lord."

None of this is to deny the existence of the "general revelation" of God in nature. The work of creation testifies to us of the power and glory of God (see Ps. 19). We can also learn something of the wrath of God—for example, in the thunderstorm and earthquake—and of the Fall. This general revelation, however, is muted, incomplete, and susceptible to misinterpretation by fallen man; it is intended by God to drive us to the specific revelation of His Word.

To reiterate, the problem comes from expecting too much of general revelation and man's ability to interpret it. Rather than relying primarily on the power of God's specific revelation, we rely on general revelation to first establish a supposed common ground with the unbeliever on the basis of reason. Only then, it is held, will he be receptive to the specific claims of God's Word. Ken Meyers provides a classic example:

> I am not ashamed of the "rhetoric" of natural law. Telling a late-twentieth-century pagan that he has disobeyed God's Word is likely to have little rhetorical power. Telling him that he has, in C.S. Lewis's terms, gone "against the grain of the universe" might well pack a bit more rhetorical punch . . . . In a culture that tends to regard all rules and all religion as merely conventional, "biblical law" language is horribly easy to ignore.[20]

Modern pagans are supposedly in a class apart from the pagans of antiquity. In this view, "The Word of God is slow and weak, duller than any two-edged sword; blunted before it can reach to the dividing

112

asunder of soul and spirit and unable to discern the thoughts and intents of the heart." I think we all know better.

OTHER ERRONEOUS STANDARDS

Political Pluralism: Majority Rule Not Enlightened by God's Word

Closely tied to majority rule is the concept of political pluralism. According to this theory, if all ideas are simply allowed to compete in the market place of ideas the truth will always or eventually prevail. The majority will validate the truth.

We have dealt with the concepts of pluralism and majority rule at some length in chapter 2 and we will encounter them again in chapter 8. Suffice it to say at this point that pluralism is the predominant religion of our time; it is an important aspect of the American civil religion. It is simply a form of polytheism: "the doctrine of a plurality of gods . . . [each] having an agency in the government of the world" (according to Webster's 1828 Dictionary). The Word of the true God thus becomes nothing more than one more voice competing for men's attention in the pantheon of the gods.

Pluralism finds expression in the doctrine of majoritarianism. Men pass judgment on the various voices—each claiming to be truth—via the ballot box. The majority determines the truth apart from any external standard. It has led in our time to such political absurdities as the Social Security system and Medicare, which now stand on the verge of bankruptcy and threaten to topple the entire economic system.

Ultimately it leads to the exclusion of the Word of God, because the Bible condemns all other standards as false. In his rebellion from God, humanistic man refuses to tolerate the authority of God's Word.

Personal Conscience Not Enlightened by God's Word

The individual conscience fares no better than the body politic in the absence of the Word of God. The conscience is sometimes held up as if it were an autonomous moral beacon. However, the human conscience is neither omniscient nor innately moral. It functions as a moral compass. The compass relies on an external force to function properly: magnetism.

Likewise the conscience is no better than the source of authority that informs it. The conscience is more than just one's personal emotions or some kind of "inner voice." A person's conscience may be informed by many things: his faith, his upbringing, the books he reads, his rebellious neighbor, etc.

Americans are often exhorted to "vote their conscience." Voting is sometimes held up as a sacred ritual, regardless of the intelligence or morality of the vote. However, it does no good to vote your conscience if the conscience is uninformed by God's Law. The prophet Jeremiah said, O LORD, "I know that the way of man is not in himself" (Jer. 10:23).

Romans 2:15 is the primary biblical reference to the conscience. This verse does not say that the law is written on the heart of the unbeliever, but rather the work of the law—namely its sense of condemnatory judgment. The unbeliever has a sense of condemnation because his life is out of sync with the image of God that is stamped on his very nature. However, the conscience of the unbeliever is a confused and darkened law unto itself. It is therefore unable to consistently inform him of what is right and wrong; at times it accuses him and at other times it excuses him.

CONCLUSION

All attempts to construct a standard for political righteousness apart from the Word of God are futile; worse than futile, they are suicidal. They spring from the misguided desire of believers to appeal to the world on the basis of an alleged common ground in common sense and human reason. They promise life but produce only death. Reliance on these erroneous standards has in fact led to the tragic collapse described in the previous chapter. Ultimately, none of them can deal with the effect of sin on man's social relations and structures. Only the redemptive work of Christ mediated through His Word is adequate for such a task. We turn to an examination of the standard for political righteousness provided by the Word of God in the next chapter.

REVIEW QUIZ

1. Who killed natural law?
   a. Charles Darwin
   b. Natural selection
   c. Thomas Aquinas
   d. Bill Clinton

2. The first principle of logic is
   a. If A=B and A=C, then B=C
   b. Every reaction has an equal and opposite reaction
   c. Human logic is fallible
   d. The logical syllogism

3. What is the only legitimate standard for civil law?
   a. Common sense
   b. Conservative philosophy
   c. Biblical common law
   d. Majority opinion
   e. Natural law
   f. Judeo-Christian heritage

4. Which law system forms the primary basis of Western civilization?
   a. Classical (Greek and Roman) law
   b. Humanistic positive law
   c. English/biblical common law
   d. Natural law
   e. Judeo-Christian law

5. Which is not a danger for the Christian?
   a. Failure to enter the political realm
   b. Entering the political realm with a standard tainted by humanistic thought
   c. Seeking to apply biblical law to the political realm

6. Who came first in the philosophical progression?
   a. Jean-Jacques Rousseau
   b. John Locke
   c. Thomas Jefferson

Discussion Guide

1. What was the error of Jehu, and how does it apply to Christian political action?

2. Is America a nation under covenant with God? What are the implications of this?

3. What are some of the false standards of righteousness that Christians have carried into the political arena?

4. Describe the first principle of logic in your own words.

5. What biblical principles should guide the campaign rhetoric of a Christian candidate?

6. What was Adam and Eve's underlying sin? What are the implications for evangelism and public debate?

7. What is the difference between natural law and general revelation?

Answer Key

   1) a   2) c   3) c   4) c   5) c   6) b

PART III
God's Blueprint for Civil Government

A few years ago my family traveled by car from the west coast to visit my mother in Iowa. One afternoon we took a slight detour to stay overnight with some friends in Pierre, South Dakota. We arose early the next morning, hoping to get a good start and make it to our destination that afternoon. After we had been on the road about an hour, it suddenly dawned on me: the sun was coming up behind us. The good news was we were making great time; the bad news was we were traveling in the wrong direction. We would have to retrace our steps, wasting about a hundred miles in the process. In our haste to make it to Iowa, we had failed to check our road map and ended up going the wrong way on the wrong road.

That embarrassing incident reminded me of the plight of American Christendom on the road back to political responsibility. On the one hand, we are quick to proclaim that "the Bible has all the answers to the problems of life." On the other hand, when pressed for specifics, we are quick to caution that the Bible is not a political text book or that the Bible does not endorse any specific political system—after all, its focus is on the "spiritual."

As a consequence, we are left with no other option but to adopt some variation of secular political philosophy, such as those in the previous chapter. There we examined and found wanting many of the false standards for political righteousness that Christians rely on today. With what are we left? When all else fails its time to take another close look at the road map. The road map for the Christian in politics, as in all else, may be found in the Word of God.

To return to our construction metaphor, a contractor relies on a roadmap of sorts in the building of a home. The plans, or blueprints, provide him with an overview of the completed project (chapter 8). The specifications page fills in the specific construction details (chapter 9).

7

THE FOUNDATION OF
POLITICAL RIGHTEOUSNESS

*W*hen King Josiah came to power the nation of Israel was in total disrepair. His reign was preceded by the very short reign of Amon and the very long and wicked reign of Manasseh. The Bible records that Manasseh was an extremely evil and murderous ruler. At this point in history Israel was at a lower level of depravity than the pagan nations that God had driven out before her (see 2 Kings 21:9–11). The nation had fallen so low that the Word of God had been totally lost to the national consciousness. Even the high priest had forgotten that a written revelation from God even existed.

REFORMATION BY THE BOOK

Into this moral cesspool was born Josiah, a boy of remarkable spirit, who assumed the throne when only eight years of age. In his eighteenth year he commissioned extensive repair for the house of the Lord, which had been grossly neglected. During the course of this construction Hilkiah the priest discovered a copy of the book of the Law, the Bible of that day.

Upon reading the Book and consulting with the priest and the prophetess Huldah, Josiah embarked on the most thorough reform in the history of Israel. He purged the land of all its idols and restored the Passover of the Lord.

His heart for God was so great that the Scripture says of him: "there was no king before him, who turned to the LORD . . . neither after him arose there any like him" (2 Kings 23:25, RSV). His greatness exceeded even that of David and Solomon because of his zeal to apply the law of God to the nation. His was a true spiritual and cultural reformation, not simply a revival limited to the internal spiritual life of the individual.

Modern America is in much the same condition as Israel before the ascent of Josiah to the throne. The Bible remains the world's number one best seller, gracing the coffee tables of many of America's living rooms. However, it is in many respects a lost book. We are clearly a society that has lost its biblical moorings. The blood of millions of aborted babies testifies against us.

In the first place, most non-believers rarely open their Bibles. Sadly, this is true of many Christians as well. In the second place, many of those Christians who do read their Bibles have been taught to read them from a very personal and privatized perspective. The hundreds of commands addressed specifically to civil rulers are either ignored as inapplicable for our day or spiritualized to the personal context.

This tendency to privatize the faith is reinforced by the emphasis of most contemporary Christian literature. A 1993 study of evangelical publishing houses found that 87.8 percent of the titles dealt with the "self" in one way or another. That included 31 percent inspirational or motivational, and another 15 percent dealing with the same themes from a new age perspective.[1]

This overwhelmingly personal emphasis has created an ingrown Christianity. Until very recently, Christianity has by-and-large buried its head in the sand to the death throes of contemporary American culture.

For example, God's directive for Moses to create a bottom-up appeals court system (see Ex. 18) might be applied by a modern Christian as a call to delegate authority on the job. While this is certainly a legitimate application, it ignores the primary application to the structure of civil government.

Such directives for rulers are sprinkled throughout the Bible. If we thereby dismiss these kinds of civil applications, the question arises, "By what standard are civil rulers to govern in today's world?" Is the government to be left to its own devices? Most believers would agree that our personal lives, our churches, even our businesses are to be governed by the Word of God. Why then do we assume that government alone is outside the purview of Scripture? Governments are faced with essentially three choices in the source of authority by which they will rule.

The first is the will of the people. The concept of democracy, in which the will of the majority is supreme, is an unbiblical (and unconstitutional) concept. Even the collective wisdom of man is insufficient to determine good and evil. Given the franchise (vote), the majority will usually abuse it for personal aggrandizement by trampling on the rights of the minority.

The second option is the wisdom of the ruler. Kings and rulers are no better when left to themselves. They likewise tend to abuse their power for the sake of personal gain. The classic biblical example is David, a man who claimed to be wiser than all his teachers because of his love for God's statutes. But even King David when left to himself by God, acted as though he were a tyrant in the matter of Bathsheba and Uriah the Hittite.

The third and only legitimate standard by which civil government in every age may rule is the Word of God. God holds civil authorities and citizens alike accountable to His Word. First Timothy 1:8–10 declares that a lawful use of God's law is to publicly restrain law-breakers. The king's responsibility is to uphold this law; the citizen's responsibility is to obey it.

> But we know that the law is good, if a man use it lawfully. Knowing this, that the law is not made for a righteous man, but for the lawless . . . for murderers . . . for whore-mongers, for them that defile themselves with mankind, for menstealers, for liars, for perjured persons, and if there be any other thing that is contrary to sound doctrine. According to the glorious gospel . . . . (1 Tim. 1:8–11)

Here we learn that Old Testament law against such crimes as murder, homosexuality, kidnaping, perjury, etc., is applicable to civil government in New Testament times. Modern governments are not left to improvise when it comes to the codification of law. They are required to look to biblical law as the model on which to pattern civil law. This is in complete accord with the glorious gospel of Christ.

123

THE LAWFUL USE OF LAW

Therefore, in our handling of Scripture we should assume continued applicability between the Old and New Testaments. In other words, the commands of the Old Testament continue to be authoritative unless specifically modified or annulled by later revelation. For example, we are told specifically in the New Testament that the Old Testament ceremonial observances were "a shadow of things to come, but the body is of Christ" (Col. 2:17).

Thus, such ritual ceremonies as sprinkling the blood of goats and bulls, circumcision, and the Jewish new moons and Sabbaths have been fulfilled; they no longer apply to us as they did to ancient Israel. All of these have been replaced or transformed in the perfect sacrifice of Christ.

On the other hand, we should assume that judicial case laws such as the requirement of double restitution for theft continue to be authoritative (see Ex. 22:4). Nowhere does the New Testament or any subsequent revelation rescind laws such as this.

Sometimes we find that the Mosaic judicials are repeated in the New Testament. For instance, in a single verse (Mark 7:10) Jesus mentioned one of the Ten Commandments and one of the case law illustrations as both being part of the command of God *not* to be rejected. These were the positive commandment to "honor thy father and thy mother" (Ex. 20:12) and the negative case law illustration: "Whoso curseth father or mother, let him die the death" (Lev. 20:9).

In addition, we find other New Testament writers appealing to Old Testament case law without apology. For example, the apostle Paul applied the case law regarding the ox treading out grain to pastoral pay in 1 Timothy 5:17–18. This is sometimes referred to as the "general equity" of the law, which is deduced from its specific cultural setting in Israel and applied to the present.

However, it is not necessary that an Old Testament command be repeated in order to be obligatory. We have, for example, no law against bestiality in the New Testament. We should rely instead on the Old Testament injunction against this crime.

Seeking to conform our personal and national life to the commands and laws of God is not legalism. On the contrary, it is obedience. Legalism has reference to a variety of manmade traditions, as per the Pharisees. There is a popular misperception that Jesus rebuked the Pharisees so harshly because of their attempted conformity to the Old Testament Law. Rather, Jesus reprimanded the Jewish religious leaders "for laying aside the commandment of God." In its place they substituted their own traditions: "In vain do they worship me; teaching as doctrines the precepts of men . . . ye hold the tradition of men, as the washing of pots and cups: and many other such like things ye do. And he said unto them, Full well ye reject the commandment of God, that ye may keep your own tradition" (Mk. 7:7–9, RSV).

The sixteenth century reformers taught that there were three lawful uses of God's law during the New Testament era. The first was to convict of sin and prepare the way for the gospel as in Romans 3:20: "by the law is the knowledge of sin." This did not mean that salvation was to be earned by works of the law, because the same verse warns that, ". . . by the deeds of the law there shall no flesh be justified in his sight."

According to the reformers, another legitimate use of God's law in the New Testament era is to provide a standard of personal righteousness for the believer. This is seen in James 1:25: "But whoso looketh into the perfect law of liberty, and continueth therein . . . this man shall be blessed in his deed."

In addition to these familiar uses, the reformers also spoke of the political use of the law of God. The commands of Scripture were to guide the civil ruler in the administration of justice within his realm. Calvin referred to this as the second function of the law:

> The second function of the law is this: at least by fear of punishment to restrain certain men who are untouched by any care for what is just and right unless compelled by hearing the dire threats in the law. But they are restrained, not because their inner mind is stirred or affected, but because, being bridled, so to speak, they keep their hands from outward activity, and hold inside the depravity . . . .
> The apostle seems specially to have alluded to this function of the law when he teaches "that the law is not laid down for the just but for the unjust . . . . "[2]

It was on this groundwork laid by the reformers that the edifice of Western liberty was erected. They taught that true liberty was impossible apart from law. Law and grace work hand in hand. Gradually the recovery of the gospel of salvation through faith worked like leaven, permeating every facet of Western culture, causing it to rise and flourish.

Conversely, Israel learned from bitter experience what it was like to live for four centuries in bondage to a nation that rejected the rule of law under God. The tyranny of Egypt was unbearable. Consequently, the case laws immediately following the Ten Commandments, given by God on Sinai, spelled out the guidelines for biblical servitude under God (see Ex. 21:1–17). Thus, wherever the Bible has gone true liberty—liberty under law—has followed.

In view of all of this, Jesus cautioned His followers not to think that He had somehow come to do away with the Old Testament. "Think not that I have come to destroy the law and the prophets," He warned, "I am not come to destroy, but to fulfil . . . . Whosoever therefore shall break one of these least commandments, and shall teach men so, he shall be called the least in the kingdom of heaven" (Matt. 5:17–19, RSV).

When the New Testament declares that the believer is "not under law" (Rom. 6:14), it means that he is not under the condemnation of the law. It does not mean that he is released from any obligation to obey the law (see Rom. 3:31; 7:12).

This is not to say that there is always a one-to-one correspondence between the way the Jewish nation of priests applied the law and the way we as converted Gentiles are to apply it. For example, what are we to do with the laws that forbid the yoking of an ox and an ass or the wearing of a mixed garment? In such instances, interpretative wisdom must first be applied to discover the appropriate meaning and application for today. In most cases, the application is unambiguous. In any event, the lack of direct correspondence at every point does not invalidate our obligation to hearken, interpret, and obey.

For example, theologian Vern Poythress assumes the abiding applicability of the law, but he warns against the risk of adopting a wooden theonomy:

> . . . the theonomists [advocates of God's law] run the danger of using the appeal to unchanging norms in order to prejudice the question of whether the great bulk of Mosaic legislation is adapted to the unique situation of Israel . . . . This move may make them underestimate the difficulty and complexity of disentangling the abiding principle from the particularity of its application to Israel.[3]

CONCLUSION

We have learned that Scripture rejects salvation by works of the law, Old Testament ceremonial observances, and manmade traditions added to the law of God. However, it upholds the lawful use of God's law as a schoolmaster to lead us to Christ and as a standard of personal and political righteousness.

Usually the application is clear and direct. However, honest men may disagree concerning the application of the law at specific points. Often this disagreement springs from the difficulty converted Gentiles face in interpreting and applying the equity of laws given originally to the Jews. However, we must not allow any lack of unanimity to dissuade us from the abiding authority of the law of God as the only acceptable standard for political righteousness.

REVIEW QUIZ

1. Which of these statements is true?
    a. Christians today are bound to obey the ceremonial laws, the case laws, and the Ten Commandments.
    b. Only the Ten Commandments are still binding on the conscience of the Christian today.
    c. The ceremonial laws have been fulfilled, but the case laws and Ten Commandments are still obligatory.

2. What is a legalist?
    a. Someone who tries to use Old Testament laws as a guideline for living the Christian life
    b. Someone who requires obedience to standards other than or in addition to the laws of God
    c. Someone who studies the history of legal theory
    d. Someone who believes that law and grace are compatible

3. To what groups does biblical law apply?
    a. Church
    b. Israel
    c. Lawyers
    d. The pagan nations
    e. All of the above

4. Which is *not* a lawful use of the law of God?
    a. Conviction of sin
    b. Means of justification through obedience
    c. Moral standard for Christian conduct
    d. Political use in civil law
    e. Both b and d

5. The Old Testament case laws:
    a. Interpret the Ten Commandments
    b. Were specific to Israel and irrelevant today
    c. Define legal sanctions for specific crimes
    d. Both a and c

6. The fact that Paul applied the prohibition against muzzling an ox to pastoral pay proves:
   a. The case laws are no longer binding today.
   b. Case law applications may be extrapolated beyond their immediate cultural context.
   c. The case laws are only binding if repeated in the New Testament.

7. Which is the most appropriate principle of biblical interpretation?
   a. The commands of the Old Testament law are presumed to be binding except where the New Testament modifies them or sets them aside in some manner.
   b. The commands of the Old Testament are presumed to be no longer binding except where the New Testament repeats or ratifies them.

8. What is the only appropriate standard for civil government today?
   a. The will of the people
   b. The Word of God
   c. The wisdom of the ruler
   d. a and b

9. The case laws were delivered after four hundred years of Egyptian bondage. They began with laws governing bond service. This proves that:
   a. Application of biblical law leads to oppression.
   b. Liberty and law are mutually exclusive.
   c. There is no liberty apart from law.

10. Which of these *is* a lawful use of God's law?
    a. Salvation through obedience to God's commands
    b. Traditional values
    c. Political use

11. Who was the greatest king in Israel?
    a. David
    b. Manasseh
    c. Hezekiah
    d. Josiah
    e. Solomon

12. In what sense is the Bible a lost book?
    a. The original text has not been recovered.
    b. Too many modern translations
    c. Privatized interpretation

13. The greatness of Western Civilization is rooted in:
    a. Free enterprise
    b. Liberty under law
    c. *E pluribus unum*
    d. Classical Greece and Rome

DISCUSSION GUIDE

1. How do the ceremonial laws differ from the case laws?

2. In what sense is the Bible a lost book today?

3. How does the New Testament handle the Old Testament case laws?

4. Why was Jesus so critical of the Pharisees? What are the lessons for us today?

5. What is the difference between legalism and obedience to the commands of Christ?

6. What are some of the lawful uses of the law of God?

7. What are some of the unlawful uses of the law of God?

Answer Key

1) c 2) b 3) e 4) b 5) d 6) b 7) a
8) b 9) c 10) c 11) d 12) c 13) b

8

THE FORM OF BIBLICAL CIVIL GOVERNMENT

*I*n his classic novel, *A Tale of Two Cities,* Charles Dickens contrasts the relative tranquility of eighteenth century London with the unrestrained anarchy of the French Revolution. At the beginning of the final epoch Charles Darney, the hero of the tale, leaves England and journeys inland toward his native Paris.

As the miles stream beneath the galloping hooves, a dreadful foreboding descends upon him. Suddenly, he is joined by an uninvited martial escort from which he cannot escape. Their mission is to turn him over for trial to the Tribunal in Paris. His crime? He is a property owner and a member of the aristocracy. As such, he is guilty of death unless proven innocent. The formerly benign French government has been transformed into a hideous monster that now draws him into its fatal embrace.

The form which civil government assumes is of vital importance to the well-being of its subjects. That form is dictated by the prevailing theology and view of God and His Word. In 1790 atheism was the prevailing theology in Paris. Thus, our study of the biblical form of civil government is more than just an academic exercise. It is a matter of life and death.

Earlier we examined those key features of biblical government that find expression in the Constitution of the United States. Let us now review some of those key features, elaborate on them, and identify several others of importance.

Covenant with God vs. Social Contract Theory

In the Bible, civil government is depicted as one means by which God rules His creation. God is seen as entering into covenant with a nation through its elected representatives. By contrast, the social contract theory of government sees people joining in a Democratic union with no reference to God or His law.

Civil authorities rule by virtue of authority delegated from God. Consequently, they are responsible to serve as His ministers, executing His wrath on wrongdoers: "There is no power but of God: the powers that be are ordained of God . . . . For he is the minister of God to thee for good . . . for he is the minister of God, a revenger to execute wrath upon him that doeth evil" (Rom. 13:1,4).

Government is not, therefore, a "social contract" as taught by Locke, Rousseau, and Jefferson in the Declaration of Independence. Civil government is established by the sovereign will of God, not the "consent of the governed."

Social Contract Theory

This is in contrast to John Locke and Jean-Jacques Rousseau. As Locke wrote in his treatise "Of the Beginning of Political Societies": "The only way whereby any one divests himself of his natural liberty and puts on the bonds of civil society is by agreeing with other men to join and unite into a community for their comfortable, safe, and peaceable living one amongst another, in a secure enjoyment of their properties and a greater security against any that are not of it."[1]

Government is therefore seen as a compact among men, with no reference to God. Locke assumed that men in their natural state are free, whereas God declares them to be slaves of sin. Community is seen as the source of peace, with no reference to the Prince of Peace. Further, Locke asserted that the *only* lawful foundation on which any government rests is the will of the majority: "And thus that which begins and actually constitutes any political society is nothing but the consent of any number of free men capable of a majority to unite and incorporate into such a society. And this is that, and that only, which did or could give beginning to any lawful government in the world."[2]

Many colonial preachers quoted Locke liberally to bolster their political teachings, and to modern ears the difference between Lockean natural law and Puritan covenantalism may seem trivial. However, the distinction does not escape constitutional historian, Edwin Corwin:

" 'The Voice of Nature is the Voice of God,' asserts one preacher; 'reason and the voice of God are one,' is the language of another; 'Christ confirms the law of nature,' is the teaching of a third. The point of view is thoroughly deistic; reason has usurped the place of revelation, and without affront to piety."[3]

Rousseau, likewise, believed that law and government were not matters of divine appointment but were based instead in the will of the people. Brown explains Rousseau's *The Social Contract* in this way: "The only valid basis for a society is for its members to agree to a social pact which will combine freedom with just government in the interests of the majority. The essay was a seminal work of modern secular, democratic thinking and played no small part in paving the way for the French Revolution."[4]

Locke predated Rousseau and clearly influenced him. Locke is also often attributed as laying the philosophical underpinnings for the American Revolution and Declaration of Independence.

Biblical Covenant Theory

By contrast, the covenant model posits the foundation of civil government in God and His Word. God is invoked as party to the covenant, His law provides the operational framework for the government, and He is the ultimate enforcer of its provisions. God is acknowledged as an active participant, not just a remote spectator as under the social compact. Thus, Joshua led the children of Israel into covenant with God following the conquest of Canaan:

> If ye forsake the LORD, and serve strange gods, then he will turn and do you hurt, and consume you, after that he hath done you good . . . . And the people said unto Joshua, The LORD our God will we serve, and his voice will we obey. So Joshua made a covenant with the people that day, and set them a statute and an ordinance in Schechem. (Josh. 24:20–25)

The great reform under King Josiah is another example, demonstrating that the national covenant with God may be reaffirmed at any point in a nation's history. The covenant was described in these words and was followed immediately by a national cleansing of all idolatrous practices: "And the king stood by a pillar, and made a covenant before the LORD, to walk after the LORD, and to keep his commandments and his testimonies and his statutes with all their heart and all their soul, to perform the words of this covenant that were written in this book. And all the people stood to the covenant" (2 Kings 23:3).

Was this national covenant limited only to Israel? Not at all. The Bible at many points assumes that all the nations were expected to submit joyfully to the yoke of God's government. For instance, "O let the nations be glad and sing for joy: for thou shalt judge the people righteously, and govern the nations upon earth. Selah" (Ps. 67:4). The Lord's attitude toward any nation is summarized in Jeremiah 18:7–8: "At what instant I shall speak concerning a nation, and concerning a kingdom, to pluck up, and to pull down, and to destroy it; If that nation, against whom I have pronounced, turn from their evil, I will repent of the evil that I thought to do unto them."

The repentance of the king of Ninevah under the preaching of Jonah is one example. Incredibly, Jonah sulked after witnessing this national revival. Too often modern evangelicals assume the same attitude in limiting the blessings and covenant of God strictly to Israel.

The Right of Revolution

If the foundation of civil government is laid by God, it follows, therefore, that the "right of revolution"—the right to overthrow an existing government—rests in God, not in man. Thus, the only legal revolution is one in which duly ordained "lesser magistrates" lead the people against a tyrannical "higher magistrate" with the blessing of the clergy.

Government that rejects its biblical purpose of restraining evil and administering justice becomes itself a violator of God's law. As such, it forfeits its biblical authority to function as a minister of God in this capacity. This does not, however, provide citizens a carte-blanche excuse to flagrantly disobey government or enter into anarchical revolutionary coups. Historically, such attempts almost invariably lead to dictatorship. Witness the rise of Napoleon following the lawless and bloody French Revolution.

Instead, the attitude of the people should be one of longsuffering under oppression, preparation for hardship, and prayer that God would raise up a deliverer. There should be a spirit of acquiescence to God's rod of discipline. Such a spirit is fostered with the recognition that in Scripture God often raised up foreign invaders to discipline His people for their disobedience. Rather than chafing under God's discipline our first response should be one of repentance and a return to His law.

The pattern of sin, judgment, repentance, and deliverance is seen repeatedly in the book of Judges. For example, when Sisera oppressed Israel they "cried to the Lord for help; for he had nine hundred chariots of iron, and oppressed the people of Israel cruelly for twenty years" (Judg. 4:3). In response, God raised up Deborah and Barak to deliver Israel.

Concerning the Christian attitude under oppression, John Calvin commented:

> That our first duty when suffering under an impious prince is to first call up the remembrance of our faults, which doubtless the Lord is chastising by such scourges. In this way humility will curb our impatience. And let us reflect that it belongs not to us to cure these evils, that all that remains for us is to implore the help of the Lord, in whose hands are the hearts of kings . . . . [5]

However, the people must resist when the civil magistrate attempts to force them into blatant violations of God's law. The biblical pattern in such cases may be individual acts of passive resistance and fervent prayer to God for deliverance. God's response to this earnest prayer will be the calling forth of the "lesser magistrate(s)" to lead the people against the "higher magistrate" who stands in violation of God's law. The lower magistrate *must* perform this duty as one who is sworn to uphold the law of God:

> . . . he raises up manifest avengers from among his own servants, and gives them his command to punish accursed tyranny, and deliver his people from calamity when they are unjustly oppressed.

> Let us not therefore suppose that that vengeance is committed to us, to whom no command has been given but to obey and suffer. I speak only of private men. For when popular magistrates have been appointed to curb the tyranny of kings . . . So far am I from forbidding these officially to check the undue license of kings . . . . [6]

Therefore, the citizenry possesses the responsibility of civil disobedience when the law of man requires disobedience to the law of God, but they do not possess the right to violently overthrow the government. However, the responsibility of the lower magistrate may extend beyond that of the citizenry when he is in a position where his superior(s) defies the law of God. In such a case, his duty is to lead the people against the lawless superior to restore the rule of God's law.

This pattern is observed repeatedly in Scripture as the people call out to God in their oppression and He raises up a deliverer to rescue them. Likewise, in the American War for Independence, we have the example of predominantly God-fearing men following their elected representatives in a defensive effort to protect their families and restore law and order to their land.

Conformity to this pattern explains in part the success of the American War for Independence. In contrast, the French Revolution was a bloody coup against lawful authority. It culminated in the Reign of Terror, with the guillotine employed to eradicate King Louis XVI and the bourgeois.

Reliance on the "lesser magistrates" is known as the biblical doctrine of interposition. This doctrine may be our best hope for deliverance as we survey the wreckage of humanist culture at this late date in America's history. Armed conflict would be the last resort. A much preferred step is to fill our state and local governments with men who will assert their biblical and constitutional authority in the face of federal and bureaucratic tyranny.

It is not overly difficult to gain control of a state legislature through a coordinated, statewide effort that concentrates on districts with a high probability of winning. The specifics of such an effort are outlined in some detail in chapter 11.

Republic, Not Democracy

The biblical form of government provides the model for what is today known as a republic, in which the people select their representatives, who then govern according to the law of God. They are not primarily accountable to the will of the people, or public opinion, as in a democracy.

Ideally, in the republican form the most godly and able men are selected as representatives. These then meet in deliberative assembly to codify law and decide cases on the basis of biblical principle apart from local or factional concern.

Republican Church Government

The republican form may be observed in both Old and New Testaments. In the church, potential leaders are *nominated*—"pick out from among you" (Acts 6:3)—by the church membership, who are in the best position to observe the individual. Qualified candidates are then *appointed* or ordained by existing church leadership (see also Acts 1:15–26).

The episcopal and congregational models are at opposite ends of a continuum of authority. Both contain elements of the biblical pattern, but both are extremes.

Congregational democracy, in which the people decide on most major issues is difficult to justify from Scripture. It is true that under the doctrine of the "priesthood of the believer," each individual has direct access to the throne of God; however, in the matter of church government, elders are chosen by the people, who then possess the authority to lead.

By contrast, the episcopal form typically follows the pattern of leaders appointed from above, rather than emerging from and approved by, the congregation. The biblical model, the golden mean of representative government, thus falls between these two extremes.

Republican Civil Government

The form of government adopted by the church often works itself out into the form of government adopted by the civil government. For example, Presbyterianism corresponds with the republican form of civil government. The American Revolution was, in fact, referred to as the "Presbyterian Revolt" in England. Likewise, Congregational church government corresponds to democratic civil government and Episcopalianism coincides with monarchy.[7]

As we have noted earlier, the republican form is also seen in the biblical model for civil government. In Deuteronomy 1:13 Moses called on the people to choose wise and understanding men whom he could appoint over them.

Thus, in both church and civil government the republican pattern is evident. The people are granted the privilege of selecting their leaders. The leaders are then appointed or sworn in (hands laid on) as if receiving also the divine stamp of approval. They then govern in response to the Word of God, not swaying with the tide of public opinion. This arrangement has been referred to by some as a theocratic republic.

The preference of some evangelical leaders for democracy in lieu of the theocratic republic model is bewildering. For example, a symposium of evangelical leaders was organized by *Christianity Today* in 1985. They summarized their proceedings in part with these words:

> Though a Christian can survive under almost any government, he strongly supports democracy as most consistent with his understanding of the purpose of government and the nature of man.

> While evangelicals seek freedom to witness to all by persuasion, they are unutterably opposed to any form of "theocracy." They desire a nation of Christians, but they are opposed to a Christian government that mandates "Christian" laws simply because they are Christian.[8]

Think about the meaning of the two words for a moment. *Demos* means "people" or "man" and *cracy* means "rule" or "law." *Theos* means "God." Thus, these evangelical leaders find themselves in the curious, and I should hope embarrassing, position of preferring the "rule of man" over and above the "rule of God."

The myth persists that somehow the rule of God's law is harsh and tyrannical. On the contrary, liberty is impossible apart from God's law. It is never a question of law versus no law. It is always a question of whose law will prevail. Will it be the law of man, which has led in this century alone to untold misery, slaughter, and tyranny, or will it be the law of God—the perfect law of liberty?

Political Fool's Gold

There is a stone monument shimmering in the lawn of the courthouse in Oregon City, Oregon. It is dedicated to the memory of William U'ren. The inscription reads as follows:

> In Honor of William Simon U'ren
> Blacksmith   Lawyer   Political Reformer
> Author of Oregon's Constitutional provision for the
> INITIATIVE, REFERENDUM, RECALL giving the people
> control of lawmaking and lawmakers and known in his
> lifetime as father of Oregon's enlightened system of

government. This memorial is dedicated in gratitude by the Oregon City Hilltop bookstore and friends and admirers on behalf of the people of Oregon, April, 1977.

Who was this man and what was the "enlightened system of government" that he introduced? U'ren was the father of the Oregon initiative, which first saw the light of day in Clackamas County, Oregon in 1902. Today the initiative is an integral part of the political scene in over half the states. What are we to make of this innovation that claims to be such an improvement on the system bequeathed to us in the U.S. Constitution?

Philosophic Objections. We have observed that in a biblical republic the people are given authority to elect their leaders, who then rule in accordance with the law of God (see Deut. 1:1–13). By contrast, the initiative process is pure democracy and a violation of biblical government and the spirit of the U.S. Constitution.

Contrary to popular opinion, our founding fathers despised democracy almost as much as they hated tyranny. Notes from the Constitutional Convention contain references to the framers denouncing the "excesses of Democracy." Elbridge Gerry said, "the evils we experience flow from the excess of democracy," and "[democracy is] the worst . . . of all political evils."[9]

After the convention, James Madison in *Federalist #10* noted that "democracies have ever been spectacles of turbulence and contention . . . and have in general been as short in their lives as they have been violent in their deaths." Earlier, Puritan clergyman John Cotton had warned, "Democracy, I do not conceive that God ever did ordain as a fit government either for church or for commonwealth. If the people be governors who shall be governed?"[10]

The founders followed the lead of Montesquieu who had written these words in *The Spirit of Laws:* "One great fault there was in most of the ancient republics, that the people had a right to active resolutions, such as require some execution, a thing of which they are absolutely incapable. They ought to have no share in the government but for the choosing of representatives, which is within their reach."[11]

This sentiment led to the inclusion of Article IV, Section 4 in the U.S. Constitution, "The United States shall guarantee to every state in this union a Republican form of government."

At this point, the founders were in accord with the republican model of government set forth in Scripture. In the ancient Hebrew republic, Moses instructed the children of Israel to "choose wise, understanding, and experienced men, according to your tribes, and I will appoint them as your heads" (Deut. 1:13, RSV).

The Old Testament model of government by representation was subsequently carried over into the New Testament, as seen in the appointment of the first deacons. Peter called on the Jerusalem church to nominate proven leaders from among their own number that he could ordain to office. "Therefore, brethren, pick out from among you seven men of good repute, full of the Spirit and of wisdom, whom we may appoint to this duty" (Acts 6:3, RSV).

In Scripture, "the people" enmasse are generally not regarded as competent to rule in civil or church government. However, they are seen as competent to identify those individuals in their midst who are competent to rule by virtue of a track record of Spirit-filled service. This is the republican or representative form of government.

The Bible reveals that the spirit of democracy is typically associated with the spirit of rebellion. For example, Korah justified his presumptuous rebellion against Moses with the words, "You have gone too far! For all the congregation are holy, every one of them, and the LORD is among them; why then do you exalt yourselves above the assembly of the LORD?" (Num. 16:3, RSV).

Unfortunately, the modern American addiction to democracy plagues us yet today in the form of the Oregon Initiative. The initiative is commonly spoken of in such glowing terms as an "innovative remaking of government," and "putting Oregon in the vanguard of progressive and enlightened politics." The initiative is clearly a throwback to direct democracy, in which the people themselves are called on to make policy decisions, regardless of their qualifications. It represents a radical departure from the republican form of government guaranteed to the states by the Constitution. It is an appeal to the mob that completely circumvents the reasoned deliberative assembly of the republican process.

The initiative is in diametric opposition to the republican, representative system, modeled in Scripture, and embodied in the American Constitution. It is in theory at least unconstitutional, since the Constitution guaranteed to every state a republican form of government. It represents a direct attack on constitutional government. The constitutions of twenty-six states that have adopted the initiative have been decimated into a "crazy quilt" of contradictions by the process.

The initiative, now called the Oregon Plan, sprang from the cultural milieu associated with the social gospel at the turn of the century. By 1908 the federal Council of Churches had issued a declaration of progressive principles which endorsed, among other things, such measures as the direct primary, the initiative, the referendum, and the recall. Yet the drive to introduce these tools for direct legislation was begun in the early 1890s by a group of spirtualists active in Clackamas County. An article by Burton J. Hendrick that appeared in *McClure's Magazine* in July, 1911, outlines the historical chain of events.

The article describes how the first inspiration for the initiative had been given by a Reverend M.V. Rork, "an ex-Unitarian clergyman, who came roaring through rural Oregon in the early '90's as the representative of the Farmers' Alliance. In western Oregon, in particular, his progress was the heralding of a new political age." [12]

In the 1890s the movement gained new impetus through a long series of weekly discussion meetings in a log cabin in Milwaukie, Oregon. These discussions were conducted under the tutelage of Seth and Alfred Luelling, local nurserymen who developed the famous "bing" cherries. Hendrick reports that, "in religion they were spiritualists; Seth Luelling's house, indeed, was the local headquarters of spiritualism long before it became the meeting place of political malcontents. The very room where the agitation for popular government in Oregon started had been for many years previously the scene of spiritualistic seances." [13] From Milwaukie, the Luellings and William U'ren carried the "gospel" of the initiative and referendum around the state.

There were clearly problems in the existing system. The last forty years of the nineteenth century were characterized by "social Darwinism"—the application of the survival of the fittest to every realm of society, especially government and politics. This theory was used to justify the growth of monopolies and unscrupulous control of government by monied interests. For example, Oregon's senior U.S. Senator at that time, John Mitchell, would use his war chest to fund the campaigns of state legislators and in return have them commit in writing to vote for him when they were elected.

Clearly, this demonstrates that even the best form of government will be abused if the people do not live in obedience to the law of God.

Instead of reforming this authoritarian situation and turning to the sovereignty and law of God, the people of Oregon swung to the revolutionary extreme by vesting lawmaking sovereignty in the people. They adopted a variation of direct democracy. The amendment was adopted by an eleven-to-one margin.

Practical Objections. How does this work itself out into practical politics? While thousands of Christians expend their energies on the initiative process, state legislatures leave hundreds of godly legislative proposals to die in committee. This includes bills that would restrict abortion, forbid the foster care of children by homosexuals, and correct unfair child-abuse laws. If the thousands of dollars and hours wasted on the initiative process had been devoted to Christian candidates, the balance of power would likely be far different in most of our state legislatures.

The number one principle of electoral politics should be to focus the mass of our resources on the republican process. We should forget about democracy as it finds embodiment in the initiative. To continue to pour our energy into the initiative is to tilt at windmills in Don Quixote fashion. On the other hand, if we are interested in slaying the real dragons that plague our state governments and taking dominion in the name of Christ, then we will devote ourselves to the republican process at the state, city, and county levels.

Constant recourse to the initiative as a cure-all for our public ills reflects a utopian faith in the inherent goodness of the individual voter. In this view, most elected officials are perverse, corrupted, and unworthy of the trust conferred by their constituents. By contrast, the "people" are held to be noble, possessed of "common sense" and native virtue, yet they somehow are betrayed and oppressed by their leaders.

The observation that we get the kind of government officials we deserve would be far closer to the truth. If corrupt leaders are in office today, it is because corrupt voters have put them there. Voters in a post-Christian society seem to prefer these kinds of leaders. To expect these same voters to make wise policy decisions is the height of folly.

Moreover, most voters have neither the time to study, nor the technical qualifications to pass judgment, on many of the issues that wind up on the ballot. The ludicrous extent to which the initiative process may be carried was seen in the 1990 California voter's pamphlet. According to the Portland *Oregonian*, it came in two volumes—a total of 220 pages—with cryptic arguments for and against twenty-eight different initiatives.[14]

Most initiatives—some say as many as nine in every ten—fail or are nullified by the judiciary. It is usually not difficult for an opponent to demonstrate or assert that some aspect of the measure is "too extreme," "goes too far," or is unconstitutional. If a seed of doubt can be planted in the voter's mind, he will most often vote against the proposal. Considering some of the crackpot ideas that make it to the ballot, we should probably be thankful for this failure rate.

Given these facts, the amount of time, money, and energy wasted on the initiative process by Christian people is appalling. If all these kingdom resources had been devoted to the training and election of godly candidates over the past decade we would probably be in a much stronger position in most of our state legislatures around the nation. To flirt with democracy in this matter is certainly not in keeping with the apostle's command to "redeem the time for the days are evil" (Eph. 5:16).

Democracy by initiative tends to undermine republican government. Elected officials often use it to excuse themselves from their responsibilities to uphold the law of God. For example, the resounding defeat of a 1990 initiative to ban all convenience abortions in Oregon will be used as an excuse by politicians in that state for inaction in the legislature for possibly a decade. Public opinion polling conducted prior to filing this initiative revealed the strong likelihood of defeat. Unfortunately, it was ignored.

Furthermore, if an initiative is passed that does not have the support of the elected officials and their appointees, they will invariably find ways to undermine, invalidate, or overturn it. The devious response of many officials in attempting to circumvent Oregon's property-tax-cutting Measure 5 in 1992 is a case in point. Home values were immediately assessed at higher values by county assessors to make up the difference.

Another example was an Oregon initiative that would require public employees to pay 6 percent of their own pensions. The immediate response of many government entities around the state was to raise salaries 6 percent, even before the popular initiative reached the ballot.

If all else fails, the attorney general can simply write a confusing ballot title with liberal use of double negatives and emotional "catch phrases" such as "free speech" or "freedom of choice." For instance, voter confusion doomed another Oregon initiative to defeat public votes on tax increases despite obvious support for the idea. According to a poll commissioned by the Portland Oregonian a week before the 1994 election: "Six out of 10 voters indicated a 'no' vote when the poll asked the exact question that will be on the ballot. However, the results flip-flopped when the effects of the measure were described to voters in a separate question in the survey." [15]

> *Ballot Question:*
> Shall the Oregon Constitution bar new or increased state and local taxes, certain fees and certain charges without prior voter approval? As of today, would you vote yes, for the measure, or no, against the measure?
>
> > Yes 35%
> > No 60%
> > Unsure.......................4%
>
> *Separate Unambiguous Question from the Same Poll:*
> There will be a measure on the ballot that would require that any new or increased state and local taxes and fees be approved by the voters. If the election were held today would you vote for this measure or against it?
>
> > Yes 61%
> > No 36%
> > Unsure 4%

Just a fluke? Here's another ballot title from the same Oregon election: "Shall state constitution say that free speech clause may not be read to ban laws against obscenity, including child pornography?" This measure also went down to ignomious defeat in spite of strong voter opposition to child pornography. Many were diverted from the real issue by the reference to free speech and the double negative.

Conservatives were snookered again after wasting thousands of dollars and hours on a year-long campaign. Does this come as any surprise? As everyone knows, government bureaucrats are masters of the fine art of composing murky syntax. Until we elect public officials whose decisions are governed by a biblical worldview, we waste valuable time and resources trying to pass "godly initiatives."

A legislature composed of principled representatives stands to make thousands of wise decisions each session. These decisions are made in the context of a deliberative assembly where the pros and cons of each proposal are debated before it is cast in final form. By contrast, a single initiative proposal is first "set in concrete," then subjected to nearly a year of public debate without possibility of amendment. The futility of this process should be obvious to all, but it is not.

The initiative continues to glitter like fool's gold in the rocky ground of political impotency. How long will American Christians remain hypnotized by its seductive lure?

The Hebrew Republic

E.C. Wines' *The Hebrew Republic* is perhaps the best commentary extant on the republican model in Scripture. Wines taught that the most conspicuous branch of government under the Hebrew Republic was the magistery, which assumed various forms, including judge, king, and military commander.[16] The magistrate—not the "just power" of government—was established by the consent of the people (see Judg. 8:22; 9:6; 2 Sam. 16:18).

The magistery combined what we know as the executive and judicial branches of government. For example, Deborah served as both military and civil head of Israel; she directed the nation in war and served in peace as judge and administrator of public affairs (see Judg. 4:4–6). Moses is another example. Under the chief magistrate was a hierarchial judicial system which presided over disputes of a lesser nature (see Ex. 18:25).

Assisting and advising the chief magistrate was a senate of seventy elders, later called the Sanhedrin, who were to help Moses bear the burden of the people. The circumstances of their appointment—to quell a rebellion—tells something of their function. The senate was established as a council of sages to advise the judge, support his authority, prevent mutinies, and check the rashness and haste of the popular assembly (see Num. 11:16–17).

The senate was assembled with one blast of the trumpet in the wilderness (see Num 10:4). A double trumpet blast was used to assemble the third branch of government, the Hebrew commons (see Num. 10:3). At many points this is referred to as the congregation, but as

Judges 20:2,7 and other passages make clear, these were representatives of the congregation or heads of families.

There may have been some overlap between the lower judiciary and the popular assembly, but as indicated in Joshua 24:1 and elsewhere, the judges and heads of tribes and clans were distinct functionaries. Many important matters of foreign and domestic affairs were referred to the assembly for debate and decision (see Josh. 9:15–21) and then turned over to the judge for execution. In 1 Samuel 14:45 the assembly even overruled the king.

All four branches, including the Hebrew oracle, are referred to in Numbers 27:2,21. In cases of extreme difficulty, such as that represented by the daughters of Zelophehad, the judge had direct access to God through the mediation of the high priest by the Urim and Thummim. God would return answer, possibly in an audible voice or by lot (see 1 Sam. 10:19–22; 14:37–42).

Democracy vs. Republic

It is important at this point to summarize some of the differences between a republic and democracy. We have seen first of all that in a republic the people's representatives make leadership decisions; in a democracy the people themselves make decisions. Thus, a republic allows for a reasoned, deliberative process in the formulation of legislation while a democracy is often swayed by the emotional appeals of political demagogues or a liberal press.

Further, in a biblical republic the law of God embodied in a written constitution is supreme, whereas in a democracy the will of the people is supreme. As a consequence, a republic is more apt to serve the broad national interest, compared to a democracy which is subject to manipulation by local partisan interest.

One of the practical benefits of the republican form is protection for the rights of the minority. By contrast, in a democracy rights are trampled, because in the absence of a Constitution, people try to manipulate the law to their own advantage. This is now the case in the United States where the terms of the Constitution are essentially ignored.

In addition, the republican form allows for union of many small political units into a vast, orderly domain; democracy is limited geographically.

RESTRICTED FRANCHISE, UNRESTRICTED FREEDOM

The Danger of an Unrestricted Franchise

The definition of citizenship is of critical importance to the very survival of a government and a culture. This is true of church government as well as civil government. Theoretically, a group of outsiders could move into a church with loose or no membership requirements and take it over. If the church has no formal membership criteria or covenant, all that is needed would be a simple majority.

The same is true of civil government. During the 1980s a pagan, Hindu religious community established itself outside the small town of Antelope in central Oregon. Thousands of devotees moved in from around the world, contributing fabulous wealth to the cult.

The cult leader was the Bagwahn Shree Rajneesh, who lived a life of opulence and decadence in the midst of the colony. He possessed a fleet of more than fifteen Rolls Royces, which his worshipers bestowed upon him. A picture in the Portland *Oregonian* showed them all lined up in the central Oregon desert. All of Oregon was in turmoil.

After a year or two, enough of the Rajneeshees had established residence in the town of Antelope to elect the mayor and city council. They thereby institutionally evicted the original inhabitants, many of whom had lived there all their lives. Their property became next to worthless and many moved away. Their way of life and unique culture was decimated by the foreign "invaders."

The same thing has happened on a much larger scale in modern America. The original settlers—the Pilgrims—had entered into a covenant with the triune God. This simple document is known to history as the Mayflower Compact. Its primary purpose was for "ye glorie of God, and advancemente of ye Christian faith . . . . "

As we all know, that purpose was diluted over the years. Many strangers moved into the country who did not share the faith of the original settlers. They became naturalized citizens and gradually displaced those who inherited the faith of the Pilgrims. After two hundred years they have repudiated the original purpose of the civil covenant, actually banning almost every vestige of the Christian faith in public life.

Because God's people have fallen away from obedience to the "whole counsel of God" as it speaks to the culture, the "stranger" has taken the reigns of leadership. As Moses warned, "The stranger that is within thee shall get up above thee very high; and thou shalt come down very low. He shall lend to thee, and thou shalt not lend to him: he shall be the head, and thou shalt be the tail" (Deut. 28:43–44).

Debt is an instrument of social control; those who control the purse strings in society wield the power in that society. Today personal indebtedness in America is at an all-time high; even many churches are head-over-heels in debt to the pagan banking system of the "stranger in our midst." American Christians have become like the salt that is "trodden under foot of men" (Matt. 5:13). The amazing thing is that many church leaders have taught that this is "the normal Christian life," and the people of God can expect nothing better this side of the Second Coming.

The Biblical Evidence for a Restricted Franchise

Could this sad story have been avoided? Does the Bible offer any guidelines for preventing the internal disintegration of a biblical society?

As a matter of fact, it does. The foreigner in Israel was known as a "stranger." The "stranger" in Israel enjoyed the same protection of the "one law" as did the Israelite. The borders were open with freedom of movement back and forth. Ruth, for example, did not have to go through "customs" when she moved from Moab to Israel. Historian J.D. Davis notes that "The stranger was not a full citizen, yet he had recognized rights and duties."[17]

Thus, the "stranger" was not allowed to participate in the civil government. He was not permitted to enter into the congregation of the Lord, sometimes for several generations. Typical were Ammon, Moab, and Egypt. The latter was barred from the congregation of the Lord for three generations. However, the Israelites were commanded to "not abhor an Egyptian," or consider him a second class resident in the land (Deut. 23:7–8).

In like manner, the descendants of Ammon and Moab were barred from the congregation for ten generations because they sought to turn the blessing of God for Israel into a curse (see Deut. 23:4–5). The "congregation" had reference to participation within the civil body politic of the nation.

Time was required before the stranger could be assimilated into the Hebrew culture and become "an Israelite indeed." He may even have been "born again" as a child of God, but he was not yet mature enough to be entrusted with leadership in the government.

Reinforcing this concept was the prohibition against strangers, or anyone in Israel, publicly proselytizing for a pagan religion (see Deut. 13). As we have seen, law is intimately intertwined with religion; a law is simply the codification of a religious principle. Therefore, subsumed within this prohibition was a ban on political activity for the stranger.

We must be careful to distill our concepts of public expression from Scripture, not from the free speech movement or even from the First Amendment. Public expression is not without restraint. Even American libel and slander laws recognize this principle, although they have been weakened in recent years. Notice, however, that the Bible does not regulate private belief—only the public promotion of that belief. Professor of American history Terril Elniff explains:

> True liberty of conscience was to believe the truth; to believe anything else was to betray true liberty of conscience . . . . Herein is the difference between the Puritan concept of liberty of conscience and the concept of toleration. New England did not require any kind of an inward faith or belief since that would have violated the principle of the liberty of conscience, but New England did refuse to tolerate other forms of belief. [18]

Thus, there is no "equal time for Satan" as under pluralism. The hypocrisy of the advocates of pluralism is seen in their bald attempts to stifle all Christian expression in public life. They are willing to allow for any religion except Christianity because they recognize it as their mortal enemy.

At this point the humanists are much more perceptive than the Christians. They realize that detente is impossible in the battle for the mind and soul of America. Two or more religious philosophies cannot coexist peacefully in a single nation; one or the other must prevail. It is ultimately a battle to the death. And when idolatrous expression is not denied influence and ostracized, as commanded by Scripture, idolatry will flourish and continue its move to destroy true religion.

What does this mean in practical terms for the New Testament era? As noted in chapter 4, the Puritans understood the Bible to place limitations on the right to hold public office and on the right to vote. Obviously these restrictions can not be imposed top-down apart from the mass conversion of society that God will one day accomplish.

The pattern for citizenship in modern America is exactly the opposite of that described above: restricted immigration and unlimited franchise. This has been a major factor contributing to the demise of America. Only with considerable difficulty is the "stranger" able to gain legal entry to the United States or any other country for that matter. Very few sanctuary nations are left in the world. Once here, however, he is granted almost automatic citizenship after waiting a few years and swearing allegiance to the government.

The biblical policy stands in stark contrast to the pluralistic, one-man, one-vote dogma of modern democratic theory. Unger describes the stranger's entry into citizenship as a formal covenant with the people of God: "Should he desire to enjoy the full rights of citizenship a stranger submitted to circumcision, thus binding himself to observe the whole law, in return for which he was permitted to enjoy to the full the privileges and blessings of the people of the covenant, (Rom. 9:4), with whom, in virtue of this right, he was now incorporated (Ex 12:48)." [19]

Thus, citizenship was first of all an ecclesiastical matter. In democratic theory the right to vote is held to be the essence of freedom. "The right to vote is very basic," said John Fitzgerald Kennedy, "if we're going to neglect that right then all our talk about freedom is hollow." [20]

Contrary to this is the testimony of Scripture which holds that a saving relationship with Christ is the essence of freedom. Jesus said, "If the Son therefore shall make you free, ye shall be free indeed" (John 8:36). But the humanist defines freedom politically, not spiritually.

In the modern humanist state the vote is viewed as a weapon to be wielded against other elements within the society. Each faction within society strives desperately to seize the reins of power for its own peculiar advantage. When regarded in this manner, the franchise (vote) is not an instrument of freedom, but of tyranny. It is scarcely less dangerous than a physical weapon in its effect.

Unrestricted Freedom

Would the Old Testament approach not lead to oppression of foreigners in a Christian nation? On the contrary, the "stranger" is singled out in the Bible along with widows and orphans as worthy of special consideration. For example, the Israelite was told to "love him as thyself; for ye were strangers in the land of Egypt" (Lev. 19:33).

This love was to find expression in law. There was to be no

discrimination against the stranger in law: "Ye shall have one manner of law, as well for the stranger, as for one of your own country: for I am the LORD your God" (Lev. 24:22). Furthermore, the underprivileged stranger was to receive special consideration in the Israelite's tithe: "At the end of three years thou shalt bring forth all the tithe . . . And the Levite . . . and the stranger, and the fatherless, and the widow, which are within thy gates, shall come, and shall eat and be satisfied . . . " (Deut. 14:28–29).

The Israelites were told to love the stranger because they themselves had been strangers in the land of Egypt in a state of terrible bondage. This great object lesson was to teach them not to treat the stranger as an abject slave. On the contrary, he was to be treated with great kindness, that he might come to know the God of Israel. He was an honored and protected resident, but not a citizen.

As a further check to injustice, oppression of the stranger was dealt with by God in a very severe manner. God pronounced a very specific curse on any who would be so callous as to "afflict them in any wise." Through Moses the Lord warned, "I will surely hear their cry, and my wrath shall wax hot, and I will kill you with the sword; and your wives shall be widows, and your children fatherless" (Ex. 22:23–24).

Violation of the spirit of this command may have been one reason God judged the first generation of Puritans in New England. It was reported that in Salem "one Thomas Oliver was employed 'to go from house to house about the town once a month to inquire what strangers do come to have privily thrust themselves into the town.' To quicken his zeal, he was to be rewarded with the fines imposed on those who defied the ordinances against entertaining newcomers."[21]

Contrary to this example, when justice, protection, and compassion is extended to the most vulnerable classes of society, the need to strive after political power becomes inconsequential. When the franchise is not viewed as a cultural weapon and freedom is guaranteed, the right to vote fades in importance for those who are not biblically authorized to exercise it.

This principle helps to explain the limitation of the franchise to male heads of households in early America. The colonists believed that when God deals governmentally with mankind via His ordained institutions—church, state, family—it is always with the covenanted head of that institution. For example, God dealt covenantally with Adam as the federal head of the human race (in Adam's fall, we sinned all) and now deals covenantally with the head of the new humanity, Jesus Christ (see Rom. 5).

Thus, when it comes to civil government, God deals with representatives of the people, not the people as a whole. Likewise, in the church he deals with elders chosen by the people, and in the family he deals with the husband. This was the rationale for restricting the vote to male heads of households. The counsel of the wife was highly regarded due to her position as vice-regent within the family, but each covenant household was granted a single vote. That vote was cast by the husband—the covenant head of household—who was governmentally responsible before God.

CONCLUSION

The fundamental form of biblical government is republican in outline. In a republic the people select their leaders, who rule in accordance with the law of God. However, the form in and of itself is lifeless if it is not animated by God. Specifically, God insists on being party to the national covenant as the ultimate enforcement authority for its laws and specifications. National blessings and cursings are associated with a nation's obedience to these laws.

Moreover, a biblical standard for citizenship must be upheld to ensure godly representation on the human side of the covenant. This is not a plank we would expect to find in the Republican Party platform. However, as the nation is converted and the great majority yield themselves to the government of the Messiah, they will eventually submit to this feature willingly.

Review Quiz

1. The social contract theory
   a. Found expression in the Declaration of Independence via the influence of John Locke
   b. Identifies the source of governmental authority in the people rather than God and His revealed law
   c. Was a reaction against the Puritan's covenant theory of civil government
   d. Imputes great authority to autonomous man and the power state
   e. All of the above

2. The initiative is a form of
   a. Republican government
   b. Anarchy
   c. Democracy
   d. Division of powers

3. In the Hebrew republic which two functions of government were usually combined?
   a. Legislative and judicial
   b. Legislative and executive
   c. Executive and judicial

4. Match the form of civil government on the left with the form of church government on the right that it most closely resembles.
   a. Republic   1. Episcopalian
   b. Democracy   2. Presbyterian
   c. Aristocracy   3. Congregational

5. The biblical remedy for an oppressive civil government is
   a. Revolution
   b. Prayer and patience
   c. Interposition
   d. b and c

6. Which of these best sums up the biblical approach to citizenship?
   a. Limited freedom, unlimited franchise
   b. One man, one vote
   c. Unlimited freedom, limited franchise

DISCUSSION GUIDE

1. In what ways does social contract theory differ from government by covenant with God?

2. Compare and contrast the biblical doctrine of interposition with the humanistic doctrine of revolution.

3. How did the French Revolution differ from the American Revolution?

4. In what ways are various patterns of church government reflected in civil government?

5. What is wrong with the initiative petition?

6. Compare and contrast the main branches in the Hebrew republic with those established under the U.S. Constitution.

7. Describe the key elements of a biblical policy of immigration.

Answer Key

   1) e   2) c   3) c   4) a-2, b-3, c-1   5) d   6) c

9

THE FUNCTION OF BIBLICAL CIVIL GOVERNMENT

*G*ulliver, in his *Travels,* found himself shipwrecked and bound to the ground by a thousand tiny cords. These cords were fastened by the diminutive race of Lilliputians who had thus enslaved him. *Gulliver's Travels* is at once a delightful children's story and an intriguing political satire. While its original target was seventeenth century England, it speaks with equal relevance to twentieth century America.

One of its themes is the danger inherent in a government that intrudes beyond its legitimate sphere of authority. By a thousand bureaucratic decrees, introduced almost imperceptibly "as they sleep," such a government enslaves its people. Satan may attack in the form of a "roaring lion" as during the French Revolution. But often he assumes the form of "an angel of light," a civil government that promises marvelous benefits—if only we will submit to its shackles.

In this chapter we will discover that biblical civil government is a relatively small institution. It has limited but authoritative power to prevent any of the various spheres of authority (business, family, labor, etc.) from harming or taking advantage of the others. It interacts with the spheres and impedes injustice among them, but it does not impose itself on any of them or assume any of their functions. Neither state nor church attempts to assume authority over the other's God-given functions.

Contrary to this, we now find government going far beyond this legitimate police function. Through excessive taxation, regulation, and outright ownership the government slowly strangles the independent spheres of activity and assumes their function. The result is gross inefficiency and loss of freedom. Education is nearly swallowed up in government control. Other activities experience varying degrees of coercion, and the church and family barely hold their own against the encroachments on an unrestrained bureaucracy.

To gain a perspective on the proper role of civil government, we must return to the Old and New Testaments of Holy Scripture. The Ten Commandments provide the foundation for our investigation. The case law interpretation of the Ten Commandments appears in Exodus 21—23, referred to by some as the Law of the Covenant. These case laws describe the specific characteristics of a society that is attempting to live in accordance with the Ten Commandments.

In some instances, the case laws are recorded in terms unique to Israel's agricultural society. Following the lead of the apostle Paul in such cases (see Deut. 25:4; 1 Tim. 5:18), we must seek to apply the general equity, principle, or meaning of the law to our specific circumstances. A number of general legal principles emerge from our study of these and other case laws, to which we now turn our attention.

JUSTICE AND TRUE COMPASSION—
THE MERCY OF THE WICKED IS CRUEL

God specifically assigns civil government the task of administering justice in society, i.e., restraining the wrongdoer and punishing those who commit crimes. Nowhere does He assign government the task of providing for the needs of the poor. To attempt such a task, government must abandon its divine assignment of administering justice, protecting life, and safeguarding property from confiscation.

This is because government becomes a perpetrator of injustice when it forcibly confiscates the property of one group in society for transfer to another group. The law is perverted and used as an agency of injustice ostensibly to "respect the person of the poor" (Lev. 19:15). It specifically violates the Eighth Commandment: "Thou shall not steal" (Ex. 20:15).

Such a perversion of justice was logically and eloquently documented by the Frenchman, Frederic Bastiat in the nineteenth century:

The law perverted! And the police powers of the state perverted along with it! The law, I say, not only turned from its proper purpose but made to follow an entirely contrary purpose! The law become the weapon of every kind of greed! Instead of checking crime, the law itself guilty of the evils it is supposed to punish! If this is true, it is a serious fact, and moral duty requires me to call the attention of my fellow-citizens to it.[1]

These words were written during and after the Revolution of February 1848. As France plunged headlong into socialism, for the most part, Bastiat's brilliant logic fell on deaf ears.

By way of contrast, the biblical state does not engage in so-called welfare activity. Rather it fosters an environment of liberty under law in which men are free to work, trade, and provide for the poor in the land. The latter is accomplished by such things as gleaning (see Lev. 19:9), poor loans (see Deut. 15:8), indentured servitude (see Lev. 25:39–40) and outright gifts. God has given this responsibility to the church and its individual members.

When government attempts to provide for the needs of the poor it can only do so by confiscating the wealth of some other part of society. This is neither justice nor compassion, for "the tender mercies of the wicked are cruel" (Prov. 12:10).

Government is assigned the specific function of maintaining justice in society. However, when the church forsakes its responsibility by neglecting care of the poor, government moves in to fill the vacuum. It then becomes an agent of injustice and engages in illegitimate confiscatory taxation and wealth redistribution (see chapter 3).

This kind of centralization is sometimes practiced in the name of Christianity. For example, the Pilgrims were required by charter to set up a common storehouse from which everyone in the colony would be given food. Unfortunately, everyone assumed that someone else would do the planting, cultivating, and harvesting. As a result, the harvest was meager, and winter was a time of starvation and desperation.[2]

Finally, Governor Bradford assigned each family individual parcels of land. He announced that everyone would be living off whatever they themselves could manage to produce. The result was a bountiful harvest and the first Thanksgiving Day celebration in the fall.

Other Christian communal societies have sprung up from time to time in America. All eventually fail because they disregard biblical principles of private ownership and stewardship. It appears that such colonies can exist and even thrive, sometimes for many years, as long as they remain small and the religious bond remains strong.

The Amana colonies in central Iowa are a good example. For many years they functioned with a common storehouse. Every year each family was assigned an equal number of coupons which they could trade in at the store. Gradually, a small percentage (never more than about 25 percent) became malingerers and the common storehouse was not sufficient to provide for everybody.

In what the natives call the Great Change of 1932, the Amanas followed in the footsteps of Plymouth. In that year the experiment in Christian socialism was disbanded and free enterprise was introduced. Amana Refrigeration and other industries were incorporated and have flourished over the years.[3]

Thus, history confirms that socialism cannot survive, even under the most ideal circumstances. Even when strong Christian charity binds members of a communistic society, the system fails eventually. How much more is it doomed to failure when the bond is nothing more than state coercion? The collapse of the bloody Soviet state in 1990 is the latest example of such folly.

RESTITUTION—MAKING SURE CRIME DOES NOT PAY

Justice is defined in Scripture by restitution. For non-capital crimes, double restitution is required: "If the stolen beast is found alive in his possession, whether it is an ox or an ass or a sheep, he shall pay double" (Ex. 22:4, RSV).

Thus, the basic principle of criminal justice is restitution.[4] In ordinary penal restitution, double restitution is the normal requirement. In Bible times, the thief was to pay back what he stole, plus what he hoped to profit. Restitution may rise as high as fivefold for a productive animal or (by extension) a tool of production (see Ex. 22:1).

This principle was applied in Puritan New England in cases of theft. For instance, when one Owen Jones was convicted "of stealing a rugg and a coate from Phillip Keane valued at twenty six Shillings," the court ordered that he make threefold restitution and "in case hee make not Satisfaction accordingly that hee bee sold."[5]

If a thief repents and voluntarily returns, he is to add a fifth part, or 20 percent to what he stole. This is seen in Leviticus 6:4–5, RSV: "when one has sinned and become guilty, he shall restore what he took by robbery . . . he shall restore it in full, and shall add a fifth to it, and give it to him to whom it belongs . . . . "

In cases of assault, the law of equivalence (see below), with possibility of substituting compensation in cases of irreparable bodily injury prevails. If bodily damage is not permanent, restitution is to include loss of time and hospital bills: "he shall pay for the loss of his time, and shall have him thoroughly healed" (Ex. 21:19, RSV). Another possible penalty is corporal punishment, to be exercised at the judge's discretion, of no more than forty blows (see Deut. 25:1–3).

The criminal owes a debt to the victim, not society. Thus, the concepts of "serving time," "public service requirements," and even "boot camps for criminals" are unbiblical and counterproductive. Any program in which the offender does not focus on repaying his victim is an exercise in futility.

Most humanistic attempts at rehabilitating criminals have ended in failure because they have failed to comprehend the biblical view of man. They have ignored the biblical prescription for restitution, focusing instead on education, psychological evaluation, and "treatment." True rehabilitation occurs only when the transgressor is confronted with responsibility for his crime and required to make amends.[6] Restitution should be paid directly to the victim, not to the victim via the state. The latter approach blurs the locus of responsibility in the criminal's mind.

If the state does not pursue restitution for the victim, it is simply not pursuing justice. The penitentiary/jail system is based on the humanistic presupposition that a criminal left to meditate on the error of his way will reform himself. As such it is patently unbiblical and a total failure. The only authorized use of a jail in Scripture is as a temporary detention facility, "till the will of the LORD should be declared . . . " (Lev. 24:12, RSV).

INDENTURED SERVITUDE—WHEN THE THIEF COMES UP SHORT

If the lawbreaker cannot afford to repay his victim he is required to work off his debt. Exodus 22:3 stipulates that "if he has nothing, then he shall be sold for his theft." The book of Philemon is evidence that this form of private, household "slavery" is still part of God's pattern for dealing with a lawbreaker in New Testament times.

As we have seen, restitution teaches responsibility by making the offender directly accountable to the victim. Restitution provides for justice by requiring the offender to repay his victim commensurate to the crime. The judges should estimate value based on the current market value of the stolen item. This should not be inflated by any supposed "psychological duress" suffered by the victim.

Biblical "slavery" is based on this principle of restitution. If the offender cannot afford repayment he must be placed into a position of indentured servitude to work off his liability.[7]

This is not chattel slavery such as practiced in the Old South, for biblical law specified rules for humane treatment and ultimate freedom at the repayment of the debt. Moreover, stealing a man for sale into permanent slavery is a crime punishable by death (see Deut. 24:7). The American South was judged by God for failing to observe principles of biblical "slavery."

The prison system, as a means of correction, is non-existent in Scripture. It was introduced to America by the Quakers, who posited that the criminal, being basically good, would surely repent if sequestered to meditate on the error of his way.

Edward Levi, attorney general under President Gerald Ford (1974–76), made this connection in a dedication speech for the Federal Bureau of Prisons Detention Center in Chicago Illinois:

> While the existence of jails dates back to medieval times, the idea of penitentiaries is modern—indeed it is American. Largely it is the product of the Quaker notion that if a wrongdoer were separated from his companions, given a great length of time to think about his misdeeds, and with the help of prayer, he would mend his ways. This late-18th-century concept was the beginning of what has come to be known as the rehabilitative ideal.[8]

The modern jail system must be replaced for it denies biblical restitution, substituting a humanistic system of penitence. The root of "penitentiary" is "penitent." Notice the strong correlation between the monastic cell (a place of meditation) and the prison cell. The concept of "debt to society" must be rejected by making the lawbreaker as directly accountable to his victim as possible.

It is ironic that many Christians have come to accept the ungodly and humanistic prison system as the norm, while they react in horror to the Bible's humane system of indentured servitude. Enslavement to the state is sanctioned, while private household "slavery" is anathema. The former reinforces irresponsibility while the latter does the best job possible of restoring the lawbreaker to a responsible position in society.

Indentured servitude is also the biblical approach to the problem of debt. The Israelite who fell upon hard economic times was permitted to sell himself as a servant, not as a slave: "And if your brother becomes poor beside you, and sells himself to you, you shall not make him serve as a slave: he shall be with you as a hired servant and as a sojourner" (Lev. 25:39–40, RSV).

However, servitude for debt was to be limited to seven years: "At the end of every seven years you shall grant a release. Every creditor shall release what he has lent to his neighbor . . . " (Deut. 15:1–2, RSV). Thus, while bankruptcy was not an option for the debt-ridden Israelite, his liability was limited to a specified time period. Historian Edmund Morgan notes that among the Puritans, "Another kind of damage which could be restored by servitude was debt. According to New England laws, when a man could not pay his debts, the creditor could exact his due (but not double or triple his due) in service."[9]

LEX TALIONIS—THE PUNISHMENT FITS THE CRIME

Contrary to popular opinion that sees biblical law as too harsh, the principle of an "eye for an eye" ensures that the punishment perfectly fits the crime. This is in contrast to humanistic law, which is either too lenient or too harsh.

The "law of retaliance" is more basically a "law of equivalence," wherein the civil magistrate ensures that conditions are restored as nearly as possible to what they were before the crime occurred.[10] Thus, the law is neither too harsh, nor too lenient—it is perfectly just.

This is in contrast to various humanistic law codes invented by men. For example, in some Islamic countries a pickpocket is punished by having his hand cut off. By contrast, in modern America guilty murderers are routinely set free with little more than a slap on the wrist. To anyone remotely familiar with the Bible these penalties are grotesquely out of proportion.

Under biblical law if a body part, such as a hand, is maliciously damaged by an assailant, justice requires that his hand, likewise, be damaged: "When a man causes a disfigurement in his neighbor, as he has done it shall be done to him, fracture for fracture, eye for eye, tooth for tooth . . . " (Lev. 24:19–20, RSV).

Such a penalty was inflicted on the pagan king Adoni-bezek and acknowledged by him as his just due (see Judg. 1:7). His thumbs and great toes were cut off even as he had dismembered seventy other kings.

However, in cases other than first degree murder, the Bible indicates that a ransom or compensation can be paid in lieu of bodily injury: "Moreover you shall accept no ransom for the life of a murderer, who is guilty of death; but he shall be put to death" (Num. 35:31, RSV). This implies that for other lesser crimes—even capital crimes such as adultery—the victim may accept monetary compensation in lieu of the physical penalty. This is an aspect of victim's rights discussed below.

Capital Punishment—Restitution to God

Some crimes are such a violent assault on the image of God in man or on biblical society that God stipulates that nothing less than death will satisfy His offended sense of justice. The death penalty is therefore the ultimate form of restitution to God.

Only when the death penalty is applied fairly and firmly in a nation does the would-be offender gain enough respect for the image of God in his neighbor to refrain from killing him. When, and if, he does murder, only the death penalty can satisfy the justice of God and provide satisfaction for the irreverent defilement of the image of God in the victim. Before God each person counts and is therefore accountable.

In addition to murder (see Lev. 24:17), the death penalty is specified for a number of crimes. This is the ultimate form of restitution. These crimes include promotion of witchcraft as an attempt to undermine biblical society (see Deut. 13). Bestiality (see Lev. 20:15), homosexuality (see Lev. 20:13), incest and adultery (see Lev. 20:10) are assaults on the family—the foundation of biblical society (see Lev. 20:10–12). Assault or repudiation of parents is an attack on the basic authority structure of society (see Lev. 20:9). Kidnapping (see Deut. 24:7) is an assault on the very person of the image of God.

Some religious crimes that carry the death penalty under the Old Testament appear to have been modified in the New Testament. For example, the Jewish Sabbath with its accompanying death penalty has been replaced by the Lord's Day in the New Testament (see Col. 2:16). The primary responsibility for enforcement also has shifted from the civil magistrate to the individual conscience (see Rom. 14:5–6).

The death penalty applies as well in cases of incorrigibility. We have learned that if the thief cannot afford compensation, he is to be sold into indentured servitude until compensation is paid in full. While indentured servitude is God's provision of grace for a repentant criminal, the Bible does not allow for the existence and growth of a permanent criminal class in society.

The incorrigible juvenile delinquent is to be put to death (see Deut. 21:18–21). This is obviously not referring to the everyday discipline of normal children. Likewise, the adult who refuses to respond to the demands of justice laid out by the civil magistrate is to be executed: "The man who acts presumptuously, by not obeying the priest who stands to minister there before the LORD your God, or the judge, that man shall die" (Deut. 17:12, RSV).

In early America this was referred to as the "three time loser" penalty. At first glance such penalties may appear cruel and heartless. However, this is misplaced mercy. "Your eye shall not pity him," declares Moses, "but you shall purge the guilt of innocent blood from Israel, so that it may be well with you" (Deut. 19:13, RSV). This kind of illegitimate mercy triggered God's judgment against King Saul.

Failure to follow through on the biblical requirement leads to the development of a permanent criminal class in society. The result is all kinds of social evil, including gang warfare, organized crime syndicates, and mob rule. God uses these means to execute an unjust society which refuses to execute the just demands of His law.

Even law-abiding citizens, who have acquiesced by their silence, find themselves besieged in their homes, afraid to walk the streets at night or in some parts of the city at any time. In the Bible the gates of the city were the place where justice was administered. But now the city, which means place of "safety" (Greek *keitai*), becomes a place of danger and violence.

The man who maliciously takes a life must forfeit his life—an extension of the law of equivalence. However, a place of sanctuary must be provided in case of accidental manslaughter, until a man may be fairly tried (see Ex. 21:12–14).

As we have seen, death is the maximum penalty, for which the victim may choose to substitute monetary satisfaction. The only exception is premeditated murder: "Moreover you shall take no satisfaction for the life of a murderer . . . " (Num. 35:31, RSV). This verse implies that monetary restitution is acceptable for some crimes that would otherwise require the death penalty.

VICTIM'S RIGHTS—THE FORGOTTEN VICTIM

We know from Psalm 51:4 that God is the ultimate "victim" of all crime. However, in most cases there is also a human victim who appears before the civil magistrate. There is a sense in which this human victim is a surrogate for God. As such, the victim has a number of unique privileges and powers in the courtroom that have been all but obliterated under the modern system. In a biblical system, the victim is much more than a passive spectator who is simply acted upon. He has a much more vigorous role to play, especially in the sentencing process.

The victim must be satisfied with appropriate restitution. However, it appears from Matthew 18:23–25 that a creditor may lawfully forgive or reduce any non-capital penalty or debt owed him. This principle extends even to some capital crimes, and it is the prerogative of the victim to choose whether or not the case should be prosecuted.

This was apparently the case when Joseph "put away" Mary for what appeared to be the capital crime of adultery. When Mary became pregnant, Joseph had no other choice than to conclude she was guilty of adultery. However, he did not insist on the death penalty as required by law, but "decided to put her away quietly." The Bible says that he was acting in the capacity of a just man in taking this action.

Likewise, God repeatedly forgave Israel for her spiritual adultery against Him, until A.D. 70. The state may not interfere with the victim's decision in this matter unless the state itself is in some way victimized.

Thus, a victim may decline to prosecute or accept a penalty less than death for some capital crimes. This may include monetary compensation in lieu of disfigurement or death, in most cases.[11] The compensation is to be proposed by the victim and finalized by the judge, as noted in the next section.

At first blush, it may appear that monetary compensation shows favoritism to the wealthy. However, it is entirely possible that a wealthy person would receive a stiffer penalty for the same crime, because the judge determines the size of the fine (see Ex. 21:22). This supposed advantage to a man of means is not due to the law, but to previous circumstances.

PENAL SANCTIONS—PENALTY BARGAINING, NOT PLEA BARGAINING

Sentencing in Scripture is seen as a give-and-take process in which the victim, the judge, and possibly even the convicted criminal are actively involved. The Bible establishes maximum penalties for a given crime, but in most cases the victim is permitted to settle for a reduced or alternative punishment such as monetary compensation.

For example, this give-and-take process is seen in the case of an accidental abortion or miscarriage in Exodus 21: 22–24. The passage stipulates that "the one who hurt her shall be fined, according as the woman's husband shall lay upon him; and he shall pay as the judges determine." This seems to indicate that the victim initially proposes an appropriate monetary punishment, and the judge(s) has the final say as to whether or not it is reasonable.[12]

A few verses later we learn that this "penalty bargaining" process extends even to capital cases short of murder.[13] The negligent owner of a notoriously dangerous ox who gores a person to death must be put to death unless the victim is willing to accept a monetary substitute: "But if the ox has been accustomed to gore in the past, and its owner has been warned but has not kept it in, and it kills a man or a woman, the ox shall be stoned, and its owner also shall be put to death. If a ransom is laid upon him, then he shall give for the redemption of his life whatever is laid upon him" (Ex. 21:29–30, RSV).

It is possible that this "penalty bargaining" process may even include the condemned criminal. For example, in cases where the victim initially calls for the maximum penalty of death or disfigurement, the condemned might be allowed to propose a monetary or service (indentured servitude) alternative.

The victim would then decide which penalty best gratifies his sense of justice. He may be satisfied to see the criminal physically maimed or put to death. In other cases, he may sense genuine repentance and call for a less stringent financial award. The latter, of course, would be more beneficial to the victim from a purely material standpoint. The judge is present for counsel and to ensure that the final determination falls within the biblical boundaries.

If justice is to be served, it is critical that the victim be satisfied with the outcome, within the parameters of biblical law. This penalty bargaining procedure stands in opposition to the humanistic plea bargaining process. In the latter the charge itself is manipulated in terms of humanistic legal definitions.

COURT PROCEDURAL RULES—SHORT AND SWEET

The death penalty is not to be administered lightly or capriciously. Proper safeguards are essential to ensure justice to the accused as well as the victim. At least two witnesses are required (see Deut. 17:6), and inquiry must be pursued until the fact of the crime is absolutely confirmed and certain (see Deut. 17:4). A good example of this is seen with the woman taken in adultery in John 8. When the witnesses against her withdrew, the case against her was dismissed.

The courtroom is the proper place for the oath; it is a tool to ensure that truth is brought to light. It is enforced by stiff biblical penalties for perjury: "The judges shall inquire diligently, and if the witness is a false witness and has accused his brother falsely, then you shall do to him as he had meant to do to his brother; so you shall purge the evil from the midst of you" (Deut. 19:18–19, RSV).

If a guilty verdict is returned in a capital case, the sentence must be executed quickly and the witness should be the chief executioner (see Deut. 17:7). Only the most hardened false witness would be able to follow through with such a requirement.

Punishment, including the death penalty, is to be administered publicly, as an object lesson to the community. Contrary to modern sociology and criminology, the Bible declares that this has a strong deterrent effect: "And the rest shall hear, and fear, and shall never again commit any such evil among you" (Deut. 19:20, RSV).

In addition, the community affirms the judgment, purging the evil from its midst. It thereby placates the wrath of God against the land polluted by blood (see Num. 35:33–34). The appearance in modern times of private execution performed by an anonymous state executioner has thus contributed to the breakdown of justice in the United States.

The need for civil expiation in cases of murder is seen in the Old Testament offering for an unsolved murder (see Deut. 21:1–9). The offering was made by the elders of the city closest to the location of the dead body. The land itself is spoken of as being defiled until the civil authorities take appropriate steps to cleanse it.

The failure of the judicial system to provide swift justice is another major contributing factor to the breakdown of law and order. Solomon, Israel's wisest judge, observed that "when sentence against an evil deed is not executed speedily, therefore the hearts of the sons of men is fully set to do evil" (Eccl. 8:11, RSV).

CONCLUSION

Restitution lies at the heart of the biblical system of criminal justice. Without restitution, justice is simply not satisfied. The centrality of this principle is seen in the death of Christ as the restitution payment for the transgressions of His people. In cases of theft the basic requirement is double restitution, with 20 percent restitution if the thief confesses voluntarily before trial.

The foregoing is obviously only a sketch of the more salient points of biblical law. We have not touched on such legal topics as marriage and divorce, usury, legal liability, seduction, pollution, and many other aspects of the law of God. Nor do we presume to have offered the final word on the topic of criminal justice. It is hoped that this brief overview will stimulate the reader to further inquiry in these areas. The Law itself is our best teacher:

> The law of the LORD is perfect, converting the soul: the testimony of the LORD is sure, making wise the simple. The statutes of the LORD are right, rejoicing the heart: the commandment of the LORD is pure, enlightening the eyes (Ps. 19:7–8).

> How I love Thy Law, O LORD, it is my meditation all the day. Thou through thy commandments hast made me wiser than mine enemies for they are ever with me. I have more understanding than all my teachers: for thy testimonies are my meditation (Ps. 119:97–99).

REVIEW QUIZ

1. What is the most effective approach to solving the gang problem in U.S. cities?
   a. Establish alternative sports/activities programs such as Street Hoops
   b. Increase the number of police patrols and gang specialists in the police department
   c. Execute incorrigible gang members

2. Who is the most appropriate person(s) to appoint as executioner in a capital case?
   a. The witnesses
   b. The condemned person's family
   c. A disguised, impartial person employed by the state

3. What is the most effective way to deal with the crime of theft?
   a. Imprison the offender so he can pay his debt to society and meditate on the error of his ways
   b. Require the offender to work on public service projects
   c. Require the offender to pay his victim twice as much as he stole
   d. Require the offender to go to a boot camp for criminals
   e. Implement programs to rehabilitate the offender

4. Restitution is central to the biblical concept of criminal justice. Under this system:
   a. The criminal repays his debt to society.
   b. The government pays restitution to the victim.
   c. The victim pays restitution to support the criminal in prison.
   d. The criminal pays double restitution to the victim.

5. (T or F) The provision for bankruptcy in American law is a workable substitute for the outmoded system of indentured servitude to repay debts.

6. Which of these was a capital crime in Israel?
   a. Prostitution
   b. Adultery
   c. Fornication between two unmarried persons

7. (T or F) With the words "He that is without sin among you cast the first stone," Jesus abolished the death penalty in the New Testament era.

8. In Scripture, how many persons are required to convict of a capital crime?
   a. One
   b. Two
   c. Three

9. In Scripture, who alone can initiate a lawsuit?
   a. The state
   b. The victim
   c. A church officer
   d. Any competent witness

10. In a biblical republic, a judge sometimes has authority to
    a. Reduce a punishment
    b. Apply *ex post facto* law
    c. Increase a punishment

11. (T or F) From the case law regarding the rebellious son in Exodus 21, we derive the principle that after a warning and a spanking young children are to be put to death for incidents of disobeying their parents.

12. Joseph's decision to "put away Mary privately" without insisting on the death penalty is strong evidence that:
    a. The death penalty for adultery has been abolished.
    b. The state may not prosecute if the victim declines to prosecute.
    c. Joseph was at bottom a soft-hearted idealist.

13. When is the state *not* authorized to initiate a lawsuit?
    a. In the case of murder
    b. When the state itself was injured by the act
    c. When the victim is alive and competent

14. No crime is specified as requiring lashing, yet the Bible limits
    lashings to no more than forty. Thus, this penal sanction
    a. is only for juvenile delinquents
    b. may be used for crimes such as disputes, prostitution, stalking,
       drunkenness, pornography, drug dealing, etc. for which no
       other penalty is specified
    c. is a relic of prediluvian civilization, now abolished because it
       constitutes cruel and unusual punishment

15. What is the purpose of biblical slavery?
    a. A necessary source of income for the slave's master
    b. A picture and warning of eternal enslavement in hell
    c. A source of inexpensive labor for public works projects such as
       Solomon's Temple
    d. Train irresponsible men to be productive members of society
    e. Both b and d

16. For which crime may no monetary satisfaction be offered, but the
    death penalty be applied?
    a. Adultery
    b. Kidnaping
    c. Murder
    d. Incorrigible son

17. Victim's rights means that
    a. The victim may decide not to prosecute.
    b. The victim may accept monetary compensation instead of the
       death penalty for a capital crime.
    c. The victim may choose the death penalty instead of monetary
       compensation for a capital crime.
    d. All of the above

18. Which of these is not a purpose of victim's rights?
    a. Extend mercy to a truly repentant criminal
    b. Incentive for criminals to deal less harshly with victims during the crime
    c. Allows for personal vengeance
    d. Provides compensation for the victim

19. The "eye for an eye" principle means that
    a. Punishment is inevitably too harsh.
    b. The punishment fits the crime.
    c. The courts dispense cruel and unusual punishment.
    d. There is a direct one-for-one correspondence between punishment and crime.

20. How much restitution is required of a law breaker who turns himself in voluntarily?
    a. An additional 10 percent
    b. An additional 20 percent
    c. An additional 50 percent
    d. Double restitution

21. The primary argument against prisons is
    a. Offender can't repay victim
    b. They are hotbeds of homosexuality
    c. They are colleges of crime

22. The "three-time loser" penalty in Scripture was
    a. Death
    b. Life imprisonment
    c. Double restitution
    d. Fourfold restitution

23. Which Canaanitic king had his thumbs and big toes cut off because he had done the same to seventy other kings?
    a. Gog
    b. Agag
    c. Adoni-bezek
    d. Achish

24. A person guilty of manslaughter
    a. is worthy of the death penalty without mercy
    b. has killed an innocent person by unwarranted or accidental
       violence
    c. is a cold-blooded murderer
    d. may escape the death penalty if a sum of money is laid on him
    e. b and d

25. Who has the primary responsibility for determining the specific
    penalty for a crime?
    a. The legislature
    b. The victim
    c. The offender
    d. The judge
    e. The jury

26. In establishing the penalty for a crime the victim is limited by
    a. The judge
    b. His conscience
    c. The maximum penalty specified by biblical law
    d. English common law precedents

27. In economic affairs there is a time limit on debt "bondage" of
    a. Seven years
    b. Ten years
    c. Forty-nine years

28. Under a biblical system of sentencing
    a. The victim may specify the punishment up to the biblical
       maximum.
    a. The criminal, who stands to lose a body part, may make a
       counter-offer.
    c. The integrity of the legal system is confirmed because the victim
       is satisfied.
    d. All of the above

29. Which of these statements best fits the biblical mode of execution in the case of capital crimes?
    a. Execution should be conducted in private in order to preserve the essential human dignity of the condemned.
    b. Execution should be public to serve as a negative example for others who may be tempted to break the law.

30. What is the best guideline for restitution in cases of theft?
    a. The appraised value of the item
    b. Thirty pieces of silver, the price paid for the Redeemer
    c. The market value of the item
    d. The victim's estimate of value

31. Which of the following is *not* a characteristic of biblical slavery?
    a. The stealing of men for purposes of sale is strictly forbidden.
    b. There were few limits placed on the master's treatment of his slave(s).
    c. Indentured servitude is morally permissible, but the Christian, as a free man in Christ, should avoid it.

32. Which sin is likened to witchcraft?
    a. Murder
    b. Unauthorized mercy
    c. Adultery
    d. a and b

33. When Jesus told the woman taken in adultery, "Neither do I condemn thee, go and sin no more," He thereby acknowledged that:
    a. The Old Testament death penalty for adultery was no longer in effect.
    b. Without witnesses she could not be lawfully convicted.
    c. The Old Covenant death penalty was too harsh under the New Covenant of grace.
    d. Text is irrelevant because not in the original.

Discussion Guide

1. If civil government curtails its welfare activity, how are the needs of the poor to be met? Be as specific as possible.

2. Compare and contrast the biblical concept of restitution to the victim and the modern concept of paying a "debt to society."

3. Compare and contrast the biblical system of indentured servitude with the modern jail system.

4. What does the concept of victim's rights refer to in Scripture?

5. Describe the process by which the specific punishment for a crime is established. How does penalty bargaining differ from plea bargaining?

6. When God instituted the death penalty, did He intend it to be temporary or permanent? How do we reconcile the death penalty with Jesus' teaching to "turn the other cheek" and the Sixth Commandment, "Thou shalt not kill"? What are some of the judicial safeguards relating to the death penalty?

7. What are the implications of the biblical principle of *lex talionis* for the criminal justice system?

Answer Key

1) c	2) a	3) c	4) d	5) F	6) b	7) F
8) b	9) b	10) a	11) F	12) b	13) c	14) b
15) e	16) c	17) d	18) c	19) b	20) b	21) a
22) a	23) c	24) e	25) b	26) c	27) a	28) d
29) b	30) c	31) b	32) b	33) b		

PART IV
Rebuilding by the Blueprint

Prior to the Normandy invasion, General Dwight Eisenhower allowed the Germans to intercept radio transmissions that misled them as to his true intentions. Consequently, the Germans were taken by complete surprise when Allied troops landed at Normandy. Centuries earlier Quintus Fabius Maximus won fame when his army triumphed over Hannibal by a strategy of exhausting the enemy and avoiding a pitched battle. In each case the strategy was different, but it was appropriate to the situation and executed to perfection.

An effective military campaign requires both effective strategy and effective tactics. To win the cultural war in which we are engaged, we must give careful attention to both. Our strategy includes the guiding principles and the global context in which we launch our campaign. Tactics, on the other hand, are specific plans to be implemented in a particular situation on a specific battlefield. To be effective, both must be animated by a sense of purpose and an absolute belief in ultimate victory. Our closing chapters address these three issues.

Switching from the military to the construction metaphor, the skill of the carpenter (chapter 11) must be brought to bear on the raw materials at hand in accordance with the plan (chapter 10). The final outcome rests in the carpenter's ability to visualize the finished project and hold that vision in his mind's eye as he works (chapter 12).

Given our current state of decline, the possibility of ever implementing the principles outlined in the preceding chapters may seem unrealistic, impractical, idealistic, even quixotic. However, we must keep the ultimate goal in sight, remembering that the power and command of God are not limited by our immediate circumstances.

10

STRATEGY

A ccording to Ephesians 6:12, the church of Christ wrestles "not against flesh and blood, but against principalities, against powers, against the rulers of the darkness of this world, against spiritual wickedness in high places." The battle for our culture and civil government is one theater of this great war. From the Bible we derive a number of "Principles of War" which when applied tend toward long-term cultural victory. These begin with a definition of the proper relationship between church and state. Failure to understand this relationship has produced untold suffering for the church and the world over the centuries, which is yet to be resolved.

SEPARATION OF CHURCH AND STATE

In the Old Testament, civil and ecclesiastical offices were established by God with distinct officers, functions, and funding. All attempts to violate these spheres, particularly by civil rulers, were severely punished by God.

For example, King Uzziah was smitten with leprosy for presuming to perform the duty of a priest (see 2 Chron. 26:16–21). Likewise, the heart of King Saul's rebellion lay in his impertinent offering of sacrifice, the prerogative of the priest (see 1 Sam. 13:8–14).

At various points in the history of Western civilization, either the church or the state has invaded and dominated the domain of the other at the expense of personal liberty. For example, during the period of the Holy Roman Empire, church and state vied for political control, and later on the state came to dominate the church.

God forbids unity of power to mankind to thwart the constant human striving to "be like God." He has parceled the authority for the necessary ordering and control of society into numerous institutional spheres which are limited to their God-ordained function.

The function of the church is to worship God and serve Him by advancing the Kingdom of God through preaching, administration of the sacraments, church discipline, and evangelism. The function of the state is to preserve human society by holding man's evil nature forcibly in check by means of law. This is primarily a negative, rather than a positive function. The civil sphere is a separate institution established to administer God's law under the direction of judges, kings, elders of the gate, and the like.

Leaders in both institutions are described as ministers of God, performing their God-ordained functions independently of one another (see Rom. 13:4). Neither institution has been authorized to assume the functions of the other. Historically, efforts to do so have produced centralization of power, loss of freedom, and corruption of the God-ordained purposes of both institutions.

The First Amendment to the U.S. Constitution forbids the federal government from having anything to do with support of a single church or government preference of one Christian creed over another. It forbids the mingling of the *function* of the civil and ecclesiastical spheres, but it does not deny the right of any Christian citizen to participate in government as a Christian.

The separation of church and state means freedom *for* religion, not freedom *from* religion. We seem to be confused on this matter because we assume that religion is the purview of the church alone. We have secularized everything not illuminated by stained glass windows.

As we have seen, almost all biblical restrictions are directed toward the state to ensure it does not abuse its power by setting itself up as God with ecclesiastical authority. On the contrary, government is enjoined to protect and promote true religion (see Rom. 13:3) or at least provide an atmosphere of freedom in which it may flourish (see 1 Tim. 2:1–4)

On the other hand, it is impossible for government to function in a godly fashion apart from the counsel and instruction of the church. The church, as the repository of the oracles of God, is to provide experts in the law of God to counsel governors. Many of her trained laymen should serve as judges and lawyers in government.

The Levites in ancient Israel were supported by the tithe to study, teach, and apply the law of God to every aspect of the nation's culture. For example, the Bible records evidence of what appears to be a Supreme Court in Israel:

> If any case arises requiring decision between one kind of homicide and another, one kind of legal right and another, or one kind of assault and another, any case within your towns which is too difficult for you, then you shall arise and go up to the place which the LORD your God will choose, and coming to the Levitical priests, and to the judge who is in office in those days, you shall consult them . . . . (Deut. 17:8–9, RSV)

Here we see the ecclesiastical and civil authority working hand-in-hand to decide difficult cases of law. Apparently the Levitical specialists in the study of God's law were present in court to advise (not displace) the civil authority in such cases.

As the evangelical church has increasingly rejected the law of God, government, in turn, has rejected the counsel and authority of God and the church. It has, in fact, assumed a hostile posture against the church by means of social security taxation, liability suits, and attempts to establish jurisdiction over the church via zoning and other local ordinances. The church has done much to aid and abet this process by voluntary submission to state incorporation and tax exemption, which necessarily limit the preaching of God's word.

A corporation is by definition a creature of the state. Thus, it is possible to argue that most evangelical churches today are state churches, by virtue of incorporation.[1] Who defines the percentage of time or money that an incorporated, tax-exempt church may devote to political and governmental matters in modern America? It is the IRS, not the Word of God, that has presumed to establish these parameters (currently 5 percent of budget).

As an independent institution under God, the church is necessarily tax immune (see Ezra 7:24). By applying to the civil government for tax exemption, the church places itself under the illegitimate authority of the government. The true status of the church is much like that of a foreign embassy in Washington, D.C.; it is an enclave of heaven on foreign soil. It functions primarily under the law of its homeland rather than of the host country.

Restoring the proper relationship between church and state is central to the reformation of civil government. The church must be reformed first as the model and example for the civil magistery. Scripture warns us that God deals first with His own people before moving to the broader culture: "For the time is come that judgment must begin at the house of God" (1 Pet. 4:17).

The doctrine of separation of church and state has both an offensive and defensive aspect. Currently, the doctrine is used against the church to exclude Christianity from any vital role in the life of the nation. With the retreat of the church we now find the state pressing the pursuit with totally illegitimate attacks on the church. Some trial lawyers cast a ravenous eye on the church as an extremely lucrative field for exploitation. For example, some churches have been taken to court for inflicting "undue psychological duress" on members in matters of church discipline.[2]

In the near future, the church will be on the defensive with little but an emasculated doctrine of church and state to defend herself. Such a position may well result in the refusal on the part of church officers to submit to demands of state officials in areas that compromise the sovereignty of Christ over the church.

Long-term, the church must take the offensive, asserting her long neglected role as counselor to the state. Government leaders are dependent on church leaders to guide them in the proper interpretation of Scripture in matters of civil justice. Church leaders and other Christian leaders must begin this process on an informal basis now by getting to know the elected officials in their area.

What are their concerns and at what points might they be perplexed? What assistance and advice can be offered? These informal meetings could lead to a more organized Bible study on the biblical role of government. As God blesses your efforts, you will see some officials come to Christ and begin to apply your biblical instruction to public policy. Just as Nebuchadnezzar became frustrated with his humanistic advisors and called for Daniel, they will begin to look to the church for advice in difficult situations.

Over time, as God anoints the public ministry of some of these converts, the church can team up with them to lead seminars, public forums, or legal symposiums. Together, these platforms afford the opportunity for believers to share the gospel and law of Christ the King in the public arena. As the power of God's law begins to permeate the legal culture and institutions in an area, the legal expertise of the church will eventually be in great demand. Judges and public officials will begin to seek the support and advice of church courts and leaders.

The church will then fulfill its biblical role as prefigured in Deuteronomy 17. Church and state will fulfill their divine assignments as separate, but cooperating institutions in the kingdom of Christ.

IMPRECATORY PRAYER

Few Christians would deny that any effective strategy of national renewal must begin with prayer. It is God who has been offended by our national disobedience and whose wrath has been provoked. Only as we appeal to Him for mercy is there any hope of reversing the judgments He has set in motion.

His judgments loom like thunderheads. We taste of them in the AIDS epidemic (see Rom. 1:27,32), in oppressive leadership and taxation, and in the impending threat of economic ruin. Our national blindness and rejection of the plain truths of God's Word is evidence that God is ripening us for judgment. If God did not spare His spiritual bride Israel for her spiritual adultery, He will certainly not spare America. In this context, the oft-quoted passage eloquently calls us to the duty of prayer: "If my people, which are called by my name, shall humble themselves, and pray, and seek my face, and turn from their wicked ways; then will I hear from heaven, and will forgive their sin, and will heal their land" (2 Chron. 7:14).

Scripture indicates God marvels at our feeble response to the priority of prayer in the face of impending judgment. "And I sought for a man among them," He said, "that should make up the hedge, and stand in the gap before me for the land, that I should not destroy it; but I found none." Because no man was there to stay the hand of God's judgment God said that He "poured out my indignation upon them; I have consumed them with the fire of my wrath . . . " (Ezek. 22:30–31).

Prayer must lie at the heart of any reformation. We find many examples in Scripture where God's agents for reform began with prayer, acknowledging their own sins and the sins of the nation. The prayer of the prophet Daniel of confession and intercession (see Dan. 9:3–19) is a classic example. He pleaded with the Almighty to vindicate His honor among the heathen in the deliverance of His people:

> Now therefore, O our God, hear the prayer of thy servant, and his supplications, and cause thy face to shine upon thy sanctuary that is desolate, for the Lord's sake. O my God, incline thine ear, and hear; open thine eyes, and behold our desolations, and the city which is called by thy name: for we do not present our supplications before thee for our righteousnesses, but for thy great mercies. (Dan. 9:17–18)

The Scripture seems to indicate that God is actively on the lookout for reasons to extend mercy, even in the face of judgment. On the eve of the Babylonian captivity He commanded these words through the prophet Jeremiah: "For if ye thoroughly amend your ways and your doings; if ye thoroughly execute judgment between a man and his neighbour; . . . Then will I cause you to dwell in this place, in the land that I gave to your fathers, for ever and ever" (Jer. 7:5–7).

Only when the groundwork of repentance has been laid are we on solid footing to beseech God to judge our enemies, rather than use them as our "rod of correction." This is the essence of imprecatory prayer that we find often in the Psalms. For example, David prayed in Psalm 59:5, "Thou therefore, O Lord God of hosts, the God of Israel, awake to visit all the heathen: be not merciful to any wicked transgressors." And earlier in Psalm 7:6, "Arise, O Lord, in thine anger, lift up thyself because of the rage on mine enemies; and awake for me to the judgment that thou hast commanded."

The essence of imprecation is an appeal to God to either convert or judge and remove His avowed enemies. It is to serve as a legal advocate in the divine halls of justice on behalf of the people of God against their persecutors. Although it is impossible to prove beyond a shadow of a doubt, the fact that most Roman emperors died a violent death may be evidence of the power of imprecatory prayer on the lips of the early Christians.

We must be careful not to let impending judgment immobilize us, however. To quote an old cliche, "we must pray as though everything depends on God, and work as though everything depends on us."

Thus, we can move confidently beyond the prayer closet as penitent soldiers to implement other principles of political reformation.

GRADUALISM

As we have seen, political action ultimately cannot succeed without evangelism and discipleship. This takes time. Too often in the Old Testament a godly king would make dramatic reforms in terms of the law of God, but it did not last because the hearts of the people were not truly with him. The rule of Christ cannot be imposed in a top-down, bureaucratic manner.

This does not mean we should neglect political action, but we must recognize that we are in an inter-generational battle and place heavy emphasis on training our children to carry on after us. Even in the conquest of Canaan God told the people of Israel "by little and little I will drive them out before you until you be increased and inherit the land" (Ex. 23:30).

Furthermore, recognition of the principle of gradualism will help us avoid rash and desperate political maneuvers. For example, a recent gubernatorial election in Oregon pitted an ultra-liberal Democrat against a "moderate" Republican. The Republican was a fiscal conservative, but a social liberal on issues such as abortion and homosexuality. He had been nominated by an 80 percent vote in a Republican primary which included about eight candidates, at least two of which were Christians. This man was quite popular statewide and was initially favored to beat the feminist Democrat handily.

About half way through the general election campaign, however, a group of conservative Christians became frustrated and impatient with the Republican's liberal social views. They proceeded to organize a convention to place a conservative Christian on the ballot as an Independent. This man had little prior political experience, was not on the primary ballot, and had virtually no chance of winning. However, his presence in the race drew about 14 percent of the vote, mostly Republican, and threw the election to the ultra-liberal Democrat.

In this case the conservative Christian served as nothing but a spoiler. His presence was extremely divisive and resulted in Oregon suffering for four years under the most liberal governor in its history. He diverted precious resources from other winnable contests in the state, including an anti-gay rights initiative promoted by this same group.

It is the belief of this writer that Christians who hold a long-term view of gradual cultural victory will be fortified against such counter-productive ventures. They will have the wisdom to recognize that we cannot win every battle and that the war will not be won in a single campaign. They will pick and choose their battles carefully and devote the bulk of their resources to the winnable campaigns that emerge during each election cycle. They will not dissipate their energy on causes that are likely to lose, no matter how emotionally appealing they may feel.

They recognize that sometimes the wisest course of action may be to simply ignore an "unwinnable" race even though participation might "send a message" to the powers that be. In some cases, they are willing to live temporarily with partial or incomplete victories. They recognize that these constitute a "political beachhead," leading to complete victory in the future. They believe that we need to stop "sending messages" and start sending Christian representatives to our state capitols and city halls.

COALITION

We must avoid the temptation of perfectionism or titanism, especially when we are still in a minority position. Titanism is the view that we must have all or nothing and we must have it now. We charge onto the public stage like a bull in a china shop and demand instant obedience to the command of God. Any attempt to cooperate with unbelievers for common goals is viewed with a jaundiced eye. In contrast, we find examples in the Bible where God permitted His people to temporarily ally themselves with unbelievers in a limited fashion to defeat a greater enemy.

For example, Abraham allied himself with the king of Sodom to rescue Lot, but he refused to accept spoil from the king. In this case, the Bible actually uses the word "ally" or "confederate" to describe the relationship (Gen. 14:13). Note that Abraham was the leader of the expedition and that he refused to allow the joint victory to lead to subsequent cultural bonding. After the battle Abraham took Lot and his goods and departed from the king of Sodom.

In captivity Daniel and Joseph served as high level advisors to unbelieving rulers. In the providence of God, Esther was united in a marriage covenant with a non-believing king in order that the Jews might defeat Haman, the committed enemy of God. In cases such as these the Bible seems to distinguish between "friendly unbelievers" and committed enemies of the kingdom. It may therefore be foolish to make vows such as "I will never vote for a candidate who supports abortion." Perhaps Francis Schaeffer said it best, "We are co-belligerents, but not allies."

Therefore, evangelical Christians may at times join forces with Roman Catholics, Mormons, and others who oppose the cultural sin of abortion. They may work within political parties with the goal of transforming those parties along biblical lines. However, it is extremely dangerous to carry this coalition beyond the limited cultural context. Such attempts at constructing a pseudo-unity inevitably lead to compromise.

Unfortunately, this kind of compromise on the part of evangelicals is occurring as an unexpected consequence of the abortion conflict. A statement of cooperation issued by leading Evangelicals and Roman Catholics in March, 1994, is a case in point. Respected Protestant signers of this document included Charles Colson, Bill Bright, Pat Robertson, and J.I. Packer.[3]

This statement assumed basic unity as brothers in Christ among Catholics and Protestants. It therefore emphasized the need for cooperation in the task of world evangelization. The fundamental, historic conflict between Catholicism and Protestantism—justification by faith alone—was ignored as the defining distinction. The conflict created by the Protestant Reformation was spoken of in embarrassing and apologetic terms.

In stark contrast, Abraham—following his confederation with the kings of Sodom to rescue Lot—went his way refusing to acknowledge any fundamental unity. Instead, he departed and paid his tithe to God, acknowledging him as the ultimate source of victory—not the coalition.

Coalition does not necessarily mean compromise and may prove very useful, but compromise must be carefully guarded against in any coalition. Like Abraham, believers should take the lead in such joint enterprises. They should communicate lovingly but firmly to the unbeliever the limited nature of the coalition and the underlying points of disunity. This is an obvious opportunity for presenting the gospel and the comprehensive claims of Christ.

OFFENSIVE

Taking the offensive means an aggressive advance against the enemy to wrest the objective from his possession. Jesus Christ has already delivered the decisive victory at Calvary. Our victory is assured, but it remains our task to move boldly forward in a mopping up operation to establish the kingdom He has inaugurated.

From the military we learn that the best defense is a good offense. A defensive posture is a passive and reactive posture. Like the famed Maginot line in World War I France, it risks being overrun because all the guns are stationary and pointed in the wrong direction. An army on the defensive cannot win the war. At best it can avoid defeat for a limited period of time. To win, the troops must be roused out of the relative safety of their foxholes and move forward to engage the enemy.

The church is to go on the offensive against Satan and we know that "the gates of hell shall not prevail" (Matt. 16:18). In the conquest of Canaan the people of God were on the offensive, and the Canaanites were holed up in their cities in a defensive posture. It took the Israelites forty years of wandering in the wilderness to learn the terrible price of failing to take the offensive when God has issued the command to move forward.

Today, of course, swords of steel have been replaced with the Sword of the Spirit, the Word of God. But the Sword must be unsheathed and used. The socialists of this century have made incredible progress by constantly probing for weaknesses in the cultural foundation. Inch by inch they have advanced their heresies until the foundation is all but destroyed. The Fabian Socialists are masters of the principle of gradualism discussed earlier.

Christians, on the other hand, have spent too much time reacting to the "brushfires" lit by the enemy: pornography, school health clinics, etc. We need to spend more time on the offensive, implementing some of the basic principles of biblical justice described earlier. We must learn to preempt the enemy and occupy the moral high ground by presenting positive biblical solutions to cultural problems. We must place greater emphasis on transforming underlying institutional structures according to the biblical pattern, as seen in chapters 8 and 9.

For example, the utter failure of the modern prison system is becoming evident to more and more people, even unbelievers. But how many Christians are actively promoting the practical biblical alternative: restitution? Sadly, very few.

MASS

Resources of time, energy, and money are limited and precious. Scarce resources are easily wasted or dissipated if an objective is not carefully defined. The army that throws itself headlong in a frontal assault against the entire enemy position is likely to be repulsed. We must carefully count the cost and weigh the likely outcome of every engagement. In the words of Jesus, "What king, going to make war against another king, sitteth not down first, and consulteth whether he be able with ten thousand to meet him that cometh against him with twenty thousand? (Luke 14:31)"

This leads to another "principle of war," the principle of "mass": The concentration of forces at the weakest point of the enemy's line to achieve a decisive breakthrough, leaving just enough troops elsewhere to keep the enemy diverted. Such a concentration of firepower at the weakest point allows for a decisive breakthrough and the opportunity to divide and conquer. For example, the book of Joshua states: "Joshua came, and all the people of war with him . . . suddenly; and they fell upon them" (Josh. 11:7).

In politics it is counterproductive to waste time on "long shots" no matter how emotionally appealing they may be. Instead time, energy, and money should be focused on districts and candidates that have a high probability of winning, even if you do not live in those districts.

The principle of mass depends on accurate information and careful analysis of the situation. We will discuss specifics of research and planning for political campaigns in the next chapter. Suffice it to say at this point that the public opinion poll is an extremely valuable tool in this regard.

In 1989, public opinion polling showed that an initiative banning abortion completely had little chance of success in Oregon. Over two-thirds of the electorate was opposed. On the other hand, polling indicated that parental notification was favored by almost the same margin.

Rather than concentrating at the weak point in the enemy line—parental notification—one group of Christians chose to ignore the poll data and launched a campaign to totally ban abortion. Another group pursued parental notification. This was a classic example of failure to honor the principle of "mass." As a consequence, pro-abortionists were able to tie the two initiatives together as "too extreme" and both were defeated by an approximate sixty-to-forty margin.

Would it not have been better to take what we can get this year, gradually enlist the public on the pro-life side, and go for the big prize when the climate of public opinion has improved? Better yet, would it not be better to forget about initiatives altogether and elect more pro-life representatives?

SURPRISE AND PURSUIT

Once the enemy is on the run, we must keep him on the run. An active pursuit requires great will and perseverance, but pursuit conserves and multiplies the fruits of victory. A pursuing army will outrun a retreating enemy and hit his unprotected flanks or overrun his disoriented rear guard.

Gideon provides a classic biblical example. Actually, Gideon's campaign against the Midianites illustrates two principles of war: 1) the principle of surprise, and 2) the principle of pursuit.

When Gideon and his band of three hundred men surrounded the sleeping enemy camp and blew their trumpets, the Midianites were so surprised that they began to kill each other. Those that were left took off in frantic flight. What did Gideon do after the initial victory? Did he sit down to rest or rest on his laurels? "And Gideon came to Jordan, and passed over, he, and the three hundred men that were with him, faint, yet pursuing them. . . . And Gideon went up by the way of them that dwelt in tents on the east of Nobah and Jogbehah, and smote the host: for the host was secure" (Judg. 8:4, 11).

In order to achieve this route, Gideon relied on the principle of surprise. The same was true of Joshua when he commanded his troops to "rise up from the ambush, and seize upon the city [Ai]: for the LORD your God will deliver it into your hand" (Josh. 8:7).

Surprise may be effected by strategic use of the elements of time, place, or method. For example, Christian Linda Smith set the stage for a surprise victory over liberal Rep. Jolene Unsoeld with a massive, last-minute write-in campaign in the 1994 Washington primary.

In the conquest of Southern Canaan, Joshua was not satisfied with the trophy of capturing the five kings. Instead he imprisoned them temporarily in a cave and ordered an immediate pursuit of the retreat-ing army: "And stay ye not, but pursue after your enemies, and smite the hindmost of them; suffer them not to enter into their cities: for the LORD your God hath delivered them into your hand" (Josh. 10:19).

We too must not be satisfied with a single election victory, no matter how many "kings" we have captured. Our task is not complete until we have brought "into captivity every thought [philosophy] to the obedience of Christ" (2 Cor. 10:5). In Joshua's day, the result of such an aggressive pursuit was that "none moved his tongue against any of the children of Israel" (Josh. 10:21).

There is always a tendency after an election victory to relax, bask in the sense of accomplishment, go home, and forget about it. Too often Christians have done just this, only to be swept out of office in the next election. This is not the time to lower our guard. Rather, it is a time to press the attack. It is a time to pray for the man whom we have just elected, to consider legislative priorities, and even to plan for the next election.

CONCLUSION

Over the centuries a number of strategic principles have evolved, which if followed tend toward success in battle. These have been systemized in numerous books and military manuals as the "principles of war." In this chapter we have attempted to demonstrate that many of these principles appear also in the Bible and may be adapted to the cultural context.

We should remember that our efforts to carry the Word of God into the civil arena are an important aspect of the Great Commission to disciple the nations. Those efforts should be directed by believers who are "as wise as serpents" in strategic application of the principles of war to politics.

In the process of working for institutional change, we will encounter many opportunities to share the gospel of Christ with individuals as well. Both objectives—institutional and individual—are complimentary, not competitive, aspects of the advancement of the kingdom of God. All of life is to be subdued by the gospel for the glory of God.

REVIEW QUIZ

1. What is the basis of all law?
   a. Legal scholarship
   b. Religion
   c. Natural philosophy
   d. Sociology
   e. b and c

2. Separation of church and state means
   a. The church has no business trying to advise the government about anything.
   b. Government must remain religiously neutral.
   c. Neither institution controls the other, but government protects the church and church advises government.
   d. Christians have no business in politics.

3. Which is *not* one of the principles of war?
   a. Mass your forces at the weak point
   b. Attack when the enemy is most apt to be surprised
   c. An impregnable defense is the best offense
   d. Pursue the enemy when he is on the run
   e. Make the enemy doubt the cause for which he is fighting

4. Which strategy is *not* biblical?
   a. Gradualism
   b. Compromise
   c. Coalition

5. Which king attempted to break down the wall of separation between church and state?
   a. David
   b. Ahab
   c. Uzziah
   d. Solomon

6. Focusing effort in the district of a vulnerable incumbent is an application of which principle?
   a. Surprise
   b. Cooperation
   c. Entropy
   d. Pursuit
   e. Mass
   f. a nd e

DISCUSSION GUIDE

1. Explain the concept of the separation of church and state.

2. In what ways is the concept of separation of church and state like a two-edged sword?

3. What is imprecatory prayer and under what circumstances is it to be employed?

4. How do the principles of war relate to the church's cultural battle? Are these principles biblical?

5. What is the difference between gradualism and compromise?

6. Under what circumstances may Christians form coalitions with non-believers?

7. How can we avoid compromising our position as we seek to build coalitions with non-believing allies?

Answer Key
1) b   2) c   3) c   4) b   5) c   6) e

11

TACTICS

*M*any excellent books and seminars discuss in detail the principles of political action and campaigning. Therefore, this chapter will not attempt to present an in-depth political action manual. Instead the focus will be on how some of these tactics have been implemented by a group of Christians—with whom the author is associated—in the state of Oregon over the past decade.

Oregon is, of course, notorious for its "liberal" or "progressive" politics. Oregonians take pride in their supposed independence and open-mindedness when it comes to politics. If you want to promote some new, half-baked political theory, Oregon is the place to start. You know you have a problem with liberalism when people who move from California complain about the "statist mentality" in Oregon.

By the late 1970s liberalism was well entrenched, and the work to reclaim lost ground seemed overwhelming. Nonetheless, progress has been measurable and encouraging. At that time, you could count the number of pro-life legislators on one hand. Both houses of the legislature were firmly in Democrat control and it was impossible to get anything even remotely resembling good legislation introduced, let alone passed. Strategically, the best opportunities seemed to lie in working for reform within the Republican party.

In 1990, after more than a decade of sustained effort, Republicans took control of the Oregon House for the first time in over twenty years. They have held it for three sessions. In the 1994 election Republicans also gained control of the state senate, which the Democrats had held for forty years. Most inside observers recognized that the prime mover behind this shift in power was the resurgence of the Christian right.

What has been accomplished with this newly won political power? Mostly gridlock! Nobody is happy. The liberal *Oregonian* newspaper complains incessantly that the schools are underfunded, that social responsibilities to future generations have been neglected. The man on the street complains that government does not accomplish anything. Pro-lifers are frustrated because there is no meaningful legislation to eradicate abortion.

But when you consider where Oregon has been, gridlock is progress. Step one is minority status, step two is gridlock, and step three (by the grace of God) is majority control.

Both the quantity and quality of legislators still hinders progress. Numbers fall just short of the working majority needed to control legislation. In terms of quality, many Christian legislators remain ignorant or only vaguely cognizant of the biblical principles of government discussed in the preceding chapters. Their thinking is still tainted by years of exposure to the contamination of humanistic social theory. Mental detoxification is needed (see Rom. 12:2), but in some cases the need is not recognized.

Furthermore, a substantial number of Oregon Christians are intoxicated by the initiative process. As documented in chapter 8, the initiative has served as a diversion of resources that has hindered progress in the direction of godly, republican government. For many Christians, the lure of the initiative—power to the people—is simply too great to resist. Unfortunately, the visibility of some of the more volatile issues has served to arouse the opposition and mitigate the strategic element of surprise in the legislature.

Still, there have been some preliminary victories. For the most part, tax increases have been stymied, much to the chagrin of the liberals. Oregon has led the nation in the passage of legislation guaranteeing the rights of home schoolers. In the 1993 session a law was passed requiring the teaching of abstinence in sex ed classes.

How specifically has all of this come to pass? A group of committed Christians—including the author—has labored in two areas: 1) getting good candidates elected in a less than ideal political climate, and 2) getting good legislation enacted. The purpose of this chapter is to encourage other believers to persevere in the battle for righteous government in their own state. Perhaps our "starts and stumbles" will provide some instruction for others. Though we do not have all the answers, by the grace of God we have taken some initial steps in the right direction.

ELECTORAL POLITICS

Research and Planning

From the beginning, strong emphasis was placed on survey research to provide information needed in strategic planning. To cut costs, many of the early polls were conducted by volunteer phone interviewers from office lines donated by Christian businessmen.

I remember in the spring of 1984 sitting around a kitchen table planning strategy and thinking up survey questions for a neophyte state legislative candidate. This particular candidate was one of the first Christians to present himself for office in those early years. On the basis of that strategy, he won the election, the next four consecutive races, and attained the chairmanship of the House Ways and Means Committee in 1992. From that powerful position he was able to block tax increases and apply strategic pressure in the passage of social legislation such as abstinence education.

The value of the political survey lies not in predicting elections, but in planning for campaigns and tracking public opinion prior to election day. To use polling data to test the political wind—and then modify your convictions accordingly—is highly improper. Rather the poll should be used to find out what issues are important to voters and develop a positioning strategy based on that information.

The candidate simply cannot convey his entire philosophy of life and government during the course of a campaign. He must narrow his message to a few key points that he drives home repeatedly. Rather than emphasizing his primary area of interest, he must talk about the electorate's primary area of interest. That is what the survey can tell him. Survey data paves the way for a strategy biblically focused to the expressed concerns of the electorate.

The opinion poll is simply a snapshot in time, and it can change very quickly, particularly down the stretch. The following line chart illustrates the use of polling over the course of a recent general election campaign. The following descriptive narrative is from the *Oregon Campaign Institute Manual.*[1]

a. *The benchmark survey, conducted in early August of 1992 showed the Republican incumbent in disfavor with a plurality of voters in this liberal district. It was clear that the contest with this well-known Democrat would be hard-fought and would probably come down to the wire.*

(AUGUST 3-8: R=33%, D=40%, ???=26%)

b. *About a month out, the impact of voter identification and targeted direct mail were having a positive impact. The incumbent had taken the lead by capturing a substantial share of undecided voters.*

(OCTOBER 2,3: R=42%, D=38%, ???=20%)

c. *By the third weekend in October, the Republican had opened a seven-point lead, with about one in every five voters still undecided. The waters were deceptively calm.*

(October 17: R=44%, D=37%, ???=19%).

d. *The following week, Bill Clinton paid a campaign visit to the largest city in the district, a university town with lots of liberal students. A tracking poll conducted the following Saturday revealed a strong coat-tail effect. The Democrat now led by five points, with one in five still undecided.*

(OCTOBER 24: R=37%, D=42%, ???=21%)

e. *About one week before the election the incumbent countered with a strong "hit piece" exposing serious ethical problems in the Democrat's business practices. Again the current of public opinion was flowing slightly in the Republican's favor. About one in every ten were waiting until the last weekend to make up their minds.*

(OCTOBER 28: R=46%, D=43%, ???=12%)

f. *The Democrat followed immediately with a defensive piece that flatly accused the Republican of being a bald-faced liar. The Democrat was the real liar, but the defense left a big question about the Republican's veracity in the mind of many voters.*

The incumbent felt that the campaign was degenerating into a mud-slinging contest. Even though a defense had been prepared, the

Republican elected not to mail it. In the absence of a credible defense, many district voters were heavily swayed by the final Democrat attack. The Republican lost by 56 percent to 44 percent on election day, the only poll that really counted.

The dramatic shifts in this race during the last two weeks of the campaign illustrate the volatility of public opinion. They tell the story of the "punch/counter punch" and how it affected public opinion right up to the last minute. This campaign dramatizes the importance of anticipating opposition attacks and getting in the final word.

ANATOMY OF A CAMPAIGN

The Volatility of Public Opinion

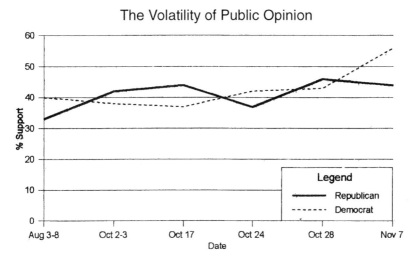

Ten to sixteen percent of the voters wait until the last weekend before deciding who to vote for. Thus, it is important to peak the campaign in the last five or six days. Tracking polls measure the impact of campaign communications both overall and within demographic segments—and thus provide information for fine-tuning the campaign message.

Attack and Defense

The example above illustrates the dramatic give-and-take that can occur during the course of a heated contest. At this point, perhaps more than any other, a Christian candidate must exercise great wisdom and restraint in the avoidance of unethical behavior. I do not believe that all negative campaigning is unethical if based on truth. The apostle Paul advised, "Take no part in the unfruitful works of darkness, but instead expose them"(Eph. 5:11, RSV). It is unethical, however, to resort to half-truth, innuendo, or character assassination.

With these cautions in mind, let us consider some principles of attack and defense that have proven to be effective in actual campaign communications.[2]

These principles of attack have proven effective:
1) The attack should be conducted by a surrogate so the candidate is perceived to be "above the fray."
2) The attack should be just strong enough to accomplish its purpose, but not too strong. It should discredit the opponent's record, but not the opponent himself. The attack should be with measured strokes to avoid a backlash of sympathy.
3) The attack should be honest, well documented, and point out the opponent's failures to live up to his campaign promises. The contrast between promise and performance should be clear.
4) The attack should take the initiative to frame the issues to your advantage. However, the communication must have the ring of truth—which it will have if it portrays conditions as they really exist.

These principles are effective in mounting a defense:
1) The defense should be made by the candidate himself, a member of his immediate family, or another respected person.
2) The defense should use concrete evidence to discredit the attack. The attacked candidate should unequivocally defend his position.
3) The defense should turn the argument back to the attacker. The response should be immediate, unless the attack is localized, in which case it should be ignored or given a local response only.
4) The defense should anticipate and plan a strategy for defusing an attack. Negatives can be turned into positives.

During the 1990 campaign one of our candidates was running a strong race, but we knew he had one potentially fatal flaw. He had been late one year in paying his taxes. Anticipating an attack on this point at the last minute, we prepared a camera-ready letter to describe the extenuating circumstances and explain that the taxes were indeed paid. The letter was printed up and ready, just in case.

Sure enough, about four or five days before the election an official-looking document appeared in every district mailbox from something called the "Ethics in Government" committee. The mailer—paid for by our opponent—described in excruciating detail the sins of our candidate in failing to pay his government dues. Immediately, our letter went in the mail and arrived the day before the election—just in time to avert a disaster. Our candidate won by several hundred votes, less than a 1-percent margin of victory.

Fundraising

Money, as everyone knows, is the "mother's milk" of politics—and the key question is "how do I get it?" In planning strategy for various campaigns, we realized that families were our natural constituency. So in the early 1980s we tried to figure out how to serve and mobilize families. The publication of the *Christian Voters' Guide* was one answer. The *Voters' Guide,* which we began to publish in 1980, compared the positions of candidates on some of the fundamental moral issues. This has proved to be an extremely helpful tool for the Christian trying to figure out how to vote.

We also compiled a computerized list of Christian families in Oregon and organized it according to political district. We then distributed the *Christian Voters' Guide* by direct mail, as well as at churches and Christian bookstores.

Oregon offers a unique political tax credit of $100 per couple for donations made to a political organization or campaign. What this means is that a family can give candidates $100 that they would otherwise have to give to the state. Every year we organized a telephone campaign to encourage our families to use their tax credit. In recent years, we have generated several hundred thousand dollars annually for pro-family and pro-life causes in this way.

Some of this money has been used to publish the *Christian Voters' Guide* before the primary and general elections. Much of it however, has been dedicated to the campaigns of Christian candidates for the state legislature.

This approach is not necessarily unique. For example, Senator H.L. "Bill" Richardson has used a similar strategy in California, with the gun issue as the key motivator:

We were not fighting the gun issue as much as we were leveraging politicians. We won a number of races in which we were the dominant financial contributor and by 1980 the Gun Owners of California were giving more to candidates than was the State Republican Party. It was joked that G.O.P. had come to stand for Gun Owners Party.

Instead of reacting, we acted. We engaged in positive confrontation on our battleground. We did not fight one campaign on the gun issue, but let the gun community finance successful political campaigns using issues germane to each race.[3]

Voter ID and Turnout

Another extremely effective tool during the last two months of a campaign is to use the telephone for voter identification and turnout. The goal of such a phone bank is to identify and turn out voters favorable to our candidates. Undecided voters are also identified.

Typically, district voters are asked two questions in a short survey format. The first pinpoints for whom they would vote "if the election were today." The second is a short list of issues they are most concerned about, such as crime, economy, abortion, or education.

Each day the candidate is provided with results of the previous evening's surveys. These provide valuable—albeit unscientific—tracking information. These reports are typically segmented demographically by party and gender.

Undecided voters are mailed a personalized, follow-up letter describing how our candidate would deal with their top issue. During the week before the election, undecided voters are recontacted to identify those who have made up their mind for our candidate.

On election day all supporters are contacted with a reminder to vote. The purpose is to ensure that every favorable voter identified in the previous phases makes it to the polls.

Economies of scale are realized when several campaigns are supported from a single, centralized phone bank. The campaigns split the expenses and may be asked to provide a few volunteers for each shift.

Our experience has been that between 60 percent and 65 percent of the campaigns participating in voter identification phone banks end up as winners. In a well-executed campaign, a voter identification program can provide the necessary margin of victory.

Our most gratifying experience to date came during the 1990 election when Republicans finally made the breakthrough to control the Oregon House. At that time we controlled the executive committee of the Multnomah County Republican Central Committee, located in Oregon's largest metropolitan area. Using that platform we organized a forty-line phone bank which supported seventeen of the targeted House races statewide.

We received partial funding from the Oregon House Caucus and the National Republican Committee. About two-thirds of our interviewer staff was volunteer, and the rest were paid. Volunteer recruiting began about six months before the start date.

The budget for this project was over $100,000; it was a monumental, one-time effort to achieve a decisive breakthrough, employing the principle of mass. However, the same basic principles can be employed on a much smaller scale by a single campaign at far less expense.

Our typical win-loss ratios held, and about 65 percent of our races won. That was enough to give the Republicans a 31-29 margin in the Oregon House and end a twenty-year period of minority status. And a majority of the new Republican legislators were Christians.

LOBBYING

Victory on the campaign trail is sweet, but victory in the legislature is sweeter. It does no good to elect good candidates, if those victories cannot be translated into good legislation. Lobbying implies persuasion. The word conjures up images of constituents "buttonholing" their legislators out in the lobby to try to change their mind just before a vote. During the course of our legislative battles, a number of biblical principles have crystallized.

Prayer

Chapter 10 noted the critical priority of prayer in all efforts to bring reformation to the nation. Another excellent biblical example of prayer in the "lobbying" context is found in the book of Nehemiah. When Nehemiah heard that the wall of Jerusalem was broken down and the remnant of his people was in great affliction and reproach, he turned first to God: "And it came to pass, when I heard these words, that I sat down and wept, and mourned certain days, and fasted, and prayed before the God of heaven" (Neh. 1:4).

Prior to 1984, the right to homeschool in Oregon was in serious jeopardy. Home schoolers were required to ask permission of the state before they could homeschool. That placed many families completely at the mercy of the educational bureaucracy.

A bill was introduced to change the requirement for permission to simple notification, and it began to wind its way through the legislative process. During public hearings on the bill it was noted that certain women drove all the way across the state to sit in the back of the hearing room. They offered not a word of testimony, however; they simply sat in the back of the room and prayed. To everyone's amazement, the bill passed both chambers of the liberal legislature and was signed into law. Everyone was amazed—everyone, that is, except the praying women.

Humility and Relationship Building

When Nehemiah had finished his prayer, he went back to his duties as cupbearer to the king with a heavy heart. Because Nehemiah had served faithfully in the king's presence for a long time, the king expressed concern when he noticed Nehemiah's distress. The king even went so far as to ask Nehemiah what he could do to help. Notice the humility with which Nehemiah responded: "And I said unto the king, If it please the king, and if thy servant have found favour in thy sight, that thou wouldest send me unto Judah, unto the city of my fathers' sepulchres, that I may build it" (Neh. 2:5).

Relationship development is one of the most important aspects of effective lobbying. When a credible image has been formed in the eyes of a legislator, he or she becomes easier to persuade in the political process.

In Oregon our group has attempted to be a servant within the Republican Party, rather than to take a strictly confrontational posture. Over a long period of time our effectiveness and hard work have earned us a position of respect and authority within the party and the state government. When it comes time to vote, we have found that legislators listen to what we have to say.

After a hundred years or so of inactivity, Christians are finally waking up to their civil responsibilities. Sometimes the temptation for a newly mobilized believer is to come in with both guns blazing, demanding immediate reform. If so, the result is usually strong opposition, polarization, and ineffectiveness.

By contrast, in the Bible God more often placed believers strategically in a position of service within the government. Over a period of time leaders such as Joseph and Daniel were elevated to positions of authority and influence. When the crisis came and people looked for answers, these leaders were ready. In the words of political activist Kevin Gottlieb, "You can't sit under the shade unless you water the trees."[4]

Credible Evidence and Persuasiveness

Finding and presenting credible testimony and evidence to support the direction you would like a piece of legislation to go is critical. A legislator must find it easy or reasonable to adopt your plan or perspective. Nehemiah sought such credible evidence to help him accomplish his goal: "Moreover I said unto the king, If it please the king, let letters be given me to the governors beyond the river, that they may convey me over till I come unto Judah" (Neh. 2:7).

A variety of evidence should be marshalled. For example, expert writings on the subject should be presented, including specialists in the field, teachers, experiential testimonies, and research. In addition, using a variety of perspectives which state the same idea will add credibility. This would include the political, economic, educational, and social dimensions of the problem, among others.

An example of this kind of effort involved a bill requiring abstinence education to be part of the public schools sex education program. We did not initiate this legislation, but we were asked to assist in getting it enacted. I hesitate to use this example because it appears to advocate "cleaning up" the government schools. However, I have chosen it to illustrate the effective application of lobbying principles, not necessarily because I would recommend it as a priority issue on which to focus. All names used in this account are fictitious.

This bill was almost pronounced "dead on arrival" because it required that abstinence education should completely replace all existing "safe-sex" curricula. While this was obviously the ideal, no legislator could be found to introduce the bill in committee in that form. Given the makeup of the legislature, the best that could be expected was to require that abstinence be taught as an alternative without excluding the other approaches. Although not ideal, this was perceived as consistent with the principle of gradualism.

However, one of our conservative legislators was adamantly against such a concession. We have learned that such "principled" stands are sometimes—not always—mere posturing. A legislator will introduce a bill simply to appease the "folks back home" but then will do nothing substantive to really push it through the system. He can then go back at election time and say, "Well, I tried, but the liberals killed it."

Our lobbyist, Karmen Smith, took a conciliatory approach. "Representative Latner," she said, "I can see that you have a real interest in this bill and are a lot more knowledgeable about it than most legislators. What can I do to help make this happen for you? What if I set up a meeting with all interested parties to see if we can work out the details on this?"

The meeting that transpired included Karmen, the conservative representative, an attorney, the head of the Department of Education, and representatives of Legislative Counsel and Planned Parenthood. Karmen started the meeting by saying, "Here's what we want to see happen." She explained our reasoning and listed the points that were not negotiable. The ensuing discussion resulted in formulation of the dual-curriculum, which everyone was at least willing to consider.

Public Support and Numbers

Many issues are determined by just a few votes—often just one. "You can have an enormous impact on that one vote if you know it's out there," says Kevin Gottlieb, "if you've done a good job vote counting ahead of time, if you're organized to get the right people to push the right buttons at the right time."[5]

Laying the groundwork described throughout the first part of this chapter will put you in a strong position to get legislation enacted. "Pushing the right buttons" involves bringing both public pressure and peer pressure to bear on key legislators.

In recent years we have made good use of the phone bank concept to generate this kind of pressure. Our phone bank contains only twelve lines, but we use it year-round to accomplish a variety of complementary tasks: fundraising, voter identification, political polling, and the mobilization of public support during the legislative session.

The abstinence bill was introduced initially in the House of

Representatives, because Republicans commanded a majority in that body and controlled key committee chairs. However, the Republican majority was only two votes, and several Republicans threatened to break ranks and vote against abstinence education.

At this point the phone bank swung into action. We first mailed a postcard to all our constituents residing in the districts of the wavering legislators. The postcard summarized the situation, gave the name of their representative, and asked the constituent to make a phone call to urge a yes vote. A few days later, we followed up with a reminder phone call to ask for a contribution and get a definite commitment to make the call to the legislator. We also asked our members if they could get a few of their friends to call as well.

Inside the capitol our lobbyist, Karmen Smith, had been working for several weeks to befriend the legislative aide of one of the more influential, liberal Republicans, Hillary Ripon-Daggett. The day before the vote, Karmen requested permission to print a support letter carrying the official seal of Representative Daggett. Karmen got right to the point: "I could get a conservative to endorse this, but your recommendation will carry a lot more weight with the moderates." Hillary glanced over it and said, "I don't really have a problem with it—go ahead." That letter appeared on the desk of every legislator the morning of the vote and permitted them to save face in supporting abstinence.

Also, for the week before the vote, calls had poured into the capitol. That show of support proved to be enough, and our bill passed the House by a narrow margin. That was the first hurdle. Still to be overcome was a 16–14 Democrat majority in the Senate, and the threat of a veto from a feminist Democratic governor.

To our surprise, a head-count showed that we had the votes for passage on the floor, and the governor stated that she would not veto the bill if it got through the Democrat Senate. Our next big obstacle was the Senate Democrat leadership.

We were able to schedule a hearing for the bill and had an out-of-state expert testify. He did a superlative job. However, the next morning we were hit with a bombshell: an announcement from the Senate president that the Education Committee had been closed—ostensibly because the end of the session was near and all substantive business had been conducted. For all practical purposes, the bill was now dead unless we could get the Committee reopened to pass it out to the floor.

Our phone bank began to focus calls on the three Democrats on the Education Committee. After several days of non-stop phone calls, two Democrats caved in and said they would support the bill. The only remaining obstacle was the committee chair.

Neither the president nor the committee chair wanted to offend Planned Parenthood by passing this bill, but neither wanted to take the blame for killing it either. When Karmen approached the chair she was met with this excuse: "I wouldn't mind hearing it, but the President has closed the committee."

So we alerted our constituents statewide to flood the Senate president's office with phone calls. After a few days, things were getting pretty hot in the President's office so he passed the potato back to the Education Committee, declaring that if they wanted to reopen the Committee and vote on it he would not stand in the way. At this point, both key players were paying us lip service but passing the buck to the other; neither was taking action to reopen the committee.

Finding ourselves stonewalled on both fronts, we decided to draft a letter on behalf of one of the Republicans on the committee to be signed by each of our supporters on the committee. The letter was addressed to the president of the Senate requesting him to reopen the committee. In a conference with the chair, Karmen asked innocently: "Since you favor the bill, how about sticking your name on this?" Trapped by her own words, she capitulated.

Even this tactic probably would have failed without the bargaining power of Christian legislators in the House, who controlled the budgetary purse strings. One key legislator shut down the entire legislature for almost two days, refusing to consider key bills the Senate Democrats wanted, if they refused to permit a vote on abstinence.

The existence of our letter from the Committee allowed the Senate president to save face in "bowing to the desire of the Education Committee." In the end the committee chair yielded to the constant pressure, and our bill sailed through the Senate and on to the governor.

That is how it often happens. The cliche is trite but true: "if they can't see the light, you have to make them feel the heat." But all the pressure in the world will not get something done without someone working on the inside to build relationships and orchestrate the action. This person must be adept at responding creatively to the flow of events, which can change very rapidly near the end of the legislative session.

Behind the Scenes Organization

As you can see, the most important part of the lobbying process takes place behind the scenes. You must make sure that you have discussed the issue with key legislators before hearings, collected evidence and witnesses to speak to the issue, made changes and compromises where warranted, and provided supportive legislators with information to assist them in fighting for your position. Your availability to answer questions or assist in any way is essential.

CONCLUSION

Effective lobbying is a process which starts years before the legislative session begins. The latest campaign technology and techniques should be used to mobilize the voter. Good candidates for election must be cultivated. Time should be invested in serving and befriending key government officials. That means treating them with respect and showing them that helping us get what we want is really in their best interests. Above all, successful lobbying includes time in prayer for God to bless our labor and use it to advance His kingdom.

REVIEW QUIZ

1. The campaign message should include
   a. The candidate's philosophy of life
   b. A few key points of greatest interest to voters
   c. As many points as can be packed into a fifteen-minute speech
   d. The candidate's bio

2. The most important use of the political poll is to
   a. Predict a winner the weekend before an election
   b. Help the candidate adjust his views in response to public opinion
   c. Identify issues of greatest concern to the voting public

3. When attacked during the course of a campaign, a candidate should always
   a. Defend
   b. Respond in kind
   c. Remain silent and above the fray
   d. a and b

4. From political polling we learn:
   a. Never overestimate the intelligence of the American people
   b. Public opinion is static and only changes slowly over a long period of time
   c. What to say and who to say it to

5. Which symbol best describes the Bible's characterization of an effective politician?
   a. A smoking gun
   b. A white flag
   c. A wash basin
   d. A sound bite

6. Who should be contacted first when organizing a lobbying campaign?
   a. The Secretary of State
   b. The Speaker of the House
   c. The Chairman of the Republican or Democratic Party
   d. The Master of the Universe

DISCUSSION GUIDE

1. What are some of the key ingredients necessary to gain control of a state legislature?

2. What is the difference between negative campaigning and comparative campaigning?

3. Compare and contrast the proper and improper use of polling data.

4. What is the difference between confrontational politics and service-oriented politics?

5. What are some of the important principles of the political attack?

6. What are some of the important principles of political defense?

7. What can we learn from Nehemiah about effective lobbying?

Answer Key
   1) b   2) c   3) a   4) c   5) c   6) d

12

THE FRUIT OF OUR LABOR

*W*ithout hope life is not worth living. Statistics show that retirees who just sit around "enjoying their retirement" die much earlier than those who continue to work or volunteer their time.

On the other hand, the presence of hope is a powerful motivation to action. Consider the incredible progress toward world domination that communism made during most of the twentieth century. The Communists were obsessed with a vision of inevitable victory. During that same period the church waned in influence, having persuaded herself that there is no hope for this world. Somehow the church lost faith in the power of the Holy Spirit to accomplish what God had commanded in the Great Commission: "Go ye therefore and make disciples of all nations" (Matt. 28:19, RSV).

Thus, eschatology, the study of last things, is not simply an ivory tower subject. Our philosophy of history and how God intends it to unfold has a powerful impact on the ebb and flow of history in our particular generation.

It is easy to yield to the temptation of despair in our political endeavors. On the one hand, the voice of secular humanism attacks and belittles all attempts of the "religious right" to involve themselves in politics. On the other hand, fellow Christians admonish us to stop wasting precious time and resources because the Second Coming is just around the corner: the "don't polish brass on a sinking ship" syndrome.

As we have seen in chapter 5, America has progressed a long way down the road to judgment. The tiny army of Christian activists currently in the field seems helpless to stem the tide of rebellion that has engulfed the nation. Even the historic Republican landslide of 1994 has not been accompanied by true national repentance and turning back to God.

Perhaps it is time to remind ourselves of the words of General Douglas McArthur when the North Koreans had his troops pinned down on the southern tip of Korea. In that desperate situation his attitude was expressed in this pithy call to arms: "They've got us surrounded, men—the poor devils don't stand a chance now."

More importantly, it is time to remind ourselves of the precious promises of the Word of God regarding the glorious destiny of the "church triumphant." In this chapter we will look in detail at some of those long neglected promises.

WHERE ARE WE GOING?

The forces arrayed against us are, of course, very powerful. From a human standpoint, the power elite at the apex of the humanist pyramid have the capacity to manipulate events to their purposes. Or so they think.

The situation today is not unlike that which has existed at many points in the past, such as the time of the Hebrew prophets. On the brink of the captivity God told Jeremiah that the men of his own city had entered into conspiracy against him because he spoke the Word of God: "And the LORD hath given me knowledge of it . . . and I knew not that they had devised devices against me, saying, Let us cut him off from the land of the living . . . " (Jer. 11:18–19).

Modern America has turned her back on God and His law. We are all guilty, from the government official to the clergy to the lowliest man on the street. As a result violence stalks our cities at night, the pestilence of AIDS "wasteth at noonday," and flood waters devour our breadbasket. In rebellious defiance, the wicked attempt to strike back. They cannot destroy God, so they strike out at the people of God.

We may be tempted to blame this disaster on a conspiracy of powerful men. Larry Abraham's *Insider Report* had this to say about the "insider elite" in the October 1993 issue.

218

An Insider elite very often has the power to stack the deck and deal themselves a winning hand . . . . In the real world of big government, big business, big labor, big media, big almost everything, the friends at the top are a very small circle. They elect presidents and prime ministers, they promote senators and parliamentarians, they own and direct the news, and with very few exceptions they create economic policies that serve their interests.

Because I believe and know these conditions to be true, I am sometimes held out as a conspiracy nut—but I should hasten to add, only by those who are too lazy or too compromised or too set in their ways to check my evidence . . . . [1]

That such a conspiracy or conspiracies exist is undeniable. They have always existed, since the rebellion of Satan and the fall of man. The satanic power and presence doubtless resides in the inner sanctum of their secret chambers. From there it emanates out to permeate and pollute every facet of our culture. This is clearly acknowledged in Scripture: "Why do the nations conspire, and the peoples plot in vain? The kings of the earth set themselves, and the rulers take counsel together, against the LORD and his anointed saying, 'Let us burst their bonds asunder, and cast their cords from us'" (Ps. 2:1–3, RSV).

However, it is critically important that we not ascribe to them a power which they do not possess. We must not stand in awe or shrink in fear at their ostensible authority over the affairs of men and nations. We must not let our hearts subscribe to the satanic version of Romans 8:28, "All things work together for evil to them that love God." To act as if this is true is a form of Satan worship.

As in all things, we should take counsel from the attitude of God when it comes to the conspiracies of men. Not only must we not fear the intrigues of the ungodly, we should view them as absurd and ludicrous.

With appropriate restraint, we should assume the outlook of God, who laughs and scoffs at them: "He who sits in the heavens laughs; the LORD has them in derision. Then he will speak to them in his wrath, and terrify them in his fury, saying, I have set my king on Zion, my holy hill" (Ps. 2:4–6, RSV).

At the right time, God will speak a word and they will be gone. A breath from His nostrils will scatter them. Consider the ease with which God, in His sovereignty, shattered the Berlin Wall. Tiny pieces of this once impenetrable barrier are now sold in curiosity shops around the world. His kingdom will come and His *will* will be done "on earth as it is in Heaven" (Matt. 6:10).

The puny attempts these conspiring rebels make at playing God cannot succeed. They are doomed. It is the height of folly for them to think that they can resist the Almighty. The kingdom of God will be established in history. It has been established by the eternal decree of God in the inner sanctum of His secret counsel chamber from eternity: "I will tell of the decree of the LORD: He said to me, 'You are my son, today I have begotten you. Ask of me, and I will make the nations your heritage, and the ends of the earth your possession. You shall break them with a rod of iron, and dash them in pieces like a potter's vessel'" (Ps. 2:7–9, RSV).

The doctrine of the sovereignty of God is critical for our spiritual well-being at this point. We must believe the Word of God when it says that all events are under His control. History moves inexorably toward the purpose He has determined. The kings of the earth will submit themselves to Christ as King of kings and Lord of lords in history: "Now therefore, O kings, be wise; be warned, O rulers of the earth. Serve the LORD with fear, with trembling kiss his feet, lest he be angry, and you perish in the way; for his wrath is quickly kindled" (Ps. 2:11–12, RSV).

In the book of Acts, Peter declares that this victory was accomplished *conclusively* with the victory of Christ on the cross. Quoting Psalm 2, Peter announced that the great conspiracy (Acts 4:25–26) came to a climax when the Gentiles and Jews joined together to crucify the Lord, "to do whatever thy hand and thy plan had predestined to take place" (Acts 4:28, RSV).

This great victory is manifesting itself *gradually* in history as the disciples of Christ carry His word to the nations. Peter went on to pray, "And now, Lord, look upon their threats, and grant to thy servants to speak thy word with all boldness" (Acts 4:29).

The task of the people of God is not complete until the kings and rulers of earth "serve the Lord with fear, and with trembling kiss His feet" (Ps. 2:11, RSV). At that point Jesus will deliver the kingdom to the Father, at which point it will be established *completely* or consummately.

Thus, we see that "all things work together for good to them who love God, who are the called according to his purpose" (Rom. 8:28). Psalm 2 closes with these words of comfort to the kings and peoples of the world: "Blessed are all who take refuge in him."

The three-fold nature of this victory is also spelled out by the apostle Paul in 1 Corinthians 15:25-28. Verse 27 says that God "hath put all things under his feet." Through the work of Christ on the cross, all things have been *conclusively* brought under the reign of Christ.

Verse 25 says, "For he must reign till he hath put all enemies under his feet." The reign of Christ involves the *gradual* defeat of Christ's enemies in history.

Finally, verse 28 declares, "And when all things shall be subdued unto him, then shall the Son also himself be subject unto him that put all things under him, that God may be all in all." At the second coming His victory is final; Christ will deliver His *completed* kingdom to God the Father.

Jesus established his kingdom at His first coming, as manifested in His power to cast out devils. Jesus told His followers that ". . . if I with the finger of God cast out devils, no doubt the kingdom of God is come upon you" (Luke 11:20). All that remains is a "mopping up" operation on the part of the Holy Spirit working through the church.

Therefore, we must go forth in the spirit and power of Elisha. One day Elisha and Israel found themselves surrounded by a great army of Syrians. From a purely human standpoint, they were doomed. Elisha's servant was at a loss: "Alas, my master! What shall we do?" "Fear not," said Elisha, "for those who are with us are more than those who are with them" (2 Kings 6:16–17, RSV).

"So the LORD opened the eyes of the young man, and he saw; and behold, the mountain was full of horses and chariots of fire round about Elisha." At the prayer of Elisha, God then blinded the Syrian army who were led as captives to the king of Israel. Instead of slaying them, Elisha commanded the king to prepare a great feast for them and release them.

Is this not a beautiful picture of the great work that God is doing in the earth today? The first task is God's: to open the eyes of His people to the greatness of His power compared to that of the enemy. The second task is also God's: to blind the eyes of the enemy and make them helpless before the people of God. Once God has paved the way, the final task is ours: to lead the enemy hosts to the King, feast them at

His banqueting table, and send them back to their nations in peace.

We must move forward with the vision of Joshua and Caleb who brought back a good report of the promised land. Even though the cities were walled and the inhabitants of the land were giants, Joshua and Caleb refused to shrink back in fear. "Let us go up at once and possess it," they said, "For we are well able to overcome it" (Num. 13:30).

Then came one of the darkest chapters in the history of the people of God. The people refused to listen to the voice of faith; instead they listened to the voice of despair: "We are not able to go up against the people, for they are stronger than we" (Num. 13:31, RSV). The result of this unbelief was forty years of wandering in the wilderness until the entire generation except Joshua and Caleb had died off. Their children then went in to conquer the land.

What will it be for this generation of Americans? Will we continue to wander in the wilderness of cultural defeat and impotence? Will God have to consign us to our graves before He raises up our children or grandchildren to accomplish our work? Or will we go forth in the spirit and power of Joshua and Caleb to subdue our culture for Christ?

WHERE ARE WE NOW?

God's Judgment in History

The foregoing optimistic view of the kingdom has been the position of many great theologians in church history. For example, Charles Spurgeon commented boldly on Psalm 72:9:

> It makes us content to be in the minority to-day, when we are sure that the majority will be with us to-morrow, ay, and that the truth will one day be carried unanimously and heartily. David was not a believer in the theory that the world will grow worse and worse, and that the dispensation will wind up with general darkness, and idolatry. Earth's sun is to go down amid tenfold night if some of our prophetic brethren are to be believed. Not so do we expect, but we look for a day when the dwellers of all lands shall learn righteousness, shall trust in the Saviour, shall worship thee alone, O God, "and shall glorify thy name." The modern notion has greatly damped

the zeal of the church for missions, and the sooner it is shown to be unscriptural the better for the cause of God. It neither consorts with prophecy, honours God, nor inspires the church with ardour. Far hence be it driven.[2]

Spurgeon spoke disparagingly of those prophetic theories which in his day were only beginning to break the soil. Today they have become a tangled thorn which threatens to choke God's vineyard. Spurgeon only built on the work of his predecessors.

For example, Gary Crampton describes John Calvin's view as "incipient post-millennialism." The doctrine of the "Chiliasts [pre-millenialists]," Calvin says is, "too childish either to need or to be worth a refutation."[3]

On the other hand, he is very optimistic regarding Kingdom growth. In fact, the second generation of Reformers, and the overwhelming majority of Puritans, taking their lead from Calvin's optimism, became strong advocates of post-millennialism. . . . On Psalm 47, he claims that Christ's Kingdom is to grow to the point where all nations will be included. The same is true of his exposition of Psalm 72.[4]

Matthew Henry echoes the same refrain regarding the Great Commission in Matthew 28. Of the command to go and disciple all nations, he explains: "That Christianity should be twisted in with national constitutions, that the kingdoms of the world should become Christ's kingdoms, and their kings the church's nursing-fathers."[5]

Typical of early American evangelists was Jonathan Edwards who spoke of the period between Christ's first and second comings as the time of the millennium. He wrote that this is ". . . most properly the time of the kingdom of heaven upon earth . . . a time wherein religion shall in every respect be uppermost in the world . . . a time of the greatest temporal prosperity . . . ."[6]

Even some of our early American politicians were animated by this vision. The following fast-day proclamation, issued by Samuel Adams as governor of Massachusetts in 1797, is a prime example. This statement is one reason why he is sometimes referred to as "the last of the Puritans" as well as "the Father of the American Revolution."

We cannot better express ourselves than by humbly supplicating the Supreme Ruler of the world that the rod of tyrants may be broken into pieces and the oppressed made free. That wars may cease in all the earth and that the confusions that are and have been among nations may be overruled by promoting and speedily bringing on that holy and happy period when the Kingdom of our Lord and Savior Jesus Christ may be everywhere established and all people everywhere willingly bow to the scepter of Him who is Prince of Peace.[7]

Eminent theologians of our own day are also embracing an optimistic view of history. For example, D. James Kennedy asks the question "Where is history going?" in his book *What If Jesus Had Never Been Born?* He finds the answer in the Old Testament passage quoted most frequently by New Testament writers:

Psalm 110:1 written by David a millenium before Christ, tells us:

The LORD said to my Lord,
"Sit at My right hand,
Till I make your enemies Your footstool."

So what is God doing in the world today? He's making the enemies of Jesus Christ a footstool for His feet! If you're an enemy of Christ, you're on the wrong side of history. You can either join Christ's side or become His footstool. Jesus is the King of kings and Lord of lords.[8]

But how does this optimistic long-range view square with the present darkness and distress that envelopes America? The certainty of the earthly victory of the kingdom of God does not exclude the possibility of temporary periods of judgment and apparent defeat. These are the result of the corporate disobedience of the people of God. The blessings and cursings are laid out in Deuteronomy 28. God warned His people: "If thou wilt not hearken unto the voice of the LORD thy God, to observe to do all his commandments and his statutes which I command thee this day; that all these curses shall come upon thee and overtake thee" (Deut. 28:15).

Then follows nearly two pages of holy writ in which the seven-fold curse of God is spelled out in graphic detail. When God's people lapse into disobedience, God takes them to the "woodshed." He often uses the "paddle" of oppressive civil government to bring them to repentance.

This was the burden of Habakkuk, who lamented that "the law is slacked, and judgment doth never go forth, for the wicked doth compass about the righteous; therefore wrong judgment proceedeth" (Hab. 1:4).

When we are tempted to think that ours is the terminal generation we should consider the words of Solomon, "Say not, 'Why were the former days better than these?' For it is not from wisdom that you ask this" (Eccl. 7:10, RSV). Consider the desperate straights and the depth of despair into which the people of God have been driven in times past. Consider the four hundred years of cruel bondage under the Egyptian taskmasters. Consider the days of Gideon when the children of Israel dwelt in caves and dens of the mountains because of the Midianite oppression (see Judg. 6:2). Consider the ruthless reign of Ahab and Jezebel, when the righteous were again forced to retreat to the caves and desert fastnesses.

Church history since the cross has added scores of examples. We must not fail to remember the Christians in the Coliseum (Rome), "The Church in the Desert" (France), and the underground church in the Soviet Union and China. These are but a small sampling from the "Hard-Times" handbook of the people of God.

In the face of great difficulty, John Owen could write: "Though our persons fall, our cause shall be as truly, certainly, and infallibly victorious, as that Christ sits at the right hand of God. The gospel shall be victorious. This greatly comforts and refreshes me."[9]

Not long before his death, Francis Schaeffer asked this critical question in the title of one of his books: *How Shall We Then Live?* More than anything else, our view of history—optimistic or pessimistic—determines how we will answer that question. It is critical that our view of history—past, present, and future—be shaped by the optimistic promises of the Word of God.

Judgment unto Death or Judgment unto Restoration?

Will God save Sodom for the sake of "five righteous"? As goes the church, so goes the nation. We have seen that a nation's culture is nothing more than the outworking of its religious faith in every aspect of life. When the church fails in her duty to transform the culture, the nation under the influence of humanism, sinks inexorably into the maelstrom of God's judgment. Some have described this as "integration into the void."

Thankfully, the mercy and grace of God abound even in the midst of judgment. Therefore, the judgment of God for His people is judgment unto restoration, not judgment unto death.

Before the captivity, Jeremiah was commanded by God to purchase a field and record it in the municipal record. Specifically, he charged Baruch to place the evidence of purchase in an earthen vessel at the court, in which it "may continue many days" (Jer. 32:14). At this time the Babylonians were already building siegeworks against the city. Jeremiah reverently questioned the purpose of God in commanding him to invest seventeen shekels of silver in a piece of land that was soon to be repossessed by the invading enemy.

Even though Jeremiah was not to enjoy this parcel for long, it was a symbol of God's merciful intention to one day establish his descendants in the land. Long-range cultural victory was assured. God told Jeremiah that He would grant repentance to His people in the captivity and restore them to their land. Their fields would once again be bought and sold. Jeremiah's field was an earnest of that promise.

The judgment and captivity were to have a two-fold purpose in the sovereignty of God. For the enemies of God this was a judgment unto death, used by God to cleanse the land of evil and restore it to rest and productivity. The same judgment was used to purify and perfect the people of God and prepare them to return to the land in total victory.

Picking up the Pieces

Likewise, penitent American Christians should continue to work, serve, and invest in the face of God's impending judgment. They may be assured that their "labor is not in vain in the Lord" (1 Cor. 15:58). We may even rejoice in the gathering clouds of judgment, knowing that the humanistic edifice of cultural evil is soon to be swept away. This assumes, of course, that we daily reform our lives in repentance for our sins and prayer for the sins of the nation.

For example, the Proverbs woman, because of her prudent preparation, is described as one who "laughs at the time to come" (Prov. 31:25, RSV). She has worked hard to lay up a store of goods for her family and for the poor, so she knows that God will take care of her when hard times come. Her husband "is known in the gates, where he sitteth among the elders of the land" (Prov. 31:23). He drew strength and encouragement to serve the community from his wife's support and prudent management of his household.

The church should not only expect and desire cultural victory in this age, it is commanded to accomplish it—through good times and bad. Although that victory may be delayed, it will not be denied. Like the patriarchs who did not receive the promise during their lifetimes (see Heb. 11:13), we may see nothing but cultural decay in our generation. Nonetheless, we receive a heritage from our forebears, add to it by a life of diligent labor, and pass it on to the next generation. By faith we know that this intergenerational effort will lead to the visible manifestation of the kingdom of Christ on earth.

Scripture states this in different ways. The church is to be salt, or preservative in the world. The church is to be on the offensive against the gates of hell. The purpose of godly civil government is to actively restrain evildoers.

This victory is not to be won by means of a holy war, but by the works and words of the believer and the community of saints. In the power of the Holy Spirit, men and nations will be persuaded of their need to turn to God. Many times it takes a crisis for them to see this need.

It was just such a crisis that gave birth to the Protestant Reformation. One of the major themes flowing out of the Reformation was the priesthood of the believer in his so-called "secular" calling. This doctrine in fact supplied the theological underpinning for the development of Western Civilization.

As this doctrine works itself out, the believer is increasingly elevated to higher levels of responsibility and authority. Through the service of diligent labor he gradually assumes dominion in his sphere of influence. The cumulative effect of this process over time is a free society, as the church moves out into the world dissolving the chains of tyranny in the process.

In one sense, work is the result of God's curse resulting from the disobedience and fall of man. With the fall of the creation, strenuous work became necessary for mere survival in the earth. This curse has extended even to the present day and prompted Paul to exhort the Thessalonians to work if they were interested in eating (see 2 Thess. 3:10).

However, work predated the fall, and God in His grace has now made the curse the very means of blessing for mankind. Consecrated work is to be the means by which men fulfil their divine mandate to subdue the earth. Frequently, in Genesis, men were distinguished by their job descriptions or titles, an indication that this was the means by which they fulfilled the dominion mandate assigned earlier (see Gen. 4:20–21).

The Bible is replete with symbolism and direct example of work-motivated people snapping the shackles of tyranny through their consecrated labor. For example, Jesus was a carpenter, Shamgar defeated the Philistines with an oxgoad, and in Zechariah, four workmen (smiths) defeated four oppressors (horns). The faithful labor of Daniel and Joseph was used of God to extend His dominion in the earth. Both were elevated by God from the depths of slavery to a position of supreme authority in Egypt and Babylon. We observe this process over and over again in the Bible.

Because of their faithfulness "on the job," believers have a platform from which to communicate the gospel of Christ to those around them. Their works as well as their words are a powerful testimony to Christ in the real-life, real-world context of the marketplace. This is the primary means that God has ordained for Christianity to permeate the culture and gradually transform it for Christ.

CONCLUSION

The patient labor and evangelism of the people of God, empowered and blessed by His Spirit will again prevail.[10] And it will be "not by might, nor by power, but by my Spirit, saith the LORD of hosts" (Zech. 4:6). This was the hope of our Christian forbearers: "Strong and certain was the conviction of the Christians that the church would come forth triumphant out of its conflicts, and, as it was its destination to be a world-transforming principle, would attain to dominion of the world."[11]

Western civilization following the Reformation is the greatest example of Christian cultural conquest we have to date. The shameful abandonment of that heritage by the church has left us in our current desperate plight. That heritage will be restored only as the church awakens to reclaim her birthright and asserts the authority of the King of kings over every sphere of life—including the political.

REVIEW QUIZ

1. What is the kingdom of God?
   a. Heaven
   b. The Spirit of God in the heart of man
   c. The millennium
   d. Christian civilization as defined by obedience to God's Word in every sphere of earthly activity

2. What is the basis for building a Christian society?
   a. Education
   b. Evangelism
   c. Political action

3. Which view of the future has tended to cause Christians to withdraw from their cultural responsibilities in the twentieth century?
   a. Post-millenialism
   b. Pan-millenialism
   c. Pre-millenialism
   d. Amillenialism

4. Which of these did/does *not* believe in the triumph of the church in history?
   a. John Calvin
   b. Matthew Henry
   c. Hal Lindsey
   d. C.H. Spurgeon
   e. Jonathan Edwards
   f. c and d

5. Which psalm outlines the biblical philosophy of history?
   a. Psalm 1
   b. Psalm 2
   c. Psalm 23
   d. Psalm 100

6. Which of these attitudes best characterizes twentieth century pre-millenialism?
   a. 10 spies: "Things can only get worse, retreat to the desert"
   b. 2 spies: "Let us go up at once and possess it"

DISCUSSION GUIDE

1. What is the kingdom of God? What are the implications for our life on earth today?

2. In what sense is Christ the King of kings?

3. How has the rise of pre-millenialism in the twentieth century church affected the American church?

4. Given the dark times in which we live, what possible basis can we have for cultural optimism?

5. Debate the biblical case for a historically optimistic eschatology versus a historically pessimistic eschatology.

6. What are the implications of the Great Commission for historical/cultural victory of the church? (see Matt. 28:19–20)

7. How does our view of the millennium affect the way we live?

Answer Key
  1) d   2) b   3) c   4) c   5) b   6) a

End Notes

PART 1: Cracks in the Foundation

1. J. Edgar Hoover, *The Birth of Our Nation and Foundation of Our Republic* (DeLand, FL: Patriotic Education, Inc., 1974), iv.
2. Gordon Stebbins, *American Constitutional and Civil Rights Union* (Longview, WA: Constitutional law class, 1979).
3. Rus Walton, *One Nation Under God* (Washington, D.C.: Third Century Publishers, 1975), 21.

CHAPTER 1 — The Promise of the Constitution

1. Robert Duncan Culver, *Toward a Biblical View of Civil Government* (Chicago, IL: Moody Press, 1974), 72.
2. Montesquieu, *The Spirit of Laws* (Colonial Press, 1900).
3. Robert B. Weaver, *The Birth of Our Nation and Foundation of Our Republic* (DeLand, FL: Patriotic Education, Inc., 1974), 61.
4. Alexander Hamilton, *The Federalist Papers* (New York: New American Library, 1961), 76.
5. Verna M. Hall, *The Christian History of the Constitution* (San Francisco, CA: Foundation for American Christian Education, 1966), 252.
6. E.C. Wines, *The Hebrew Republic* (Uxbridge, MA: The American Presbyterian Press, 1980), 14.
7. James Madison, *The Federalist Papers* (New York: New American Library, 1961), 241.
8. Thomas Cuming Hall, *The Religious Background of American Culture* (Boston, MA: Little, Brown & Co., 1930), 184–185) as cited in Gary DeMar, "America's Deep Roots: Seeing the Forest for the Trees" in *"Biblical Worldview"* (June 1995), vol 11, no. 6, 12.
9. John Adams, *The Earliest Diary of John Adams,* ed. L.H. Butterfield (Cambridge, MA: Harvard University Press, 1966), I:35.

CHAPTER 2 — The Problem with the Constitution: The Original Document

1. Verna M. Hall, *The Christian History of the Constitution,* 204.
2. Edwin S. Corwin, *The "Higher Law" Background of American Constitutional Law* (Ithaca and London: Cornell University Press, 1955), 65.
3. Hall, *The Christian History of the Constitution,* 253.
4. Ibid., 38.
5. Ibid.
6. Max Farrand, ed., *The Records of the Federal Convention of 1787* (New Haven, CT: Yale University Press, 1966), I, 452.
7. John Eidsmoe, *Christianity and the Constitution* (Grand Rapids, MI: Baker Book House, 1987), 360.
8. John Witherspoon, *An Annotated Edition of Lectures on Moral Philosophy,* ed. by Jack Scott (Newark: University of Delaware Press, 1982), 45.
9. James Madison, *The Federalist Papers,* 81.
10. Rus Walton, "Letter From Plymouth Rock," *Plymouth Rock Foundation,* (November, 1983), 1

11. Ebenezer Burgess, *Dedham Pulpit,* 127; quoted by Thomas Jefferson Wertenbaker, *The Puritan Oligarchy* (New York, NY: Grosset & Dunlap, 1947), 70.

12. Hall, *The Christian History of the Constitution,* 254.

13. Witherspoon, *Lectures on Moral Philosophy.*

14. James C. Hefley, *America: One Nation Under God* (Wheaton, IL: Victor Books, 1975), 20.

15. Farrand, *The Records of the Federal Convention of 1787,* 310.

16. Isaac Kramnick, "Assaults by Christians on American Leaders Aren't at All New," *The New York Times* (1994).

17. Ibid.

18. Frank A. Rexford and Clara L. Carson, *The Constitution of Our Country* (New York, NY: American Book Company, 1926), 138.

19. Paul F. Boller, Jr., *George Washington and Religion* (Dallas, TX: Southern Methodist University Press, 1963), 34.

20. Ibid., 75.

21. Hugo Tatsch, *The Facts about George Washington as a Freemason* (New York, NY: Macoy, 1931), 43.

22. Washington to G.W. Snyder, 1798; quoted by John C. Fitzpatrick, ed., *The Writings of George Washington from the Original Manuscript Sources, 1745–1799* (Washington, D.C.: U.S. Govt. Printing Office, 1931–1944), XXXVI:453.

23. Quoted by Victor L. Smith, "An Analysis of the Religious Beliefs of George Washington," senior paper submitted to History Department, Dr. David Poteet, Oral Roberts University, Tulsa, Oklahoma, 1982, 51.

24. Quoted by John Eidsmoe, *Christianity and the Constitution* (Grand Rapids, MI: Baker Book House, 1987), 125.

25. Forrest McDonald, *E Pluribus Unum: The Formation of the American Republic, 1776–1790* (Indianapolis, IN: Liberty Press, [1965] 1979), 259–60.

26. Norine Dickson Campbell, *Patrick Henry: Patriot and Statesman* (Old Greenwich, CT: Devin-Adair, 1969), 338.

27. Farrand, *The Records of the Federal Convention of 1787,* 250, 258.

28. Edmund S. Morgan, *The Birth of the Republic 1763–89* (Chicago, IL: The University of Chicago Press, 1977), 150.

29. Ibid., 145, 154.

30. Hamilton Abert Long, *The American Ideal of 1776* (Philadelphia, PA: Your Heritage Books, Inc., 1976), 18.

31. Ibid., 176.

32. John Eidsmoe, *Christianity and the Constitution* (Grand Rapids, MI: Baker Book House, 1987), 306.

33. Long, *The American Ideal of 1776,* 184.

34. Ron Paul, *Survival Report,* vol. IX, no. 11 (November 15, 1993), 3.

35. Cleon Skousen, *Miracle of America* (Salt Lake City, UT: The Freeman Institute), 22–24.

36. Rus Walton, "America's Christian Heritage," no. 9. *Plymouth Rock Foundation.*

37. Otto Scott, *The Secret Six: John Brown and the Abolitionist Movement,* (repr.) Uncommon Media, (P.O. Box 69006, Seattle, WA 98168) 97–98.

CHAPTER 3 — The Problem with the Constitution: Amendments and Judicial Misinterpretations

1. Dan M. Fox, *Contemporary's New GED* (Chicago, IL: Contemporary Books, 1987), 275.
2. Madison, *The Federalist Papers,* 262, 263.
3. Edward S. Ellis, *The Life of Davy Crockett* (Philadelphia, PA: Porter & Coates, 1884).
4. For an example of this faulty view, see R.J. Rushdoony, *Institutes of Biblical Law* (The Craig Press, 1973), 281–284.
5. Long, *The American Ideal of 1776,* 113.
6. Carroll Quigley, *Tragedy and Hope,* (New York, NY: Macmillan, 1966).
7. Carl Brent Swisher, *American Constitutional Development* (Cambridge, MA: The Riverside Press, 1943), 125.
8. Steve Wilkins, *America: The First 350 Years* (Forest, MS: Covenant Publ., 1988), 125.

CHAPTER 4 — From Plymouth to Philadelphia – The Decline from Puritanism

1. Peter Marshall and David Manuel, *The Light and the Glory* (Old Tappan, NJ: Fleming H. Revell Company, 1977), 120.
2. Terrill Irwin Elniff, *The Guise of Every Graceless Heart* (Vallecito, CA: Ross House Books, 1981), 36.
3. John Cotton, "Copy of a Letter from Mr. Cotton to Lord Say and Seal in the Year 1636," *The Puritans,* ed., Perry Miller and Thomas H. Johnson (2 vols.; rev. ed.; New York, NY: Harper and Row, 1963), I, 213.
4. *Suffolk Court Records,* 631, 886, 1014, 1015, 1066; quoted by Edmund S. Morgan, *The Puritan Family* (New York, NY: Harper and Row, Publishers, 1966), 111.
5. Thomas Jefferson Wertenbaker, *The Puritan Oligarchy* (New York, NY: Grosset & Dunlap, 1947), 77.
6. Perry Miller, *The New England Mind* (Cambridge, MA: Harvard University Press, 1954), 190.
7. Ibid., 191.
8. Wertenbaker, *The Puritan Oligarchy,* 252.
9. John Frame, *The Doctrine of the Knowledge of God* (Phillipsburg, New Jersey: Presbyterian & Reformed Publishing Company).
10. James Turner, *Without God, Without Creed – The Origin of Unbelief in America* (Baltimore, MD: Johns Hopkins University Press, 1985).
11. Terrill, Irwin Elniff, *The Guide of Every Graceless Heart* (Vallecito, CA: Ross House Books, 1981), 66-67.
12. Wertenbaker, *The Puritan Oligarchy,* 220.
13. Ibid., 216.
14. Ibid., 337–338.
15. Steve Wilkins, *America: the First 350 Years,* 30.
16. Ibid., 32–33.
17. Richard Bushman, *From Puritan to Yankee: Character and the Social Order in Connecticut, 1690–1765* (Cambridge, MA: Harvard University Press, 1967), 206.
18. Francis Schaeffer, *How Should We Then Live?* (Old Tappan, NJ: Fleming H. Revell Company, 1976), 79–119.
19. John Demos, "Families in Colonial Bristol, Rhode Island: An Exercise in Historical Demography," *William and Mary Quarterly,* 3rd Ser., XXV (Jan. 1968), 56.

20. Whitney Cross, *The Burned-Over District: The Social and Intellectual History of Enthusiastical Religion in Western New York, 1800–1850* (Ithaca, NY: Cornell University Press, 1950).
21. Ibid., 356.
22. Gregg Singer, *Colonial Presbyterianism and the Great Awakening* (Mount Olive, MS: Mount Olive Tape Library), audio tape message.

PART II: A Collapsing Superstructure

1. Matthys Levy and Mario Salvadori, *Why Buildings Fall Down* (New York, NYL W.W. Norton & Company, 1992), 224.

CHAPTER 5 — From Philadelphia to the Present — the Descent into Judgment

1. H. Edward Rowe, *Save America* (Old Tappan, NJ: Fleming H. Revell Company, 1976), 72–73.
2. Russel B. Nye, *William Lloyd Garrison and the Humanitarian Reformers* (Canada: Little, Brown, & Company, 1955), 48.
3. *1995 World Almanac.*
4. *1993 World Book Encyclopedia.*
5. Otto Scott, *The Secret Six* (Columbia, SC: Foundation for American Education, 1979), ii.
6. Paul deParrie, "John Brown and the Judgment of God," *Life Advocate,* (March 1995), 24.
7. Robert Allen Hill and Olaf John, *Your Children: the Victims of Public Education* (Van Nuys, CA: Bible Voice, Inc., 1978), 5.
8. William Ebenstein, *Great Political Thinkers: Plato to the Present, 4th edition* (New York, NY: Hoht, Rinehart and Winston, Inc.), 734–735.
9. John P. Foley, ed., *The Jeffersonian Cyclopedia* (New York, NY: Funk & Wagnel Company, 1900), 663.
10. Robert L. Dabney, *Discussions, Vol IV* (Harrisonburg, VA: Sprinkle Publications, 1979), 280.
11. Herbert Schlossberg, *Idols for Destruction: Christian Faith and its Confrontation with American Society* (Nashville, TN: Thomas Nelson, Inc., 1983), 16–17.
12. Hefley, *America: One Nation Under God* (Wheaton, IL: Victor Books, 1975), 90.
13. Norman F. Dacey, *How to Avoid Probate* (New York, NY: Macmillan Publishing Company, 1990), 22.
14. Ibid., 25–28.
15. Ron Paul, *Survival Report* (Houston, TX: Ron Paul & Associates, Inc., 1993), 6.
16. Bureau of Justice Statistics Bulletin, *Criminal Victimization 1992* (Washington, D.C.: U.S. Department of Justice, 1992), 6.
17. Bureau of Justice Statistics Bulletin, *Felony Sentences in the United States, 1990* (Washington, D.C.: U.S. Department of Justice, 1990), 1.
18. Don S. McAlvany, *The McAlvany Intelligence Advisor,* (October, 1993), 14.
19. Reported by American Information Newsletter from *The Wanderer,* (Sept. 30, 1993), 201 Ohio St., St. Paul, MN 55107.
20. The Associated Press, September 20, 1993.
21. Reported by American Information Newsletter from *Doctors for Disaster Preparedness* (September, 1993), 2509 N. Campbell Ave., Box 272, Tucson, AZ 85719.

22. *New York Times* (September 25, 1993).
23. Don S. McAlvany, *The McAlvany Intelligence Advisor* (October, 1993), 3.
24. Ibid., 5.

CHAPTER 6 — Remodeling without a Blueprint

1. Daniel V. Davis, *Christians Can Be Persuasive* (Denver, CO: Persuasion Seminar, 1986), 1.
2. Cornelius Van Til, *The Defense of the Faith* (Phillipsburg, NJ: Presbyterian and Reformed Publishing Co., 1955), 8.
3. Richard L. Pratt, Jr., *Every Thought Captive* (Phillipsburg, NJ: Presbyterian and Reformed Publishing Company, 1979) 37.
4. Schaeffer, *How Should We Then Live?* 110.
5. James Forrest, "The Religious Basis for Fundamental Law: In the Search for National Unity" in *The Christian Focus,* vol. 4, no. 3 (Fall 1979), 9.
6. Marvin Olasky, "Decisive, Not Devisive," in *World Magazine,* vol. 9, no. 11 (July, 1994), 30.
7. John W. Whitehead, *The Stealing of America* (Westchester, IL: Crossway Books, 1983), 31–32.
8. Carl Henry, *World,* vol. 9, no. 29 (December 24, 1994), 28.
9. Harold Berman, *Law and Revolution: The Formation of the Western Legal Tradition* (Boston: Harvard University Press, 1983).
10. Robert L. Dabney, *Discussions* (Harrisonburg, VA: Sprinkle Publications, 1979), 496.
11. Sally D. Reed, "The NEA: Ruining Education in America," *Conservative Digest,* vol. 11, no. 1 (January, 1985), 16.
12. Ron Paul, *Survival Report,* vol. IX, no. 11 (November 15, 1993), 6.
13. Michael P. Farris, *The Home School Court Report,* vol. 6, no. 2 (Spring, 1990), 1.
14. Ibid.
15. David Reinhard, "How Should Christians Practice Politics?" Portland *Oregonian* (January 19, 1995), editorial page.
16. William Blackstone, *Law of Nature,* commentaries.
17. Colin Brown, *Philosophy and the Christian Faith* (London: Inter-Varsity Press, 1969), 138.
18. C.S. Lewis, *Mere Christianity* (New York, NY: Macmillan Publishing Co., Inc., 1952), 19.
19. Don Richardson, *Peace Child* (Ventura, CA: Gospel Light/Regal Books, 1976).
20. Ken Meyers, "Natural Law Without Shame," *Table Talk* (May, 1994), 61.

CHAPTER 7 — The Foundation for Political Righteousness

1. David Wells, *No Place for Truth* (Grand Rapids, MI: Erdmans, 1993), 142, 143, 175.
2. John Calvin, *Institutes of the Christian Religion* (Philadelphia, PA: The Westminster Press, 1960), 2.7. 10–11.
3. Vern Poythress, *The Shadow of Christ in the Law of Moses* (Brentwood, TN: Wolgemuth and Hyatt, Publishers, Inc., 1991), 325.

CHAPTER 8 — The Form of Biblical Civil Government

1. John Locke, *The Second Treatise of Government* (New York , NY: The Liberal Arts Press, Inc., 1952), 54.

2. Ibid., 56.
3. Corwin, *The "Higher Law" Background of American Constitutional Law* (Ithaca, NY: Cornell University Press, 1955), 75.
4. Brown, *Philosophy and the Christian Faith,* 83.
5. Calvin, *Institutes of the Christian Religion,* 4.20.29.
6. Ibid., 4.20.30.
7. E.C. Wines, *The Hebrew Republic,* iv.
8. Kenneth S. Kantzer, "Summing Up: An Evangelical View of Church and State," *Christianity Today* (April 1985), 28.
9. Morgan, *The Birth of the Republic 1763–89,* 137.
10. John Cotton, "Copy of a Letter from Mr. Cotton to Lord Say and Seal in the Year 1636," *The Puritans,* eds. Perry Miller and Thomas H. Johnson, 2 vols., rev.ed. (New York, NY: Harper and Row, 1936), I, 209–212.
11. Montesquieu, *The Spirit of Laws* (Colonial Press, 1900).
12. Burton J. Hendrick, "The Initiative and Referendum and How Oregon Got Them," *McClure's Magazine* (July 1911).
13. Ibid.
14. "Taking the Initiative and Gagging on It," Portland *Oregonian* (November 11, 1990).
15. Gail Kinsey Hill, "Four Money-Related Initiatives Struggling for Votes in New Poll," Portland *Oregonian* (November 5, 1994).
16. E.C. Wines, *The Hebrew Republic,* 145.
17. J.D. Davis, *Illustrated Davis Dictionary of the Bible* (Nashville, TN: Royal Publishers, Inc., 1973), 788.
18. Terril Irwin Elniff, *The Guise of Every Graceless Heart* (Vallecito, CA: Ross House Books, 1981), 87.
19. Merrill F. Unger, *Unger's Bible Dictionary* (Chicago, IL: Moody Press, 1966), 376.
20. Marchette Chute, *The First Liberty* (New York, NY: E.P. Dutton & Co., Inc., 1969), 314.
21. Urian Oakes, *New England Pleaded With,* 41; quoted by Wertenbaker, *The Puritan Oligarchy,* 68.

CHAPTER 9 — *The Function of Biblical Civil Government*

1. Frederic Bastiat, *The Law* (Irvington-on-Hudson, NY: The Foundation for Economic Education, Inc., 1979), 5.
2. Peter Marshall, *The Light and the Glory,* 141.
3. Joan and John Zug, *The Amanas Today* (Monticello, IA: Julin Printing Co., 1974).
4. *Illustrated Davis Dictionary of the Bible,* 770.
5. *Suffolk Court Records,* 631, quoted by Edmund S. Morgan, *The Puritan Family* (New York, NY: Harper & Row, Publishers, 1966), 111.
6. Jay E. Adams, *Competent to Counsel* (Grand Rapids, MI: Baker Book House, 1970), 152–153.
7. Mendelsohn, "Slavery in the Ancient Near East" in *The Biblical Archeologist IX,* 4 (1946), 74–88.
8. Roger F. Campbell, *Justice Through Restitution, Making Criminals Pay* (Milford, MI: Mott Media, 1977), 63.
9. *Essex Court Records,* VI, 393, 394, 395; VII, 324–325; VIII, 441; quoted by Morgan, *The Puritan Family,* 112.
10. *Unger's Bible Dictionary,* 903.
11. Ibid.

12. Matthew Poole, *Matthew Poole's Commentary on the Holy Bible* (McLean, VA: MacDonald Publishing Company), 163.
13. Matthew Henry, *A Commentary on the Whole Bible* (Iowa Falls, IA: World Bible Publishers), 368.

CHAPTER 10 — Strategy

1. Kirk Coffia, "Christian Churches Should Be Unincorporated to Please God, Not Just to Avoid Additional Trouble With Government," reprinted from the "Plumbline" in *The Correspondent* (October, 1989), 13.
2. Shelby Sharpe, "The Coming Nuclear Attack on Christianity in America" in *Chalcedon Report,* no. 291 (October 1989), 3.
3. "Cooperation, Not Communion," *World,* vol. 9, no. 3 (April 9, 1994), 10.

CHAPTER 11 — Tactics

1. *The Oregon Campaign Institute Manual* (Salem, OR: Oregon Campaign Institute, 1994).
2. Dennis Woods, *Principles of Attack and Defense as Seen by the Perception Analyzer* (Portland, OR: Columbia Information Systems, 1989), video.
3. Senator H.L. "Bill" Richardson, "Winning Through Confrontation and Positive Politics," *Conservative Digest,* (May/June 1988), 101.
4. Kevin C. Gottlieb, "The How and Why of Personal Political Involvement," *Life Association News* (November 1985), 88.
5. Ibid., 86.

CHAPTER 12 — The Fruit of Our Labor

1. Larry Abraham, *Insider Report* (Phoenix, AZ: Publishers Management Corporation, 1993), 4.
2. C.H. Spurgeon, *The Treasury of David.*
3. Calvin, *Institutes of the Christian Religion,* III:25:5.
4. W. Gary Crampton, *What Calvin Says* (Jefferson, MD: The Trinity Foundation, 1992), 102–103.
5. *Matthew Henry Commentary* (Iowa Falls, IA: World Bible Publishers), 446.
6. Jonathan Edwards, *The History of Redemption* (Evansville, IN: The Sovereign Grace Book Club, 1959), 319–325.
7. Quoted by John Eidsmoe, *The Miracle of Philadelphia* (Mt. Olive, MS: Mt. Olive Tape Library, Inc.)
8. D. James Kennedy and Jerry Newcombe, *What If Jesus Had Never Been Born?* (Nashville, TN: Thomas Nelson Publishers, 1994), 245.
9. John Owen, "The Use of Faith, if Popery Should Return Upon Us, 1680," *The Works of John Owen, 1851,* vol 9, 507–508.
10. J. Marcellus Kik, *An Eschatology of Victory* (Phillipsburg, NJ: Presbyterian and Reformed Publishing Co., 1971), 16.
11. J.A.W. Neander, *History of the Christian Religion and Church,* trans. Joseph Torrey, 1851, vol 2, 395–96.

Bibliography

PHILOSOPHY AND PRESUPPOSITIONAL APOLOGETICS

Becker, Carl L. *The Declaration of Independence: A Study in the History of Political Ideas.* New York: Vintage Books, 1958.

Bellah, Robert N. "Civil Religion in America." *The Religious Situation: 1968.* ed. Donald R. Cutler. Boston: Beacon Press, 1968.

Blumenfeld, Samuel. *Is Public Education Necessary?* San Diego, CA: The Paradigm Company, 1989.

Brown, Colin. *Philosophy and the Christian Faith.* (London: Intervarsity Press, 1969.

Campbell, Colin. "Our semi-pagan forebears." *Atlanta Constitution.* June 29, 1994. C6.

Cassirer, Ernst. *The Philosophy of the Enlightenment.* Princeton, NJ: Princeton University Press, 1951.

Clark, Gordon H. *Logic.* Jefferson, MD: The Trinity Foundation, 1985.

Davis, Daniel V. *Christians Can Be Persuasive.* Denver, CO: Persuasion Seminar, 1986.

Elniff, Terril Irwin. *The Guise of Every Graceless Heart.* Valleoito, CA: Ross House Books, 1981.

Engel, Morris S. *With Good Reason.* New York: St. Martin's Press, 1982.

Frothingham, O.B. *Transcendentalism in New England: A History.* Gloucester, MA: Peter Smith, 1965.

Grant, George P. *Philosophy in the Mass Age.* Vancouver, B.C., Canada: Copp Clark, 1959.

Guinness, Os. *The Gravedigger File: Papers on the Subversion of the Modern Church.* Downers Grove, IL: Intervarsity Press, 1988.

Hay, Denys (ed.). *The Age of the Renaissance.* New York: McGraw-Hill, 1967.

Hofstadter, Richard. *Social Darwinianism in American Thought, 1860-1915.* New York: Oxford University Press, 1976.

Jefferson, Thomas. *The Life and Morals of Jesus of Nazareth: Jefferson's "Bible."* Intro. Cyrus Adler. Washington, D.C.: Government Printing Office, 1904.

Knight, Stephen. *The Brotherhood: The Secret World of the Freemasons.* United States of America: Dorset Press, 1986.

Kock, Adrienne. *The American Enlightenment.* New York: Braziller, 1965/

Locke, John. *The Second Treatise of Government.* New York: The Liberal Arts Press, 1952.

McDonald, Forrest. *Novus Ordo Seclorum: The Intellectual Origins of the Constitution.* Lawrence, KS: University Press of Kansas, 1985.

Notaro, Thom. *Van Til and the Use of Evidence.* Philadelphia, PA: Presbyterian & Reformed Publishing Company.

Orr, John. *English Deism: Its Roots and Fruits.* Grand Rapids, MI: William B. Eerdmans, 1934.

Pierard, Richard V. *The Unequal Yoke: Evangelical Christianity and Political Conservatism.* Philadelphia, PA: Lippincott, 1970.

Pratt, Richard L. *Every Thought Captive.* Philadelphia, PA: Presbyterian and Reformed Publishing Company, 1979.

Schaeffer, Francis. *How Should We Then Live?* Old Tappan, NJ: Fleming H. Revell Company, 1976.

Schlossberg, Herbert. *Idols for Destruction: Christian Faith and Its Confrontation with American Society*. Nashville, TN: Thomas Nelson Publishers, 1983.

Rushdoony, R.J. *The Messianic Character of American Education*. Nutley, NJ: The Craig Press, 1963.

Van Til, Cornelius. *The Defense of the Faith*. Phillipsburg, NJ: Presbyterian and Reformed Publishing Company, 1955.

Witherspoon, John. *An Annotated Edition of Lectures on Moral Philosophy*. Newark: University of Delaware Press, 1982.

AMERICAN HISTORY

Andrews, Charles M. *The Colonial Background of the American Revolution*. Rev. ed. New Haven, CT: Yale University Press, 1931.

Boller, Paul F. *George Washington and Religion*. Dallas, TX: Southern Methodist University Press, 1963.

Boyd, Julian P., et al. *Fundamental Testaments of the American Revolution*. Washington, D.C.: Library of Congress, 1973. [Includes essays on Paine's *Common Sense*, the Declaration of Independence, the Articles of Confederation, and the Treaty of Paris of 1783.]

Bradford, M.E. *A Worthy Company: The Dramatic Story of the Men Who Founded Our Country*. Wheaton, IL: Crossway Books, [1982], 1988.

Brooks, Van Wyck. *The Flowering of New England, 1815-1865*. New York: Modern Library, 1941.

Bushman, Richard L. *From Puritan to Yankee*. Cambridge, MA: Harvard University Press, 1967.

ed. *The Great Awakening: Documents on the Revival of Religion, 1740-1745*. New York: Institute of Early American History and Culture, 1970.

Campbell, Norine Dixon. *Patrick Henry: Patriot and Statesman*. New Haven, CT: Yale University Press, 1966.

Cross, Whitney. *The Burned Over District: The Social and Intellectual History of Enthusiastic Religion in Western New York* (Ithaca, NY: Cornell University Press, 1950.

DeMar, Gary. *America's Christian History: The Untold Story*. Atlanta, GA: American Vision, Inc., 1995.

Eidsmoe, John. *Christianity and the Constitution*. Grand Rapids, MI: Baker Book House, 1987.

Hall, Verna M. *The Christian History of the American Revolution*. San Francisco: CA: Foundation for American Christian Education, 1976.

Heath, Dwight B., ed. *A Journal of the Pilgrims at Plymouth: Mourt's Relation*. New York: Corinth.

Jordan, James. *The Failure of the American Baptist Culture*. Tyler, TX: Geneva Divinity School, 1982.

Marshall, Peter and David Manuel. *The Light and the Glory*. Old Tappan, NJ: Fleming H. Revell Company, 1977.

Mather, Cotton. *On Witchcraft: Being the Wonders of the Invisible World*. Reprint ed. Mount Vernon, NY: Peter Pauper Press, n.d.

McDonald, Forrest. *A Constitutional History of the United States*. New York: Franklin Watts, 1982.

Miller, Perry, and Johnson. *The Puritans*. New York: American Book Co., 1938.

Montgomery, John Warwick. *The Shaping of America*. Minneapolis, MN: Bethany Fellowship, Inc., 1976.

Morgan, Edmund S. *The Birth of the Republic, 1763–89*. Chicago: University of Chicago Press, 1956.

North, Gary. *Political Polytheism: The Myth of Pluralism*. Tyler, TX: Institute for Christian Economics, 1989.

Nye, Russel B. *William Lloyd Garrison and the Humanitarian Reformers*. Canada: Little, Brown, & Company, 1955.

Scott, Otto. *Robespierre: the Voice of Virtue*. New York: Mason & Lipscomb Publishers, 1974.

   The Secret Six: John Brown and the Abolitionist Movement. Reprint. Uncommon Media: P.O. Box 69006, Seattle, WA 98168.

Singer, C. Gregg. *A Theological Interpretation of American History*. Philadelphia, PA: Presbyterian and Reformed Publishing Company, 1964.

Tatsch, J. Hugo. *The Facts about George Washington as a Free Mason*. New York: Macoy, 1931.

Tooqueville, Alexis de. *Democracy in America*. New York: Oxford University Press, 1974.

Weisberger, Bernard A. *They Gathered at the River: The Story of the Great Revivalists and Their Impact upon Religion in America*. Boston: Little, Brown, 1958.

Weiss, Benjamin. *God in American History: A Documentation of America's Religious Heritage*. Grand Rapids, MI: Zondervan, 1966.

Wertenbaker, Thomas Jefferson. *The Puritan Oligarchy*. New York: Scribner, 1947.

Wilkins, Steve. *America: The First 350 Years*. Monroe, LA: Covenant Publications, 1988.

Winslow, Ola Elizabeth. *Samuel Sewall of Boston*. New York: Macmillan, 1964.

Zug, Joan and John. *The Amanas Today*. Monticello, IA: Julin Printing Company, 1974.

GOVERNMENT, LAW, AND THE BIBLE

Bahnson, Greg L. *Theonomy in Christian Ethics*. Nutley, NJ: The Craig Press, 1977.

Bastiat, Frederic. *The Law*. Irving-on-Hudson, NY: The Foundation for Economic Education, Inc., 1979.

Berman, Harold J. *Law and Revolution: The Formation of the Western Legal Tradition*. Cambridge, MA: Harvard University Press, 1983.

Campbell, Richard. *Justice Through Restitution: Making Criminals Pay*. Milford, MI: Mott Media, 1977.

Chilton, David. *Productive Christians in an Age of Guilt Manipulators.* Tyler, TX: Institute for Christian Economics, 1981.

Clark, H.B. *Biblical Law.* 2nd ed. Portland, OR: Binfords & Mort, 1944.

Cornelison, Isaac A. *The Relation of Religion to Civil Government in the United States of America: A State Without a Church, but Not Without a Religion.* New York: G.P. Putnam's Sons, 1895.

Corwin, Edward S. "The 'Higher Law' Background of American Constitutional Law." *Harvard Law Review.* XLII. 1928–1929, 149–85, 365–409.

Culver, Robert Duncan. *Toward a Biblical View of Civil Government.* Chicago, IL: Moody Press, 1974.

Dillon, John F. *The Laws and Jurisprudence of England and America: Being a Series of Lectures Delivered before Yale University.* Boston: Little, Brown, 1895.

Donor, Colonel V. *The Samaritan Strategy.* Brentwood, TN: Wolgemuth & Hyatt Publishers, Inc. 1988.

Dorchester, Daniel. *Christianity in the United States.* New York: Phillips and Hunt, 1888.

Farrand, Max. *The Records of the Federal Convention of 1887.* New Haven, CT: Yale University Press, 1966.

Hall, Thomas Cuming. *The Religious Background of American Culture.* Boston: Little, Brown, and Company, 1930.

Kelly, Douglas. *The Emergence of Liberty in the Modern World: The Influence of Calvin on Five Governments from the 16th through 18th Centuries.* 1992.

Montgomery, John Warwick. *The Law Above the Law.* Minneapolis, MN: Bethany Fellowship, Inc., 1975.

Morris, B.F. *The Christian Life and Character of the Civil Institutions of the United States.* Philadelphia, PA: George W. Childs, 1864.

North, Gary. *Tools of Dominion.* Tyler, TX: Institute for Christian Economics, 1990.

Poythress. *The Shadow of Christ in the Law of Moses.* Brentwood, TN: Wolgemuth and Hyatt, Publishers, Inc. 1991.

Rossiter, Clinton. "Introduction." *The Federalist Papers.* New York: New American Library, 1961.

Rushdoony, R.J. *The Institutes of Biblical Law.* Phillipsburg, NJ: Presbyterian and Reformed Publishing Company, 1973.

Thorpe, Newton. *The Federal and State Constitutions, Colonial Charters, and Other Organic Laws of the States, Territories, and Colonies.* 7 vols. Washington, D.C.: 1909.

Wines, E.C. *The Hebrew Republic.* Uxbridge, MA: The American Presbyterian Press, 1980.

THE CHURCH TRIUMPHANT IN HISTORY AND CULTURE

Adams, Jay. *The Time Is at Hand.* Nutley, NJ: The Presbyterian and Reformed Publishing Company, (1966) 1970.

Boettner, Loraine. *The Millennium.* Philadelphia, PA: The Presbyterian and Reformed Publishing Company, 1957; revised, 1984.

Brown, Harold O.J. "The Passivity of American Christians." *Christianity Today.* January 16, 1976. pp. 7–10.

Chilton, David. *Paradise Restored.* Fort Worth, TX: Dominion Press, 1987.

Crenshaw, Curtis. *Dispensationalism Today, Yesterday, and Tomorrow.* Memphis, TN: Footstool Publications, 1985.

Josephus, Flavious. *The Jewish War.* Edited by Gaalya Cornfeld. Grand Rapids, MI: Zondervan Publishing House, 1982.

Kennedy, D. James. *What If Jesus Had Never Been Born?* Nashville, TN: Thomas Nelson Publishers, 1994.

Kik, Marcellus. *An Eschatology of Victory.* Nutley, NJ: The Presbyterian and Reformed Publishing Company, 1971.

Kuyper, Abraham. *Lectures on Calvinism.* Grand Rapids, MI: William B. Eerdmans Publishing Co., 1931.

Lee, Francis Nigel. *The Central Significance of Culture.* Nutley, NJ: The Presbyterian and Reformed Publishing Company, 1976.

Lewis, C.S. *The Weight of Glory and Other Addresses.* New York: Macmillan Publishing Co., 1980.

Murray, Iain. *The Puritan Hope: A Study in Revival and the Interpretation of Prophecy.* Edinburgh, Scotland: The Banner of Truth Trust, 1971.

Vanderwaal, Cornelis. *Hal Lindsay and Bible Prophecy.* St. Catherines, Ontario: Paideia Press, 1978.

Scripture Index

Subject Index

gradualism 181, 189, 192
                196, 197, 210, 221
imprecatory prayer ...187, 188, 197
mass 193, 196, 197, 207
objective 193
offense ....xi, 186, 191, 192
                196, 206
positioning 201
surprise 181, 200
surprise and pursuit ..194, 195–197
suffrage.................................11
super collider............................107
superstructure...............................75
Supreme Court ....xiv, 19, 27, 43, 46
            53, 54, 56, 79, 108, 185
survival of the fittest 143
swearing-in.......................................11
sweeping clause...............................45
sword..................8, 78, 113, 153, 192
Syria....................................221
tactics, campaign..................181, 199
    attack........................203–205, 216
    defense 69, 168, 202–205, 214
                216
tariffs 2
Tatsch, J. Hugo 31
taxation 1, 200, 201, 204
    church immunity 59
    church tithe.......................50, 153
    confiscatory..........50, 51, 161, 187
    direct..48
    flat rate income 50, 57
    graduated income...........48, 49, 51
                57, 79, 80
    head tax 49, 50, 57
    illegitimate.....................47, 48, 90
    inheritance 48, 49, 57
    political tax credit.....................205
    power to collect 44, 46, 47
    property..................48, 49, 81, 145
    proportional 48, 49, 50
    resistance 50
    sales.............................50, 57
    Social Security..........................185
    temple..............................49
    10 percent limit 50, 57

temperance..................................7, 69
temple 81
Thanksgiving...............................161
theft, legalized........................82, 160
theology 69, 133
thief..162
Thompson, Bill.............................107
tithe..191
Tower of Babel..........................6, 15
treaties 12, 35, 39
trumpet...........................147
truth ....xii, 83, 98, 101, 110, 113
            123, 151, 187, 204, 222
tyranny, tyrannical 1, 6, 10, 21
        34, 36, 38, 50, 52, 59, 63, 67, 77
        80, 126, 136–138, 140, 141, 152
                224, 227, 228
unbeliever, unbelief 112, 114
                191, 198, 222
University....................................202
    Harvard................................66, 67
    Princeton 13, 22, 28
Unsoeld, Jolene 194
Urim and Thummim...................148
Utopia......................................69, 144
U'ren, William....................140, 143
Van Til, Cornelius 98
vengeance....................................175
vice-regent....................................154
victory............181, 183, 190–192, 194
            195, 200, 207, 217, 220, 221
                225–227
Vietnam..86
violence 111, 176, 218
Virginia...24
Virginia Compact.............................39
Vision ....xiii, xiv, 68, 105, 181, 217
Voltaire..28
Walton, Rus....................................26
war....................8, 147, 189, 192, 193
    Between the States..........36, 54, 77
                90, 91, 92
    cultural.....................................181
    First World..............................192
    for Independence 70
    gang 167, 172

ABOUT THE AUTHOR

Dennis Woods makes his home in Clackamas, Oregon, with his wife and three homeschooled children. He is the president and owner of Target Marketing Services, a telemarket/market research company. He is also the former director of telemarketing for the Oregon Christian Coalition. Additionally, he is a journeyman carpenter and has served as an officer of artillery in the United States Army. Educational attainments include a master's degree in education, a bachelor's in journalism, and completion of the graduate program at Multnomah Bible College in Portland, Oregon.

Active in Oregon politics since 1976, Mr. Woods has conducted nearly two hundred political surveys, with primary focus on Oregon legislative campaigns. His most satisfying political accomplishment came in 1990 when he co-managed a forty-line voter identification phone bank supporting seventeen key Republican House Races in Oregon. About 65 percent won, contributing to Republican takeover of the Oregon House for the first time in twenty years—the only legislative chamber in the nation to switch from Democrat to Republican that year.